Psychological Assessment of Adult Posttraumatic States

Psychotherapy Practitioner Resource Book Series

Kenneth S. Pope, Series Editor

Psychological Assessment of Adult Posttraumatic States
   John Briere
Recovered Memories of Abuse: Assessment, Therapy, Forensics
   Kenneth S. Pope and Laura S. Brown

Psychological Assessment
of
Adult Posttraumatic States

John Briere

AMERICAN PSYCHOLOGICAL ASSOCIATION
WASHINGTON, DC

Published by
American Psychological Association
750 First Street, NE
Washington, DC 20002

Copies may be ordered from
APA Order Department
P.O. Box 92984
Washington, DC 20090-2984

In the UK and Europe, copies may be ordered from
American Psychological Association
3 Henrietta Street
Covent Garden, London
WC2E 8LU England

Typeset in Palatino by G & S Typesetters, Inc., Austin, TX

Printer: Data Reproductions Corp., Rochester Hills, MI
Cover Designer: Berg Design, Albany, NY
Technical/Production Editor: Ida Audeh

Library of Congress Cataloging-in-Publication Data
Briere, John.
    Psychological assessment of adult posttraumatic states / by John Briere.
        p.   cm.
    Includes bibliographical references and index.
    ISBN 1-55798-403-4 (alk. paper)
    1. Post-traumatic stress disorder—Diagnosis.   2. Stress (Psychology)—Testing.   I. Title.
    RC552.P67B75   1997
    616.85'21—dc21   96-52132
                                                                          CIP

Printed in the United States of America
First Edition

This book is dedicated to Murray Wexler, PhD, Chief of Psychological Services at Los Angeles County—University of Southern California Medical Center from 1960 to 1993. Although he liked to tell young psychologists that "the business of life is trouble," he was, and is, an inspiration far beyond that partial truth.

Contents

Acknowledgments

Many people reviewed early parts or versions of this book and offered helpful suggestions. These include Judith Armstrong, Laura S. Brown, Etzel Cardeña, Eve Carlson, Mary Ann Dutton, Carol Edwards, Diana Elliott, William E. Foote, Donald R. Freedheim, Cheryl Lanktree, Ken Pope, and Patricia Kirkish. Others offered specific advice or information on a topic covered in this volume or provided feedback regarding my description of a measure they developed. These include Ellen Berah, Jon Conte, Dano Demaré, Sherry Falsetti, Edna Foa, David Foy, James High, Terrence Keane, Dean Kilpatrick, Fran Norris, Laurie Pearlman, Benjamin Saunders, Rod Shaner, and Rachel Yehuda. Despite this wealth of assistance, I alone am responsible for any errors that remain.

Thanks also go to the very capable and helpful staff at the American Psychological Association Books Department, including Ida Audeh, Julia Frank-McNeil, Judy Nemes, and Mary Lynn Skutley. I thank my editor and colleague Ken Pope for initiating this project and, more broadly, for his consistent attention to those whom our culture seemingly has abandoned. As usual, thanks to Ron Shaner and Rita Ruiz for their friendship and support during this project.

Finally, I thank Cheryl Lanktree for her intellectual stimulation and unflagging partnership.

Introduction

The study and treatment of posttraumatic stress is a relatively recent phenomenon, especially when compared to other, more traditional areas of psychological research and clinical practice. Although there have been anecdotal reports of the psychological effects of wars and natural disasters throughout recorded history, much of our empirically validated information on the impacts of interpersonal violence (e.g., rape, assault, or child abuse) and other traumatic events has been published in the 1980s and 1990s. As a result, until recently the mental health professional had far less access to clinical data regarding posttraumatic stress than was available regarding conditions such as anxiety, depression, or psychosis. Fortunately, the number of empirical studies of psychological trauma has increased dramatically in the last decade, and a number of validated trauma-specific assessment devices have been developed.

The current book was written in response to this burgeoning of new information and the growing need for integrative analyses of posttraumatic disturbance and its measurement. It is intended as a practical, empirically grounded guide to the assessment of traumatic events and associated posttraumatic states. As such, it addresses phenomena such as acute stress disorder (ASD), posttraumatic stress disorder (PTSD), stress-related psychotic states, various dissociative reactions and symptoms, and what has been referred to as *complex PTSD* (J. L. Herman, 1992a) or *self-trauma disturbance* (Briere, 1996a), an amalgam of posttraumatic, cognitive, and personality-related symptoms that often arise from more extreme and chronic traumatic events. In this regard, *posttraumatic states* is used in this book to refer to any enduring psychological response to an overwhelming life experience, as opposed solely to the presence or absence of dichotomously defined PTSD. This book also reviews assessment approaches to what has been called the "Criterion A" domain, that is, the specific traumatic events that underlie a given posttraumatic response. Thus, both adult traumas and enduring child abuse experiences are considered as they relate to adult post-traumatic distress and disorder.

Not covered in this book is the new and largely experimental topic of psychophysiological and neuroendocrinological assessment of trauma effects. PTSD (and possibly ASD) often are accompanied by a variety of altered biopsychological parameters, including cortisol hypersuppression in response to low dose dexamethasone (Yehuda et al., 1993), flashback stimulation by yohimbine (Southwick et al., 1993), and the presence of habituation-resistant startle responses (Ornitz & Pynoos, 1989); however, none of these indicators is sufficiently reliable or accurate to justify its use in individual diagnosis at this time (R. Yehuda, personal communication, June 22, 1996).

This volume is divided into three sections: etiology and phenomenology, general assessment issues, and specific assessment approaches. The first section outlines the sorts of events and processes that can produce posttraumatic difficulties and the specific form these symptom outcomes can take. The second considers general principles that should be adhered to in the assessment of posttraumatic states and discusses additional historical and environmental variables that should be evaluated as well, because of their potential to moderate or exacerbate posttraumatic response. The last section describes interview-based, projective, and objective measures that have been used to evaluate posttraumatic states. This includes not only generic psychological tests such as the Rorschach and versions of the Minnesota Multiphasic Personality Inventory (MMPI; Butcher, Dahlstrom, Graham, Tellegen, & Kaemmer, 1989; Hathaway & McKinley, 1943) and the Millon Clinical Multiaxial Inventory (MCMI; Millon, 1983, 1987, 1994), but also newer trauma-specific measures. The Appendix to this book contains an example of a detailed psychological assessment, written by clinical psychologist Diana Elliott, who specializes in trauma and forensic issues.

Although children also experience a variety of difficulties in response to major stressors, the current volume is limited to adult posttraumatic responses. Readers seeking information specific to the assessment of traumatized children should consult Carlson (in press), Friedrich (1994, in press), Nader (1996), and Saigh (1989).

I approached the writing of this book with equal amounts of excitement and trepidation. The excitement arose from the importance of the topic and the tremendous progress made in this area over the last few years. Even being a very small part of this movement has been immensely stimulating and rewarding for me, both as a clinician and as a behavioral scientist. The trepidation, on the other hand, comes from the complexity and unfinished nature of this topic. Researchers have yet to fully understand the nature of traumatic events, let alone the breadth of posttraumatic response, and our assessment approaches to this area are truly works in progress. Very little said in this book can be etched in stone; unlike books in some other areas, those written on traumatic stress require almost constant updating because the explosion of information on this topic is so great. As a result, this volume should not be seen as a definitive statement on the assessment of posttraumatic states, but rather as one view of where we are right now and what clinical practice might arise from that perspective.

Etiology of Posttraumatic States

The idea that stressful events can produce enduring, negative psychological states seems obvious to most people. Yet, it has only been in the last two decades that mental health professionals have acknowledged posttraumatic stress as a valid psychological condition. Previously, individuals suffering from the effects of overwhelming stressors either were seen as not experiencing a psychological disorder or were given the diagnosis listed in the *Diagnostic and Statistical Manual of Mental Disorders* (2nd ed.; *DSM-II*; American Psychiatric Association, 1968) as *adjustment reaction to adult life* or in the first edition of the *DSM* (*DSM-I*; American Psychiatric Association, 1952) as *gross stress reaction.* Both of these diagnoses, however, referred to transient responses to acute stress that could be expected to diminish rapidly when the stressor was terminated. As a result, prior to the third edition of the *DSM* (*DSM-III*; American Psychiatric Association, 1980), any individual who experienced significant symptomatology (e.g., flashbacks or hyperarousal) that continued well beyond the traumatic event was thought to have some other, more serious disorder. It was not until *DSM-III* that the diagnosis *posttraumatic stress disorder* (PTSD) was created, wherein a potentially chronic symptomatic response to a previous trauma was seen as primarily (although not exclusively) the result of a stressor—not as an intrinsic reflection of premorbid psychopathology.

Although formal professional awareness of posttraumatic stress is quite recent, on another level it has been acknowledged by clinicians and lay people for centuries, primarily with reference to the effects of war. For example, some version of posttraumatic stress has been variously described since World War I as "shell shock," "combat fatigue," "soldier's heart," and "combat neurosis" (Davidson & Foa, 1993). In fact, Trimble (1981) noted that post-traumatic syndromes arising from natural and human-caused disasters were acknowledged as early as the 1600s.

Definition of Trauma

As opposed to most other nonorganic psychiatric disorders, a determination of posttraumatic stress requires evaluation of etiology as well as phenomenology. Specifically, because both the third revised edition and the fourth editions of the *DSM* (*DSM-III-R*, American Psychiatric Association, 1987, and *DSM-IV*, American Psychiatric Association, 1994, respectively) require the presence of a major stressor (referred to as *Criterion A*) before a diagnosis of PTSD can be made, the clinician must assess not only symptoms of stress but also the nature of the stressor. Although this might appear to be a simple matter of listing those events known to produce posttraumatic stress, the wide variety of adverse circumstances extant in our culture defies easy cate-gorization. Moreover, it is now clear that an event that produces posttraumatic stress in one individual may not do so for another. For this reason, *DSM-III*, *DSM-III-R*, and *DSM-IV* have defined more broadly and parametrically the minimal requirements for a PTSD-level stressor. This definition has changed with each *DSM* edition, theoretically as a result of increasing knowledge about trauma and posttraumatic conditions.

In the spirit of acknowledging the importance of the precipi-tating stressor, as opposed to solely a pathologic predisposition in the individual, *DSM-III* required only that the trauma satisfy two conditions: that it be of sufficient severity that it would evoke "significant symptoms of distress in most people" and that it be outside the range of normal human experience (p. 236). *DSM-III-R* added to this definition the statement that the stressor is "usually experienced with intense fear, terror, and helplessness" (American Psychiatric Association, 1987, p. 247) and that the trauma may also include hearing about or witnessing (as opposed to solely experiencing) stressful events. Both *DSM-III* criteria were eliminated in *DSM-IV*, however, because (a) as noted previously, response to stressors is highly variable across individuals; and (b) many relevant stressors (e.g., war, rape, or child abuse) are, unfortunately, well within the realm of normal experience for some individuals. Instead, *DSM-IV* provides the following definition of *trauma*:

> [D]irect personal experience of an event that involves actual or threatened death or serious injury, or other threat to one's physical integrity; or witnessing an event that involves death, injury, or a threat to the physical integrity of another person; or learning about unexpected or violent death, serious harm, or threat of death or injury experienced by a family member or other close associate (Criterion A1). The person's response to the event must involve intense fear, helplessness, or horror (or in children, the response must involve disorganized or agitated behavior) (Criterion A2). (p. 424)

DSM-IV provides a nonexhaustive list of typical stressors, including combat, sexual and physical assault, robbery, being kidnapped, being taken hostage, terrorist attack, torture, disasters, severe automobile accidents, and life-threatening illnesses, as well as witnessing death or serious injury by violent assault, accidents, war, or disaster. Also included is childhood sexual abuse, even if it does not involve threatened or actual violence or injury (an exception to the otherwise prevailing rule). A more detailed consideration of common traumatic stressors is presented in the next section of this chapter.

Perhaps most significant of the *DSM-IV* changes to Criterion A is that of the victim's subjective response to the potentially traumatic event. Although generally supported by the *DSM-IV* field trials, addition of this criterion may be problematic. First, the criterion is, in fact, subjective, in the sense that both victim and clinician may have difficulty determining whether the fear, horror, or helplessness was sufficiently "intense" to qualify. Second, there is insufficient research available to determine whether a stressor must evoke these specific responses (at a specific level of intensity) in order to be traumatic or PTSD producing (March, 1993). Third, subjective reports of distress are easily affected by emotional avoidance, including dissociation. For example, if an individual reports numbing and depersonalization (but not horror, fear, or helplessness) after a major stressor, is it reasonable to consider the stressor nontraumatic? Similarly, it is not at all uncommon to encounter trauma victims who initially deny any negative response to what they later acknowledge were aversive events. Ironically, the posttraumatic avoidance symptoms of such individuals may cause them to miss the subjective response criterion and to be viewed as nontraumatized in *DSM-IV*.

Regardless of its ultimate logic, the subjective response criterion (A2) is currently a requirement for PTSD and thus must be assessed. It is likely that the rate of PTSD in the general population decreases under A2 because only more extreme stressors (and more expressive or vulnerable individuals) qualify for the diagnosis—regardless of the existing level of reexperiencing, avoidance, and hyperarousal symptoms associated with a given traumatic event.

Specific Stressors Known to Produce Posttraumatic States

As noted in *DSM-IV*, many events are potentially traumatic, but a smaller subset of these are cited regularly in the literature as producing posttraumatic states. Several of these more common stressors are described briefly below, both in terms of their incidence and potential posttraumatic effects. Unlike their characterization in previous *DSM* editions, these (and other) traumatic events are often well within the range of human experience. In fact, several surveys suggest that 39%–75% of people in the general population have experienced at least one major traumatic stressor (Breslau, Davis, Andreski, & Peterson, 1991; Elliott, 1995; Kessler, Sonnega, Bromet, Hughes, & Nelson, 1995; Norris, 1992; Resnick, Kilpatrick, Dansky, Saunders, & Best, 1993).

Disasters

Disasters are especially traumatic events that may affect large numbers of people. They may be divided into two types: those caused by nature (e.g., avalanches, earthquakes, floods, hurricanes, tornadoes, volcanic eruptions) and those caused by humans (e.g., explosions, large fires, nuclear accidents, toxic spills). As noted by Ursano, Fullerton, and McCaughey (1994), a significant proportion of Americans have experienced such events:

> Between 1965 and 1985, 31 states experienced five or more presidentially declared disasters. Between 1974 and 1980, 37 major catastrophes occurred in the United States. From October 1979 to September 1980, over 688,000 persons and 90,000 different families received emergency care following a disaster. . . . In 1990 alone, there were 35 presidentially declared disasters which involved 585 counties; over $2 billion were obligated by the Federal Emergency Management Agency to assist the victims of these disasters. (p. 4)

Because disaster can occur in many forms, its psychological impacts are varied. However, most research on disaster effects suggests that acute stress disorder (ASD), PTSD, other anxiety disorders, dissociation, psychosomatic symptoms and somatoform disorders, and depression are typical sequelae (e.g., Freedy, Shaw, Jarrell, & Masters, 1992; Koopman, Classen, Cardeña, & Spiegel, 1995; Norris, Phifer, & Kaniasty, 1994; Shore, Tatum, & Vollmer, 1986).

Large-Scale Transportation Accidents

Transportation accidents involve events such as airline crashes, train derailments, and maritime accidents. These events often involve multiple victims and high fatality rates. Although the incidence of such events is not readily determined, the literature on traumatic stress cites a number of transportation-related traumatic events (e.g., Bartone & Wright, 1990; Hagström, 1995; Lundin, 1995; Raphael, 1977; E. M. Smith, North, McCool, & Shea,

1990; Yule, 1992). A review of these studies suggests impacts similar to those of disasters, including PTSD, anxiety, and depression. The rates of PTSD for plane crash survivors may be typical: P. Sloan (1988) found that 54% of those who lived through a chartered plane crash had PTSD soon after the event, and 10%–15% still had PTSD 1 year later.

Emergency Worker Exposure to Trauma

Because emergency workers often encounter extremely traumatic phenomena, such as grotesque death, dismemberment, disfigurement, and mortal injury, it is not surprising that those who help the traumatized may become traumatized themselves. Among those known to be at risk for trauma-related stress are firefighters and other rescue workers (e.g., Bryant & Harvey, 1996; Lundin & Bodegard, 1993; McFarlane, 1988), paramedics and other emergency medical workers (e.g., Marmar, Weiss, Metzler, Ronfeldt, & Foreman, 1996; I. H. Sloan, Rozensky, Kaplan, & Saunders, 1994), individuals involved in the identification and handling of deceased trauma victims (e.g., Taylor & Frazer, 1982; Ursano & McCarroll, 1990), emergency mental health or crisis intervention workers (e.g., Berah, Jones, & Valent, 1984; Hodgkinson & Shepherd, 1994), and law enforcement personnel (Sewell, 1993). Psychotherapists who treat trauma survivors may also develop a form of "vicarious traumatization" (Pearlman & Saakvitne, 1995) or "PTSD by proxy" (Briere, 1996b).

The effects of trauma on emergency workers tend to involve psychological reactions to the actual stressor, such as PTSD, dissociation, shock, and depression (e.g., Berah et al., 1984; Bryant & Harvey, 1996; Marmar et al., 1996), responses to feelings of helplessness and frustration in the face of seemingly "unfixable" medical–psychological injuries or injustice (e.g., Raphael, 1981; Sewell, 1993), and repeated contact with survivors' extreme distress (e.g., Hodgkinson & Shepherd, 1994).

War

Until recently, much of the study of posttraumatic stress has been the study of war-related psychological disturbance. In fact, the appearance of PTSD as a diagnostic category in *DSM-III* reflected in large part the need to categorize the effects of the Vietnam war on combat veterans (Weathers, Litz, & Keane, 1995). Among those wars wherein posttraumatic difficulties have been described are the American Civil War and World Wars I and II, as well as "conflicts," "police actions," and other combat situations in countries or regions such as Korea, Vietnam, the Persian Gulf, Israel, Armenia, the Falklands, Somalia, and Bosnia.

War involves a very wide range of violent and traumatic experiences, including immediate threat of death or disfigurement, actual physical injury, witnessing injury or death of others, involvement in injuring or killing others (both combatants and civilians), witnessing or participating in atrocities, acts of rape, capture, and prisoner-of-war experiences such as confinement, torture, and extreme deprivation. Furthermore, as noted by Weathers et al. (1995):

> Each war poses its own hardships that color the experience of combatants and produce unique effects on long-term psychological adjustment. Wars differ with respect to climate . . . , terrain . . . , methods of warfare . . . , and types of weapons used. Also, wars may be fought on domestic or foreign soil, and they may be popular or unpopular. Finally, the experience of war may be very different depending on combatants' branch of service . . . and specific duties . . . (p. 107)

Because of the variability of traumatic exposure and its context, war may produce a wide variety of psychological effects, including dissociative responses, depression, generalized anxiety, chronic guilt, aggression, suicidality, and substance abuse (e.g., Bremner, Steinberg, Southwick, Johnson, & Charney, 1993; Kardiner & Spiegel, 1947; Kubany, 1994; Kulka et al., 1990). Most typically, however, PTSD is described as the major sequel of combat.[1] The incidence of PTSD for most wars is nearly impossible to

---

[1] Z. Solomon (1993a, 1993b) suggested that there is often a "combat stress reaction" (CSR) that occurs prior to or instead of the development of PTSD. CSR is thought to include anxiety, dissociation, guilt, exhaustion, hyperarousal, loss of control, and disorientation.

ascertain because the clinical data on them typically antedate the development of modern PTSD criteria. With regard to the Vietnam war, however, Kulka et al. (1990) estimated that the current prevalence of PTSD for Vietnam theater veterans is 15% for men and 9% for women, whereas the lifetime prevalence for PTSD in this group is 31% for men and 27% for women. These rates are even higher for those with more combat exposure.

Rape and Sexual Assault

Modern definitions of rape and sexual assault vary considerably across and within legal, clinical, and research contexts. Koss (1993, p. 199) cited Searles and Berger (1987) in defining *rape* as "nonconsensual sexual penetration of an adolescent or adult obtained by physical force, by threat of bodily harm, or when the victim is incapable of giving consent," where penetration is typically defined as "sexual intercourse, cunnilingus, fellatio, anal intercourse, or any other intrusion, however slight, of any part of a person's body, but emission of semen is not required" (Michigan Stat. Ann., 1980). This type of "reform" statutory definition is a significant advance on earlier legal definitions that often restricted rape to vaginal penetration of a woman who was not married to the perpetrator. The definition of sexual assault typically involves any forced sexual contact short of rape, although some authorities consider sexual assault to include any forced sexual contact, including rape.

Using definitions similar to these, the lifetime prevalence of rape against women in the United States is generally thought to be somewhere between 14% and 20% (see reviews by Kilpatrick & Resnick, 1993, and Koss, 1993), although some studies report higher or lower figures. There does not appear to be a widely accepted prevalence rate for sexual assault of women, partially because of definitional and methodological issues. Rape and sexual assault rates for males are also unclear, probably because society has only recently become aware that men can be rape victims (Stermac, Sheridan, Davidson, & Dunn, 1996). Nevertheless, several studies suggest that between 5% and 10% of all sexual assault victims are men (Forman, 1982; Kaufman, Divasto, Jackson, Voorhees, & Christy, 1980; Stermac et al., 1996). Because of the shame and secrecy typically associated with being a victim of rape or sexual assault in many cultures, it is likely that some victims do not identify themselves as such in research studies. As a result, the above prevalence rates are probably underestimates.

The psychological effects of rape appear to be wide-ranging, including fear, anxiety, anger, depression, low self-esteem, reduced social functioning, somatic symptoms, sexual difficulties, substance abuse, dissociative symptoms, and PTSD (e.g., Dancu, Riggs, Hearst-Ikeda, Shoyer, & Foa, 1996; Golding, 1996; Kilpatrick & Resnick, 1993; Koss, 1993; Koss & Harvey, 1991; Resick, 1993; Rothbaum, Foa, Riggs, Murdock, & Walsh, 1992; J. M. Siegel, Golding, Stein, Burnam, & Sorenson, 1990). Two longitudinal studies of rape victims presenting to emergency rooms suggest that symptoms of PTSD are very common soon after the assault and often decrease in frequency as time passes. Rothbaum et al. (1992) found that 94% of their sample of rape victims met symptomatic criteria for *DSM-III-R* PTSD an average of 13 days after the assault, 65% met full PTSD criteria after an average of 35 days, and 47% still had PTSD at 94 days. Similarly, Kramer and Green (1991) found that 73% of the rape victims they studied met *DSM-III* criteria for PTSD 6 to 8 weeks after the assault. Some rape victims appear to experience posttraumatic difficulties for an indefinite period of time (Gilbert, 1994). Kilpatrick and Resnick (1993), for example, reported that 13% of the rape victims they studied still had PTSD approximately 15 years after being raped.

Spouse or Partner Battery

Spouse or partner battery (also known as *wife battering, spouse abuse,* or *domestic violence*) may be defined as "assaultive behavior between adults in an intimate, sexual, theoretically peer, and usually cohabiting relationship" (Ganley, 1981, p. 8). Included in this definition are four forms of battering: (a) physical, (b) sexual, (c) destruction of property and pets, and (d) psychological (Ganley, 1981; Stordeur & Stille, 1989). Most research (and some clinical) definitions focus primarily on physical maltreatment, however, as well as sexual victimization when it is not subsumed under sexual assault. Furthermore, although there is little doubt that men can be beaten by their wives or partners (e.g., Straus, Gelles, & Steinmetz, 1980), most physical injuries appear to be caused by men against women (Schwartz, 1987).

Current data on the epidemiology of wife battering (used hereinafter to refer to physical violence against a wife or cohabiting female sexual partner by a man) typically use the Conflict Tactics Scale (CTS; Straus, 1979) as a measurement instrument. The CTS asks individuals to indicate whether they engaged in a number of specific violent or abuse behaviors during a dispute in the prior year. Two large general population studies (Schulman, 1979 [described in D. G. Dutton, 1992]; Straus et al., 1980) indicated that severe assaults against wives (e.g., kicking, biting, hitting with a fist, beating up, using a knife, firing a gun) were reported on the CTS for between 9% and 13% of couples. If the definition included any violence against wives (e.g., slapping, pushing, shoving), the rates increased to between 21% and 28%. A more recent survey by Straus and Gelles (1985) suggested that wife battering has decreased to some extent (21% less reports of severe violence and 7% less total violence) of late, as also suggested by a similar study of Canadian couples (Kennedy & Dutton, 1989). D. G. Dutton (1992) warned, however, that this reduction may represent, in part, reduced self-disclosure of violence as wife battering becomes more socially unacceptable.

The psychological effects of wife battering frequently have been described in terms of a "battered woman syndrome" (e.g., L. E. Walker, 1984, 1991). Clinical descriptions of this syndrome generally refer to symptoms of PTSD, as well as depression, fearfulness, guilt, poor self-image, and learned helplessness (Houskamp, 1994). More recent empirical studies generally support this symptom list (especially with reference to PTSD), as well as documenting greater somatization, substance abuse, cognitive distortions, and various anxiety disorders (e.g., Astin, Lawrence, & Foy, 1993; Astin, Ogland-Hand, Coleman, & Foy, 1995; Cascardi, O'Leary, Lawrence, & Schlee, 1995; M. A. Dutton, Burghardt, Perrin, Chrestman, & Halle, 1994; M. A. Dutton, Hohnecker, Halle, & Burghardt, 1994; Follingstad, Brennan, Hause, Polek, & Rutledge, 1991; Gleason, 1993; Houskamp & Foy, 1991).

Torture

Torture has been defined by the United Nations (reproduced in Vesti & Kastrup, 1995, p. 214) as "any act by which severe pain or suffering, whether physical or mental, is intentionally inflicted on a person for such purposes as obtaining from him [sic] or a third person information or confession, punishing him for an act he has committed or is suspected of having committed, or intimidating him or a third person." Although this definition is quite broad, it does not include other, less intrinsically political acts such as random torture of citizens by invading military forces (wherein the only basis for "punishment" is being a citizen of an enemy country), the abduction and subsequent sexual torture of women for sadistic gratification, or the ongoing physical and sexual torture that sometimes occurs in severe domestic violence.

Regardless of function or context, the actual methods of torture involve both physical and psychological techniques. Physical torture activities include beatings; near strangulation; electric shocks; insertion of objects into bodily orifices; various forms of sexual abuse and assault; crushing or breaking of bones and joints; and exposure to extreme heat, cold, or chemical corrosives. Psychological methods include sensory deprivation, threats of death or mutilation, forced nakedness and sexual exposure, mock executions, being made to feel responsible for the death or injury of others, sleep deprivation, and being forced to engage in grotesque or humiliating acts.

The incidence of torture is not known, although Amnesty International (1992) estimated that more than 60 nations currently sanction the use of torture, or at least tacitly allow it. Torture victims are thought to be dramatically overrepresented among refugees (Baker, 1992), although such individuals are rarely questioned about a potential torture history when they come in contact with American mental health systems.

The psychological effects of torture are diverse, partially because of the many types of torture and the various contexts in which it occurs. At the very least, torture has been associated with PTSD, depression, anxiety disorders, sleep disturbance, sexual problems, psychosis, somatic symptoms, and suicidality (Allodi & Cowgill, 1982; Baker, 1992; El Sarraj, Punamaki, Salmi, & Summerfield, 1996; Engdahl & Eberly, 1990; Kinzie & Boehnlein, 1989; Melamed, Melamed, & Bouhoutsos, 1990; Mollica, Wyshak, & Lavelle, 1987; Tennant, Goulston, & Dent, 1986; Van Velsen, Gorst-Unsworth, & Turner, 1996).

Child Abuse

Childhood sexual and physical abuse is unfortunately quite prevalent in North American society. Child protective agencies determined that more than 1,000,000 children had been abused or neglected in 1994 alone, and more than 1,100 were killed (U.S. Department of Health and Human Services, 1996). These statistics may be substantial underestimates because they rely on (a) incidents reported to agencies, and (b) incidents that were accompanied by sufficient evidence to warrant a determination of abuse. Studies of retrospective child abuse reports by adults in the general population (e.g., Bagley, 1991; Elliott & Briere, 1995; Finkelhor, Hotaling, Lewis, & Smith, 1989; Russell, 1983; Timnick, 1985; Wyatt, 1985) suggest that approximately 25% to 30% of women and 15% of men report sexual abuse as children, and approximately 10% to 20% of men and women report experiences congruent with definitions of physical abuse. Probably because of the negative effects of such abuse and associated family dysfunction, several recent studies suggest that approximately 35–70% of female mental health patients (according to clinical setting) self-report a childhood history of sexual abuse, if asked (e.g., Briere, Woo, McRae, Foltz, & Sitzman, in press; Briere & Zaidi, 1989; Bryer, Nelson, Miller, & Krol, 1987; Chu & Dill, 1990; Craine, Henson, Colliver, & MacLean, 1988).[2]

As might be predicted, the literature in this area indicates that adults abused as children, as a group, exhibit a wide range of psychological and interpersonal problems (see reviews by Berliner

---

[2]Equivalent data on male mental health patients are largely unavailable at this time, although clinical experience suggests that the incidence of sexual and physical abuse is elevated in this group as well.

& Elliott, 1996; Briere, 1992a; Briere & Runtz, 1993; Finkelhor, 1990; Kolko, 1996; Neumann, Houskamp, Pollock, & Briere, 1996; Polusny & Follette, 1995). Apropos of the focus of this book, these include symptoms of chronic PTSD (e.g., Cheperon & Prinzhorn, 1994; Craine et al., 1988; Gregg & Parks, 1995; Rowan, Foy, Rodriguez, & Ryan, 1994; B. E. Saunders, Villeponteaux, Lipovsky, Kilpatrick, & Veronen, 1992) and dissociative symptomatology (Briere & Elliott, 1993; Briere & Runtz, 1990a; Chu & Dill, 1990; DiTomasso & Routh, 1993; Nash, Hulsey, Sexton, Harralson, & Lambert, 1993). Also present may be more Axis II-like problems in personal identity, interpersonal boundaries, and affect regulation (Briere, 1992a; Cole & Putnam, 1992; Elliott, 1994b; McCann & Pearlman, 1990). Together, the various sequelae of childhood maltreatment fit well with the notion of *complex PTSD* outlined in chapter 2, although even that broad diagnosis cannot accommodate all of the abuse effects described in the research literature.

General Determiners of Posttraumatic Response

Specific stressor types aside, the extant trauma literature suggests that the amount of posttraumatic symptomatology an individual experiences is a function of at least four broad variables: characteristics of the stressor, variables specific to the victim, subjective response to the stressor, and the response of others to the victim. None of these variables exists independently of the others. For example, certain victim characteristics (e.g., sex, socioeconomic status, lower psychological functioning) may increase the likelihood of interpersonal victimization and potentially limit the amount of social support or clinical intervention available to the victim during and after the event. Similarly, traumatic events may combine with victim variables and posttrauma social response to determine the individual's subjective interpretation of the stressor. As a result, it may be difficult to tease out the relative contributions of specific traumatic events, preexisting psychological or demographic variables, and social system response to the victim when attempting to determine the specific etiology of a given posttraumatic psychological state. As is noted in later chapters, the complexity of these relationships supports the use of multiple measures and assessment foci when evaluating trauma-related phenomena.

Characteristics of the Stressor

A number of stressor characteristics appear to affect posttraumatic outcome. Together, these characteristics are thought to reflect a general construct sometimes referred to as *stressor magnitude* or *stressor intensity*. March (1993) reviewed 19 studies where intensity of the stressor was examined in terms of PTSD status and found that in 16 of them "stressor magnitude (was) directly proportional to the subsequent risk of developing PTSD" (p. 40). Unfortunately, because many studies in the literature examined the presence or absence of PTSD rather than the intensity of PTSD symptoms, somewhat less can be said about the relationship between stressor magnitude and severity of PTSD. Where intensity is also studied, however, the same relationship tends to occur. Variables that appear to increase stressor magnitude, and thus the likelihood or severity of PTSD, include presence of life threat (e.g., Kilpatrick & Resnick, 1993; Kilpatrick, Saunders, Veronen, Best, & Von, 1987; Resnick et al., 1993), physical injury (e.g., Foy, Resnick, Sipprelle, & Carroll, 1987; Helzer, Robins, & McEvoy, 1987; Kilpatrick et al., 1989; Ursano et al., 1994), extent of combat exposure during war (Card, 1987; Goldberg, True, Eisen, & Henderson, 1990; Helzer et al., 1987; Kulka et al., 1990), witnessing death (Green, Grace, Lindy, Tichener, & Lindy, 1983; Saigh, 1989; Ursano, Fullerton, Kao, & Bhartiya, 1995; Ursano & McCarroll, 1994), degree of violence during sexual assault (Sales, Baum, & Shore, 1984), intentional acts of violence (as opposed to noninterpersonal events; American Psychiatric Association, 1994; Elliott, 1993; Green, Grace, Lindy, Gleser, & Leonard, 1990), grotesqueness of death (Green et al., 1983; Helzer et al., 1987; Zaidi & Foy, 1994), loss of a friend or loved one (Breslau & Davis, 1987; Green, Grace, Lindy, & Gleser, 1990; Shore et al. 1986), unpredictability and uncontrollability (Foa, Zinbarg, & Rothbaum, 1992), and sexual (as opposed to nonsexual) victimization (Breslau et al., 1991).

Although there appears to be a linear relationship between

extent or severity of the stressors and subsequent posttraumatic response, in many cases this association is not especially large in magnitude and applies more to group data than to specific individuals. Thus, for example, two people who underwent the same stressor (e.g., an earthquake or fire) may differ significantly in terms of their posttraumatic response. One individual may develop ASD, followed by PTSD, whereas another may experience few short- or long-term effects. Moreover, two stressors may appear objectively equivalent (e.g., two assaults of seemingly equal severity), yet have remarkably different impacts on those involved.

Beyond any unmonitored differences between apparently equivalent events, this variability in posttraumatic symptomatology generally arises from the three sets of phenomena noted earlier: victim characteristics, subjective appraisal, and social response. Although this analysis focuses more on those phenomena associated with a negative outcome, it is also true that the extent to which a stressor produces major effects is partially a function of the internal and external resources on which the victim can draw (Briere, 1996a). Such resources are often the "flip side" of the negative mediators presented below (e.g., psychological health vs. preexisting distress or disorder, adaptive coping responses vs. use of denial or avoidance, biologic resilience vs. a genetic predisposition toward posttraumatic stress, and a positive social support system vs. social isolation or stigma). These factors not only tend to decrease the effects of potentially traumatic stressors, they are no doubt related to reports of more positive posttraumatic outcomes, such as increased internal capacities or greater empathy (e.g., Affleck, Tennen, Croog, & Levine, 1987; McMillen, Zuravin, & Rideout, 1995; Thompson, 1985).

Victim Variables

As noted by Yehuda and McFarlane (1995), recent research reveals a number of predisposing or antecedent factors that increase the likelihood that a given stressor produces PTSD. In fact, they concluded that the multiplicity of victim-level risk factors for PTSD "appears to call into question the most fundamental assumption of PTSD as potentially occurring in any individual as a result of exposure to traumatic stress" (p. 1708). Although it probably would be erroneous to consider PTSD and related posttraumatic states solely as disorders of inadequate stress tolerance, certain variables clearly are associated with a likelihood of posttraumatic disturbance. These appear to include gender (Breslau et al., 1991; Davidson, Hughes, Blazer, & George, 1991; Green, Grace, Lindy, Gleser, & Leonard, 1990; Shore et al., 1986; Ursano & McCarroll, 1994; Wilkenson, 1983), age (Atkeson, Calhoun, Resick, & Ellis, 1982; McCahill, Meyer, & Fishman, 1979), race (Kulka et al., 1990; Ruch & Chandler, 1983), socioeconomic status (Atkeson et al., 1982; Cohen & Roth, 1987; Davidson et al., 1991; Kulka et al., 1990), previous psychological dysfunction or disorder (Breslau et al., 1991; Helzer et al., 1987; Kulka et al., 1990; McFarlane, 1989), less functional coping styles (Penk, Peck, Robinowitz, Bell, & Little, 1988), family dysfunction and history of psychopathology (Breslau et al., 1991; Davidson et al., 1991; Foy, Sipprelle, Rueger, & Carroll, 1984), and genetic predisposition (Goldberg et al., 1990; True et al., 1993). As noted later in this chapter, however, several of these variables (e.g., sex and race) substantially increase the likelihood of exposure to trauma (especially interpersonal violence) in the first place, thereby potentially confounding risk factors for PTSD with those for experiencing traumatic events.

Also relevant to an individual's response to traumatic stressors is his or her previous history of other aversive events. Generally, those who have experienced previous traumas—perhaps especially if they have not sufficiently processed or resolved them—are prone to exacerbated reactions to current traumas (e.g., Davidson et al., 1991; King, King, Foy, & Gudanowski, 1996; McFarlane, 1989; Roth, Wayland, & Woolsey, 1990). This phenomenon is even more likely if the previous trauma and the current one are similar in important respects. In some instances, the restimulated earlier trauma may summate with the current reaction, thereby producing, in a sense, a "double PTSD," with symptoms from multiple traumas simultaneously present. In other cases, the previous response may interact with the current reaction in such a way that the current response is extreme or especially exacerbated.

As an example of previous trauma effects (as well as their complexity), a number of studies indicate that childhood abuse is a significant risk factor for subsequent victimization as an adult (Alexander & Lupfer, 1987; Briere et al., in press; Cloitre, Tardiff, Marzuk, Leon, & Portera, 1996; Follette, Polusny, Bechtle, & Naugle, 1996; Runtz, 1987; Wind & Silvern, 1992; Wyatt, Newcombe, & Riederle, 1993). Because both types of maltreatment can produce posttraumatic difficulties, current symptomatology in a given individual with childhood and adulthood victimization experiences may represent (a) the effects of the more recent sexual or physical assault, (b) the chronic effects of childhood abuse, (c) the additive effects of childhood abuse and adult assault (e.g., flashbacks to both childhood and adult victimization), or (d) the exacerbating interaction of child abuse and adult assault (e.g., especially severe, regressed, dissociated, or even transiently psychotic responses).

Apropos of the relationship between multiple trauma effects, Zaidi and Foy (1994) reported that individuals with child abuse experiences were considerably more likely to develop PTSD in response to adult combat experiences than were those without a history of abuse. Follette et al. (1996) found that the greater the number of childhood and adult traumas, the greater the amount of immediate trauma-related symptomatology reported. Similarly, incest victims who are then subsequently sexually abused by their therapists may be more likely than those not abused by their therapist to develop especially high levels of posttraumatic disturbance (Magana, 1990; Pope, 1994). Finally, repeated adult traumas may have exacerbating or additive effects; for example, two sexual assaults over a relatively short period of time may produce a compound rape reaction on the second (or last) occasion (Burgess & Holmstrom, 1979; Kilpatrick et al., 1987; Ruch & Leon, 1983). Thus, the client's recent and remote trauma history must be taken into account before symptoms can be attributed solely to a given event.

The various victim variables outlined above, although often found to affect posttraumatic outcome, do not inevitably do so. In fact, the majority of variables described in this section as potential mediators of posttraumatic states have been found in at least one study to have no significant relationship to posttraumatic outcome. Among the potential reasons for this variability may be (a) the characteristics of the sample studied (e.g., race might not emerge as an important mediator of posttraumatic outcome in university students, yet might be an important variable among combat veterans); (b) methodological issues such as restriction of range in the mediating variable or insufficient statistical power (both of which can mask mediator effects); (c) the traumatic event under investigation (e.g., rape vs. a natural disaster); and (d) the instrument or procedure used to assess posttraumatic outcome (e.g., a PTSD scale vs. a diagnostic impression formed during an emergency room evaluation).

Furthermore, not all victim variables operate in the same manner across their entire range, nor is such pretrauma mediation necessarily independent of the specific trauma considered. For example, although it is sometimes found that older people are more susceptible to posttraumatic stress following sexual assault than are younger individuals (e.g., Atkeson et al., 1982), other research suggests that childhood sexual abuse—by virtue of its potential to disrupt development and elaborate over time may be especially traumagenic (Briere, 1992a). Thus, it may be that within adulthood, relative youth provides some protection from sexual victimization, whereas over the life span sexual traumas may be more disruptive and distress producing when they occur in childhood as opposed to later in life. In a similar vein, women are often understood to be more vulnerable to the development of posttraumatic states (e.g., Breslau et al., 1991), but recent research suggests that men may be more likely than women to develop posttraumatic outcomes in response to sexual assault or domestic violence (Briere, Elliott, Harris, & Cotman, 1995; Elliott & Mok, 1995). In such circumstances, it may be better to consider the interaction between these various potential trauma mediators and the trauma in question, as opposed to merely considering mediators across traumatic experiences.

Finally, it appears that several of the risk factors for PTSD noted in this section are also risk factors for traumatic (Criterion A) events per se. Breslau, Davis, and Andreski (1995), for example, found that past exposure to traumatic events, neuroticism, extraversion, and being Black were all predictive of *exposure* to a PTSD-level traumatic event. Similarly, Kessler et al. (1995) found that women in the general population were more likely than men to be exposed to events that, in their study, were most likely to produce PTSD (e.g., rape, childhood sexual abuse, adult physical assault). As a result, at least part of the reason why women and people of color in North American culture have higher rates of PTSD (and other posttraumatic states, such as dissociation) is probably due to social inequities that increase their risk of victimization.

The relationship between risk factors for trauma exposure and PTSD is exemplified by the National Vietnam Veterans Readjustment Study (Kulka et al., 1988) data on race differences for PTSD. In that investigation, the rate of PTSD in veterans was considerably lower for Whites (14%) than for Hispanics (28%) or Blacks (19%). However, Hispanics and Blacks were also more likely to be exposed to higher combat stress than Whites. When differences in level of combat exposure were controlled statistically, the race difference in PTSD between Whites and Blacks disappeared, and the White–Hispanic difference decreased significantly.

In combination, these race and sex data suggest that "vulnerability factors do not increase their influence merely by increasing the likelihood of [PTSD] in persons exposed to environmental stress. The way in which they influence disorder is in part by increasing the likelihood of exposure to adverse experiences" (Breslau et al., 1995, p. 534).

Subjective Reaction

As described earlier, the victim's subjective response to the potential stressor is given substantial credence by *DSM-IV*, to the point that the negative event is not deemed a stressor or trauma unless subjective horror, fear, or helplessness is reported. Although the use of such responses as an inclusion criteria is problematic, there is little doubt that posttraumatic stress is more likely (and perhaps more intense) when the individual reports greater perceived threat or danger (Green, Grace, & Gleser, 1985), helplessness (Frye & Stockton, 1982; Mikulincer & Solomon, 1988), suffering or being upset (Speed, Engdahl, Schwartz, Eberly, & Raina, 1989), terror (Holloway & Fullerton, 1994), and horror or fear (American Psychiatric Association, 1987). Presumably, other negative responses, such as shame and feelings of degradation, also increase the risk of posttraumatic reactions (Wong & Cook, 1992).

The implication of these findings is that those who interpret a traumatic experience more negatively are more at risk for posttraumatic difficulties, partially because of cognitive predispositions (e.g., the tendency to view life events as outside of one's control or to perceive challenges as threats) and partially because of the specific nature of the trauma (i.e., stressors vary according to the extent that they would motivate negative appraisal in most people). Unfortunately, the subjective response criterion is implicitly circular with respect to psychological symptomatology. By requiring that the trauma be associated with reports of obvious, immediate distress, the revised Criterion A becomes, in part, a symptom category rather than a stressor criterion. As a result, its association with other psychological symptoms is nearly assured.

As a result of these factors, the *DSM-IV* subjective response criterion (Criterion A2) probably involves a complex combination of stressor, victim, and outcome characteristics. For example, one individual may respond to an event with horror or helplessness (or both) because the event itself is horrific and overwhelming, whereas another might respond in a similar manner to a much lower magnitude stressor because of negative cognitive schema arising from previous child abuse experiences (McCann & Pearlman, 1990). A third person might report terror regarding a trauma and posttraumatic symptoms following it partially as a function of his or her generally low threshold for emotional reactivity. To compound the complexity of subjective response, such attributions are almost always reported after the traumatic event and its impacts have occurred (March, 1993). As a result, Criterion A2 may be further mediated by phenomena that occur after the event, such as the level of perceived support from others, subsequent negative or positive events, the effects of posttraumatic symptomatology, financial or interpersonal influences, or the results of professional intervention.

Social Response, Support, and Resources

As is reported in the interpersonal violence literature, posttraumatic states may vary in intensity as a function of the level of social acceptance and support that follow the stressor. However, social response to the victim is not independent of trauma characteristics or victim variables. Some traumatic events appear to be more socially acceptable than others (e.g., a victim of a hurricane or earthquake may be seen as more innocent and worthy of compassion than a rape or "gay bashing" victim), and certain trauma survivors are more likely to receive prejudicial treatment than others (e.g., racial minorities, gay men and lesbians, undocumented immigrants, prostitutes, the homeless). This correlation between certain traumas, victims, and social variables may especially produce reports of shame, guilt, or self-hatred in victims of certain crimes (e.g., Chan, 1987; Hardesty & Greif, 1994; Lisak, 1994).

Holding social prejudice constant, however, it appears that posttrauma support by family members, friends, helping professionals, and others can mediate the intensity of posttraumatic stress. Such support includes accepting (vs. rejecting) responses after the trauma disclosure, nurturance from loved ones, an absence of stigmatization or blame by others, and availability of helpers and agencies after a traumatic experience. In this regard, posttrauma social support appears to reduce the effects of disaster (Joseph, Yule, Williams, & Andrews, 1993; Madakasira & O'Brien, 1987), rape (see Steketee & Foa, 1987, for a review), being battered in a domestic relationship (Astin et al., 1993; Kemp, Green, Hovanitz, & Rawlings, 1995; Tan, Basta, Sullivan, & Davidson, 1995), and war and combat (J. A. Fairbank, Hansen, & Fitterling, 1991; Green, Grace, Lindy, Gleser, & Leonard, 1990; Z. Solomon & Mikulincer, 1990; Z. Solomon, Mikulincer, & Waysman, 1991).

Despite this general relationship between support and resilience, Meichenbaum (1994) cited the work of Green (1994) and S. D. Solomon and Smith (1994) in noting that very high levels of social support may interfere with recovery from trauma, especially for women. In this regard, S. D. Solomon and Smith

(1994, p. 188) concluded that "for females, in particular, too much involvement has its costs." Although the basis for this relationship is unclear, one possibility is that women who are actively embedded in social environments are especially required by prevailing gender roles to be supportive of others—a phenomenon that might produce significant role strain when the woman herself needs extensive support from the interpersonal environment.

More generally, some writers (e.g., Hobfoll, Dunahoo, & Monnier, 1995) have suggested that the trauma victim's overall level of social (as well as physical and psychological) resources, before and after the trauma, is an important moderator of his or her response to a given stressor. Hobfoll (1988) noted that traumatic events not only produce stress, they may also precipitate *loss spirals*, wherein the victim becomes more dependent on (and consuming of) social resources after a major stressor, eventually resulting in depletion of these resources, leading to additional stressors, greater vulnerability, and more stress responses. A stressor that affects an entire community (e.g., a natural disaster) may reduce social and physical resources at the same time that it traumatizes individuals, thereby producing more severe reactions (Norris & Thompson, 1995). When the stressor is more confined to the individual level (e.g., a rape or miscarriage), initial social support may decrease if the victim does not recover in a time span expected by the social milieu, leading to victim perceptions of abandonment and rejection and, ultimately, potentially more severe stress responses.

Summary

As suggested in this chapter, the notion of what constitutes a traumatic event is less straightforward than might be envisioned. The initial intent of *DSM-III* was to define stressor characteristics, relatively independent of the victim, that were of sufficient intensity to produce a posttraumatic response in almost anyone. However, recent research suggests that the extent to which an event is traumatic is determined by the interaction between trauma magnitude and a range of victim variables that serve as relative risk factors for the development of posttraumatic stress. This interaction is further mediated by concurrent and postevent variables such as social status, level of social support and resources, and postevent attributions regarding the stressor.

It is clear that the interactionist view of traumatic events has provided greater precision to a clinical understanding of post-traumatic states. Among other things, this perspective increases the likelihood that the clinician will consider the stressor, the individual, and the individual's social network when evaluating the etiology of posttraumatic states. As has been found in other areas of mental health, the interactionist model suggests that posttraumatic stress rarely exists in a vacuum and that the individual's responses to upsetting events must be considered within the context of his or her environment, resources, and life history.

On the other hand, the growing awareness of predisposing and moderating victim variables in PTSD response should not be used to discount the inherently traumatic nature of many events. Regardless of mediating victim and environmental phenomena, some events are intrinsically traumatic—acts of tremendous intrusion that negatively affect almost all of those who experience them. If these stressors are considered traumatic only when they produce a formal *DSM-IV* posttraumatic stress disorder, there is a danger that the pain and lasting distress of many trauma survivors (i.e., those whose symptoms do not fit precisely into existing PTSD criteria) may be discounted. In contrast, the broader view of posttraumatic disturbance offered in the following chapters takes into account various types of disturbance, including subthreshold PTSD, ASD, dissociation, and interpersonal sequelae, and thus implicates a wider range of potentially traumatic events.

2

Symptomatology and Phenomenology

This chapter outlines a variety of posttraumatic presentations, some of which have achieved the status of "disorder" in *DSM-IV*. It should be reiterated, however, that many individuals' trauma-related difficulties do not fit into any specific *DSM-IV* category—in part because of the idiosyncratic relationship between specific traumatic events, those individual and social variables outlined in the previous chapter, and the wide variety of potential posttraumatic outcomes. As a result, it is not especially helpful to define the clinical significance of a given person's posttraumatic disturbance in terms of meeting the criteria for a specific *DSM-IV* stress category.

Described below are two general types of posttraumatic responses: stress disorders and dissociative disorders. Also presented are a sample of culturally bound stress responses and several disorders that may arise from traumatic events in some people. In several instances, these latter posttraumatic responses include patterns of symptomatology that, although frequently described by trauma workers, have not been codified in *DSM-IV*.

The Stress Disorders

DSM-IV recognizes three stress disorders: two as anxiety disorders (acute stress disorder [ASD] and posttraumatic stress disorder [PTSD]) and one as a psychotic disorder (brief psychotic disorder with marked stressor[s] [BPDMS]). In addition, some writers have suggested the existence of "complex PTSD" (J. L. Herman, 1992a, 1992b) and "posttraumatic depression" (e.g., Davidson, 1994), although neither is a *DSM-IV* diagnosis.

Acute Stress Disorder

The diagnosis of ASD is new to *DSM-IV*, although its symptoms have been recognized for some time by trauma-specialized clinicians and researchers (Koopman et al., 1995). For example, many of the symptoms of ASD have been described as the "impact" or "response" phase of a crisis state (see Forster, 1992, for a review). Moreover, the diagnosis *acute stress reaction* has existed for several years in the *International Classification of Diseases and Related Health Problems, Tenth Edition* (ICD-10; World Health Organization, 1993). The primary function of this diagnosis is to recognize and codify those psychological reactions to an acute stressor that occur relatively immediately, as opposed to those that endure long enough to justify a diagnosis of PTSD.

According to *DSM-IV*, "[t]he essential feature of Acute Stress Disorder is the development of characteristic anxiety, dissociative, and other symptoms that occurs within 1 month after extreme traumatic stressor" (American Psychiatric Association, 1994, p. 429). To be categorized as ASD, the relevant symptoms must last for at least 2 days but not exceed 4 weeks in duration. The specific symptoms of ASD are presented in Table 1. This disorder is noteworthy for its similarity to PTSD, except that it may be diagnosed more acutely and includes considerably more dissociative symptomatology. In fact, one recommended name for this new *DSM-IV* diagnostic category was "brief reactive dissociative disorder" (Cardeña, Lewis-Fernandez, Bear, Pakianathan, & Spiegel, 1996). Especially prominent dissociative features may be psychic numbing and detachment, as well as depersonalization or derealization. In some cases, the poor concentration and reduced attention span found in some individuals with ASD may be labeled as dissociative symptomatology when, in fact, it also represents difficulties in cognitive processing associated with hyperarousal.

Table 1

DSM–IV Diagnostic Criteria for Acute Stress Disorder

A. The person has been exposed to a traumatic event in which both of the following were present:
  (1) the person experienced, witnessed, or was confronted with an event or events that involved actual or threatened death or serious injury, or a threat to the physical integrity of self or others
  (2) the person's response involved intense fear, helplessness, or horror.

B. Either while experiencing or after experiencing the distressing event, the individual has three (or more) of the following dissociative symptoms:
  (1) A subjective sense of numbing, detachment, or absence of emotional responsiveness
  (2) a reduction in awareness of his or her surroundings (e.g., "being in a daze")
  (3) derealization
  (4) depersonalization
  (5) dissociative amnesia (i.e., inability to recall an important aspect of the trauma)

C. The traumatic event is persistently reexperienced in at least one of the following ways: recurring images, thoughts, dreams, illusions, flashback episodes, or a sense of reliving the experience; or distress upon exposure to reminders of the traumatic event.

D. Marked avoidance of stimuli that arouse recollections of the trauma (e.g., thoughts, feelings, conversations, activities, places, people).

E. Marked symptoms of anxiety or increased arousal (e.g., difficulty sleeping, irritability, poor concentration, hypervigilance, exaggerated startle response, motor restlessness).

F. The disturbance causes clinically significant distress or impairment in social, occupational, or other important areas of functioning or impairs the individual's ability to pursue some necessary task, such as obtaining necessary assistance or mobilizing personal resources by telling family members about the traumatic experience.

G. The disturbance lasts for a minimum of 2 days and a maximum of 4 weeks and occurs within 4 weeks of the traumatic event.

H. The disturbance is not due to the direct physiological effects of a substance (e.g., drug abuse, a medication) or a general medical condition, is not better accounted for by Brief Psychotic Disorder, and is not merely an exacerbation of a preexisting Axis I or Axis II disorder.

Although not included in *DSM-IV* diagnostic criteria, individuals with ASD sometimes demonstrate labile affect and evidence of psychomotor agitation or retardation. Also present in some instances, especially when the stressor is severe or the victim is especially vulnerable psychologically, may be some near-psychotic symptoms. These may include transient cognitive loosening, briefly overvalued ideas involving persecution or outside control, and auditory hallucinations with trauma-related content. When psychotic features are prominent, however, the appropriate diagnosis is usually brief psychotic disorder, as noted later in this chapter.

Because ASD is a frequent—and thus "normal"—response to overwhelming trauma (Cardeña, Holen, et al., in press), it may be argued that codifying it as a psychiatric disorder is inappropriate. However, the severity of some ASD responses and the disorder's ability (by definition) to impair social and occupational functioning seems to justify its inclusion in *DSM-IV* (Koopman et al., 1995).

Posttraumatic Stress Disorder

PTSD has been available as a diagnosis since *DSM-III*, although some version of its essential premise existed in *DSM-I* ("gross stress reaction") and *DSM-II* ("adjustment reaction of adult life"). It is interesting that the *DSM-I* diagnosis was more similar in many ways to current criteria than the intervening *DSM-II* (Wilson, 1994). As is also true for ASD, *DSM-IV* PTSD criteria require an initiating stressor involving direct personal experience or direct witnessing "of an event that involves actual or threatened death or serious injury or other threat to . . . physical integrity" or learning of similar events that happened to a family member or close associate (American Psychiatric Association, 1994, p. 424). As noted previously, the most substantial changes from *DSM-III-R* to *DSM-IV* are (a) the elimination of the former's description of trauma as outside the range of normal human experience and (b) the new requirement that the victim's response to an aversive event must involve intense fear, helplessness, or horror before it can be considered traumatizing.

As presented in Table 2, the symptoms of PTSD are divided into three clusters: reexperiencing of the traumatic event, avoidance of trauma-relevant stimuli and numbing of general responsiveness, and persistent hyperarousal. Typically, reexperiencing takes the form of flashbacks and intrusive thoughts or memories of the trauma, as well as considerable distress on exposure to internal or external stimuli reminiscent of the event. Avoidance may be cognitive (e.g., "pushing" upsetting thoughts, feelings, or memories out of one's mind), behavioral (e.g., avoiding activities, people, or places that are reminiscent of the stressor), or more dissociative (e.g., amnesia for all or parts of the stressor, detachment, and numbing). Hyperarousal may present as "jumpiness" (a lowered startle threshold), irritability, sleep disturbance, or attention–concentration difficulties. It appears that intrusive–reliving PTSD symptoms are the first to fade over time, whereas avoidant and hyperarousal symptoms typically are more enduring (e.g., McFarlane, 1988).

A diagnosis of PTSD requires 30 days of symptom duration and does not include as much dissociative symptomatology as a diagnosis of ASD. The disorder does not have to appear within a certain time period after the trauma; in some instances "there may be a delay of months, or even years, before symptoms appear" (American Psychiatric Association, 1994, p. 426). ASD often serves as the prodromal diagnosis for PTSD (Koopman et al., 1995). In such instances, the initial dissociative symptoms may have waned, or they may persist but be irrelevant to the later PTSD diagnosis.

As is noted more extensively below under "complex" PTSD, *DSM-IV* acknowledges that the associated features of PTSD—especially following interpersonal victimization—often include not only dissociation, but also cognitive distortions and more Axis II-like difficulties. As a result, a detailed assessment for PTSD also considers these common sequelae.

As might be expected from the frequency of North Americans' exposure to traumatic events (see chapter 1), the lifetime prevalence of PTSD in the general population is significant. Several studies indicate that approximately 7% to 12% of Americans have had (or will have) PTSD at some point in their lifetimes

Table 2

DSM–IV Diagnostic Criteria for Posttraumatic Stress Disorder

A. The person has been exposed to a traumatic event in which both of the following were present:
   (1) the person experienced, witnessed, or was confronted with an event or events that involved actual or threatened death or serious injury, or a threat to the physical integrity of self or others
   (2) the person's response involved intense fear, helplessness, or horror. NOTE: In children, this may be expressed instead by disorganized or agitated behavior.

B. The traumatic event is persistently reexperienced in one or more of the following ways:
   (1) recurrent and intrusive distressing recollections of the event, including images, thoughts, or perceptions. NOTE: In young children, repetitive play may occur in which themes or aspects of the trauma are expressed.
   (2) recurrent distressing dreams of the event. NOTE: In children, there may be frightening dreams without recognizable content.
   (3) acting or feeling as if the traumatic event were recurring (includes a sense of reliving the experience, illusions, hallucinations, and dissociative flashback episodes, including those which occur on awakening or when intoxicated). NOTE: In young children, trauma-specific reenactment may occur.
   (4) intense psychological distress at exposure to internal or external cues that symbolize or resemble an aspect to the traumatic event
   (5) physiological reactivity on exposure to internal or external cues that symbolize or resemble an aspect of the traumatic event

C. Persistent avoidance of stimuli associated with the trauma and numbing of general responsiveness (not present before the trauma), as indicated by three or more of the following:
   (1) efforts to avoid thoughts, feelings, or conversations associated with the trauma
   (2) efforts to avoid activities, places, or people that arouse recollections of the trauma
   (3) inability to recall an important aspect of the trauma
   (4) markedly diminished interest or participation in significant activities
   (5) feelings of detachment or estrangement from others
   (6) restricted range of affect (e.g., unable to have loving feelings)
   (7) sense of foreshortened future (e.g., does not expect to have a career, marriage, children, or a normal life span)

D. Persistent symptoms of increased arousal (not present before the trauma), as indicated by two or more of the following:
   (1) difficulty falling or staying asleep
   (2) irritability or outbursts of anger

(continued)

Table 2 (continued)

---

(3) difficulty concentrating
(4) hypervigilance
(5) exaggerated startle response

E. Duration of the disturbance (symptoms in Criteria B, C, and D) is more than 1 month

F. The disturbance causes clinically significant distress or impairment in social, occupational, or other important areas of functioning.

Specify if: Acute: if duration is less than 3 months
              Chronic: if duration is 3 months or more
Specify if: With Delayed Onset: if onset of symptoms is at least 6 months after the stressor.

Reprinted with permission from the *Diagnostic and Statistical Manual of Mental Disorders, Fourth Edition.* Copyright 1994 American Psychiatric Association.

(e.g., Breslau et al., 1991; Kessler et al., 1995; Norris, 1992), although lower rates (as small has 1%) have been reported in studies with seemingly less sensitive methodologies or assessment instruments (e.g., Davidson et al., 1991; Helzer et al., 1987). Most research suggests that women are approximately twice as likely as men to have PTSD at some point in their lives. For example, Kessler et al. (1995) estimated the lifetime prevalence of PTSD to be 10% for women and 5% for men, which is similar to Breslau et al.'s (1991) estimates of 11% and 6%, respectively.

Brief Psychotic Disorder With Marked Stressor(s)

BPDMS appeared in *DSM-III-R* as brief reactive psychosis. In *DSM-IV*, however, the focus is on the time frame of the disorder, not its etiology; as a result, the clinician can apply the diagnosis when there is no stressor (i.e., brief psychotic disorder without marked stressors) or where stressors exist (BPDMS). Brief psychotic disorder also may be diagnosed with postpartum onset, which may or may not be trauma related. In the case of marked stressors, the precipitating event is generally equivalent to that of ASD or PTSD, although *DSM-IV* is less specific here and more reminiscent of *DSM-III*—noting that "psychotic symptoms develop shortly after and apparently in response to one or more events that, singly or together, would be markedly stressful to almost anyone in similar circumstances in that person's culture" (American Psychiatric Association, 1994, p. 302).

BPDMS is noteworthy because the psychotic episode often begins abruptly and may be quite florid in nature. The diagnosis requires at least one of four psychotic symptoms (delusions, hallucinations, disorganized speech, or grossly disorganized or catatonic behavior), although often several are present simultaneously. Like other acute psychotic episodes, BPDMS is often accompanied by extreme agitation, emotional distress, and confusion. *DSM-IV* lists suicide attempts as an associated feature and notes that those with this disorder may require close supervision. Duration of BPDMS ranges from 1 day to less than 1 month. If symptoms persist beyond this range, the diagnosis changes, often to schizophreniform disorder, mood disorder with psychotic features, or some other more chronic psychotic condition (e.g., schizophrenia).

Although it might appear that BPDMS would be easily discriminable from ASD or PTSD, this is not always the case. Some instances of posttraumatic stress may include what appear to be transient psychotic symptoms (see, e.g., Pinto & Gregory, 1995), and some individuals with BPDMS may present with relatively mild psychotic symptoms and more prominent ASD ones (e.g., pervasive flashbacks and other reliving experiences or substantial dissociative disturbance). Some writers (e.g., Davidson, 1994), in fact, consider BPDMS to be a variant of ASD and PTSD. Moreover, others have suggested that the extreme dissociative responses found in some posttraumatic psychotic reactions justify a combined diagnostic label (e.g., van der Hart, Witztum, & Friedman's, 1993, notion of a *reactive dissociative psychosis*).

Beyond the three formal posttraumatic stress diagnoses, at least two other stress-related syndromes have been suggested by trauma clinicians and researchers. Complicating the issue is a much-debated concern: Given the significant psychiatric comorbidity associated with ASD and PTSD (e.g., Davidson & Fairbank, 1993; Kulka et al., 1990), how does one determine whether a given symptom presentation is due to separate but concurrent disorders (e.g., PTSD with a coexisting psychosis or depression) or, instead, reflects a broader unitary syndrome of which PTSD or ASD symptoms are only a subset? Apropos of this issue, Helzer et al. (1987) found in their general population study that nearly 80% of the individuals with PTSD either had some additional psychiatric disorder or had a lifetime history of some other disorder. Similarly, Kessler et al. (1995, p. 1055) found in a large general population sample that "a lifetime history of at least one other disorder was present in 88.3% of the men with lifetime PTSD and 79% of the women with lifetime PTSD." On the other hand, various writers have made a good case for mixed or complex posttraumatic disorders that includes a number of other cognitive, affective, or interpersonal symptoms (e.g., J. L. Herman, 1992a; Kroll et al., 1989).

Posttraumatic Depression

A number of clinicians and researchers have noted a tendency for posttraumatic and depressive symptoms to arise from the same stressor (e.g., Pickens, Field, Prodromidis, Pelaez-Nogueras, & Hossain, 1995; Wilkenson, 1983; Winfield, George, Swartz, & Blazer, 1990; Yehuda, Kahana, Southwick, & Giller, 1994). Moreover, a number of studies indicate significant comorbidity between PTSD and depression (see Davidson & Foa, 1993, for a review, and a recent general population study by Kessler et al., 1995). Although neither group of studies proves the existence of a posttraumatic depression per se, they do suggest that events severe enough to produce posttraumatic stress can also produce or exacerbate depressive symptoms.

In commenting on the relationship between posttraumatic and depressive symptoms, J. L. Herman (1992a) noted:

> Protracted depression is reported as the most common finding in virtually all clinical studies of chronically traumatized people . . . Every aspect of the experience of prolonged trauma combines to aggravate depressive symptoms. The chronic hyperarousal and intrusive symptoms of PTSD fuse with the vegetative symptoms of depression . . . The dissociative symptoms of PTSD merge with the concentration difficulties of

depression. The paralysis of initiative of chronic trauma com-
bines with the apathy and helplessness of depression. The disruptions in attachments of chronic trauma reinforces the isolation and withdrawal of depression. The debased self image of
chronic trauma fuels the guilty ruminations of depression.
And the loss of faith suffered in chronic trauma merges with
the hopelessness of depression. (p. 382)

When posttraumatic and depressive symptoms arise in tandem
from the same traumatic events, victims often report themes of
loss, abandonment, isolation, and irrevocable life change. Some
victims appear to present with a "dissociative depression" (Briere, 1995c), wherein apathy and numbness appear to combine
with dysthymia to produce a singular level of avoidance and
nonresponsivity. Also evident may be preoccupation with loss,
alternately presenting as cognitive distortions and ruminations,
and intrusive thoughts and images.

Complex PTSD

Perhaps the best known of the non-*DSM-IV* posttraumatic presentations is that of complex PTSD or, when PTSD symptoms
are excluded, "disorder of extreme stress, not otherwise specified" (J. L. Herman, 1992b; van der Kolk, Pelcovitz, & Roth, 1995).
This syndrome is thought to arise from severe, prolonged, and
repeated trauma, almost always of an interpersonal nature. Examples of such stressors are torture, captivity as a prisoner of
war or concentration camp internee, extended child abuse, and
chronic spouse abuse. Such traumatic processes (as opposed to
single catastrophic events) have been associated with a wide variety of subsequent symptoms, including intrusion, avoidance,
and hyperarousal, but also dissociation, somatization, affective
changes (i.e., increased anxiety, depression, anger, and affective
instability), identity and boundary disturbance, affect regulation
problems, chronic involvement in dysfunctional relationships,
and self-injurious or self-defeating behaviors (e.g., Briere, 1992a;
Briere & Runtz, 1987; Browne & Finkelhor, 1986; Dutton & Painter,
1981; Elliott & Briere, 1992; Engdahl & Eberly, 1990; J. L. Herman,
Perry, & van der Kolk, 1989; Kroll et al., 1989; Tennant et al., 1986;
van der Kolk, Perry, & Herman, 1991).

Perhaps one of the more significant components of complex PTSD is its inclusion of symptoms and difficulties often associated with Axis II disorders. By including characterological sequelae, such as disruptions in interpersonal relatedness, identity, boundary, and affect regulation, complex PTSD approximates Horowitz, Weiss, and Marmar's (1987) notion of a posttraumatic personality disorder. It also calls upon recent research regarding the probable relationship between childhood trauma and borderline personality disorder (e.g., Briere & Zaidi, 1989; J. L. Herman et al., 1989). This inclusion of personality features is in relative opposition to the traditional (*DSM*) notion of the distinction between Axis I and Axis II disorders.

Because complex PTSD includes so many divergent symptoms, the diagnostic criteria for such a disorder would be equally complex. The criteria for disorders of extreme stress used in the *DSM-IV* field trials, for example, included the following major categories: alteration in regulation of affect and impulses, alterations in attention or consciousness, somatization, alterations in self-perception, alterations in perception of perpetrator, alterations in relations with others, and alterations in systems of meaning (Pelcovitz et al., in press). As suggested earlier, it is not clear that all those symptoms found to relate to victimization experiences necessarily represent a unitary set of posttraumatic outcomes as opposed to antecedent or comorbid clinical phenomena or preexisting risk factors for posttraumatic stress (Briere, 1992c; Yehuda & McFarlane, 1995). Nevertheless, the central message implicit in complex PTSD is important: It is unlikely that chronic interpersonal violence or maltreatment effects reside exclusively in PTSD or ASD, or even solely on Axis I. Instead, prolonged trauma appears to lead to a variety of symptoms in a number of different areas.

Although the issue of mixed posttraumatic disorders is unlikely to be resolved in the near future, it is likely that different types of stressors, varying on dimensions such as chronicity, intrusion, life endangerment, locus (e.g., intrafamilial vs. environmental), and intentionality (e.g., torture vs. natural disaster), as well as different victim variables, can produce different manifestations of posttraumatic disturbance. Whether these different responses can comprise a single disorder, each require their own diagnosis, or should just be described as associated features of

ASD or PTSD is unclear. However, it is important that the clinician be cognizant of the complexity of posttraumatic response, in order to avoid evaluating formal ASD or PTSD symptoms alone in the traumatized individual.

The Dissociative Disorders

Whereas posttraumatic stress typically involves three related components (i.e., the simultaneous presence of reexperiencing, avoidance, and hyperarousal symptoms), dissociation is a more singular phenomenon at the disorder level. Dissociative amnesia, for example, relates primarily to the psychogenic loss of access to historical information, and dissociative identity disorder reflects the coexistence of multiple personality states or identities in the same individual. Despite this nosological simplicity, however, dissociative response is more complex than might be assumed. In fact, it may be misleading to use the term *dissociation* as though it refers to a single psychological phenomenon. It is likely, for example, that sensory anesthesia differs from psychic numbing and that depersonalization is quite different from fugue states or multiplicity. For this reason, it may be helpful to see the dissociative disorders as relatively separate entities, sharing only the most basic underlying mechanism: the defensive alteration in consciousness or experience as a way to reduce contact with emotionally distressing (typically trauma-related) stimuli (Briere, 1992a). The specific way in which this avoidance is accomplished by a given individual, as well as the extent of that avoidance, determines what dissociative disorder diagnosis he or she receives, if any. Even this definition is subject to debate, however, because it assumes that dissociative phenomena are intrinsically defensive. Cardeña (1994, p. 25) suggested that at least some "[d]issociative alterations may happen automatically and unwittingly, for instance, when an individual encounters even a benign stimulus that is associated with a traumatic event." Ultimately, research may indicate that some forms of dissociation serve defensive psychological functions, whereas others (e.g., numbing) arise as reflexive neurobiological responses to overwhelming stress.

Despite this heterogeneity, some writers offer definitions of dissociation that encompass all its various forms and do not specify function. Nemiah (1993, p. 107), for example, defined dissociation as "the exclusion from consciousness and the inaccessibility of voluntary recall of mental events, singly or in clusters, of varying degrees of complexity, such as memory, sensations, feelings, fantasies, and attitudes." Putnam (1993) stated that dissociation is

> a process that produces a discernible alteration in a person's thoughts, feelings, or actions so that for a period of time certain information is not associated or integrated with other information as it normally or logically would be (West, 1967). This process, which is manifest along a continuum of severity, produces a range of clinical and behavioral phenomena involving alterations in memory and identity that play important roles in normal and pathologic mental processes. (p. 1)

DSM-IV similarly notes that dissociation represents "a disruption in the usually integrated functions of consciousness, memory, identity, or perception of the environment" (American Psychiatric Association, 1994, p. 477).

This wide definitional net is accompanied by controversy regarding the psychophysiologic and functional basis of dissociation. As noted by Steinberg (1994c), "contemporary reviews relate dissociation to a variety of phenomena, including habitual and automatic activities, parallel processing, neuropsychophysiologic state-dependent learning, and divisions between executive and monitoring functions or between mental representations of the self and representations of experience, thought, and action" (pp. 59–60).

Although the mechanisms whereby dissociation may take place are unclear, less in doubt is its frequent posttraumatic etiology. Each of the dissociative disorders (other than the residual category dissociative disorder not otherwise specified), for example, are linked in *DSM-IV* to traumatic events, albeit not always exclusively. Among the stressors related to dissociative symptoms in the trauma literature are child abuse (e.g., Anderson, Yasenik, & Ross, 1993; Briere & Runtz, 1990a; Chu & Dill, 1990; Elliott & Briere, 1992; B. Sanders, McRoberts, & Tollefson,

1989), concentration camp internment (e.g., Jaffe, 1968; Neiderland, 1968), combat (e.g., Branscomb, 1991; Sargant & Slater, 1941; Z. Solomon, Mikulincer, & Bleich, 1988), sexual and physical assaults (e.g., Briere et al., 1995; Elliott & Mok, 1995; Hillman, 1981), natural disasters (e.g., Cardeña & Spiegel, 1993; Valent, 1984; Wilkinson, 1983), and other life-threatening events (e.g., Noyes & Kletti, 1977). This trauma–dissociation relationship probably explains the prominence of dissociative symptoms in ASD and, to a lesser extent, in PTSD.

Because dissociation is a frequent response to trauma, a comprehensive, trauma-relevant diagnostic evaluation must consider dissociative symptoms and disorders as well as posttraumatic ones. Generally, there appear to be five major forms of dissociative disturbance—amnesia, fugue states, derealization, depersonalization, and identity alteration—four of which correspond to modern (*DSM-IV*) diagnoses. Each of these disorders is described briefly below, along with its diagnostic criteria. As was described for posttraumatic stress, however, some victims may present with significant dissociative symptomatology without satisfying diagnostic criteria for a specific dissociative disorder, although they may receive a residual diagnosis of dissociative disorder not otherwise specified.

Dissociative Amnesia

DSM-IV refers to dissociative amnesia as "an inability to recall important personal information, usually of a traumatic or stressful nature, that is too extensive to be explained by normal forgetfulness" (American Psychiatric Association, 1994, p. 478). In *DSM-III* and *DSM-III-R* this disorder was named *psychogenic amnesia*. *DSM-IV* identifies five forms of memory disturbance that may occur in this disorder:

☐ *localized amnesia*, in which "the individual fails to recall events that occurred during a circumscribed period of time . . . (e.g., the uninjured survivor of a car accident in which a family member has been killed may not be able to recall anything that happened from the time of the accident until two days later)" (p. 478);

- □ *selective amnesia*, in which "the person can recall some, but not all, of the events during a circumscribed period of time (e.g., a combat veteran can recall only some parts of a series of violent combat experiences)" (p. 478);
- □ *generalized amnesia*, involving rare circumstances wherein a person has no memory for his or her entire life;
- □ *continuous amnesia*, in which a person is unable "to recall events subsequent to a specific time up to and including the present" (p. 478); and
- □ *systematized amnesia*, involving a "loss of memory for certain categories of information, such as all memories relating to one's family or to a particular person" (p. 478).

A review of medical journals published around World Wars I and II suggests that psychogenic amnesia (then considered primarily a symptom of hysteria) was a broadly accepted concept among combat physicians and was frequently documented in reports of war effects (e.g., Henderson & Moore, 1944; Parfit & Gall, 1944; Sargant & Slater, 1941; Thom & Fenton, 1920; Torrie, 1944). Henderson and Moore (1944), for example, reported that of the first 200 war-related cases admitted to a military hospital for psychiatric reasons, 5% had amnesia for combat-related events. Similarly, Torrie (1944) found that 9% of 1,000 individuals with war-related "anxiety neurosis and hysteria" had symptoms of amnesia. In a study of war stress in 1,000 individuals admitted to a neurological hospital unit, Sargant and Slater (1941) reported that "severe" war stress ("prolonged marching and fighting under heavy enemy action") produced amnesia for war events in 35% of patients, whereas "moderate" stress (e.g., "experiences like periodical dive-bombing at home bases and aerodromes") resulted in amnesia for 13% of patients (p. 758).

Other traumatic events, such as torture, confinement in concentration camps, physical assaults, and rape, also have been linked to dissociative amnesia (see Loewenstein, 1993, for a review). Tromp, Koss, Figueredo, and Tharan (1995) found that, when compared to other unpleasant memories, women's memory of adult rape experiences were significantly "less clear and vivid, contained a less meaningful order, were less remembered, and were less thought and talked about" (p. 607). In a study of trauma and memory in a large sample of the general population,

Elliott (1995) found that individuals reported periods of incomplete or absent memories for a wide variety of traumatic experiences, ranging from war to accidents to instances of sexual or physical assault.

Most recent research in this area, however, has been concerned with amnesia for severe childhood abuse experiences. A number of studies of clinical and nonclinical individuals have found either (a) that a substantial proportion of those who report childhood trauma experiences (especially sexual abuse) also describe periods of partial or complete amnesia for said traumas (Briere & Conte, 1993; Elliott & Briere, 1995; Feldman-Summers & Pope, 1994; J. L. Herman & Schatzow, 1987; Loftus, Polonsky, & Fullilove, 1994; Williams, 1995), or (b) that some individuals with independently established histories of childhood sexual abuse do not report any memory of these experiences during follow-up as adults (Williams, 1994).

Despite such data, some writers (e.g., Loftus & Ketcham, 1994; Ofshe & Watters, 1993) asserted that there is no (or almost no) such phenomenon as psychogenic or dissociative amnesia for childhood traumas. Although there is little doubt that some reports of recovered memories of abuse are invalid, the position of Loftus and others (i.e., that the entire notion of posttraumatic amnesia is a myth) appears to have limited empirical or clinical support. Beyond the literature on stress- and combat-related amnesia, the last three diagnostic and statistical manuals (*DSM-III*, *DSM-III-R*, and *DSM-IV*) have each referred to the existence of dissociative amnesia, with *DSM-IV* noting that amnesia for traumatic events can also occur in ASD, PTSD, and somatization disorder (American Psychiatric Association, 1994, pp. 425, 429, 446).

The existence of dissociative amnesia does not, however, rule out the likelihood of confabulated memory in some instances. Furthermore, as *DSM-IV* noted, "[t]here is currently no method for establishing with certainty the accuracy of [recovered memories] in the absence of corroborative evidence" (p. 481). As a result, the clinician must approach any given report of memory recovery (or any other uncorroborated historical statement) with some level of care, neither ruling in nor ruling out such reports without due consideration of all relevant information.

Finally, the potential presence of amnesia for a traumatic event does not necessarily mean that the memory of that event will ever be recovered. If memory of the event was not encoded initially or was encoded in a fragmentary way, there would be no memory (or coherent version of memory) to retrieve. For example, if an individual was overwhelmed by extreme arousal associated with the trauma, or the event occurred prior to the offset of infantile amnesia, or extreme peritraumatic dissociation interfered with perception and thus encoding, one would not expect memories of the trauma to exist in a coherent form. Implications of this possibility include the likelihood that (a) not all nonorganic amnesia is dissociative; (b) when dissociation is relevant to amnesia, it may occur at the encoding level as well as during retrieval; and (c) not all amnesia is potentially responsive to attempts at memory recovery (e.g., through hypnosis or drug-assisted interviews) during the assessment process.[1]

Dissociative Fugue

As described by *DSM-IV*, dissociative fugue involves "sudden, unexpected travel away from home or one's customary place of daily activities, with (an) inability to recall some or all of one's past. . . . This is accompanied by confusion about personal identity or even the assumption of a new identity" (American Psychiatric Association, 1994, p. 481). Significant symptom-related distress or impairment also must be present.

Contrary to earlier clinical belief, the taking on of a partially or completely new identity, without knowledge of the old one, is relatively uncommon in fugue states (Riether & Stoudemire, 1988). In this regard, *DSM-III-R* probably incorrectly required the assumption of a new identity for a fugue diagnosis, thereby causing fugue sufferers who were amnestic for their past identity but who did not take a new one to be diagnosed with dissociative disorder not otherwise specified (Loewenstein, 1993). Fortunately, as noted in the *DSM-IV* definition, *DSM-IV* does not require the development of a new identity for the fugue diagnosis, thereby improving the coverage of this diagnosis as well as increasing its usage.

---

[1] Aggressive memory recovery techniques may not resolve amnesia during assessment and may lead to inaccurate or confabulated recollections. In addition, inappropriate use of such techniques may be problematic in the treatment of posttraumatic disturbance (Briere, 1996a, 1996b).

As noted in *DSM-IV* and by various authors (e.g., Cardeña et al., 1996; Riether & Stoudemire, 1988), fugue states often begin after a significant trauma or stressful life events. Putnam (1985) suggested that this disorder may be more common during wartime or major natural disasters, perhaps especially those requiring forced relocation. Loewenstein (1993) added that "[f]actors related to avoidance of responsibility may be quite prominent in many of these cases, with sexual indiscretions, legal difficulties, financial problems, or fear of anticipated combat being part of the clinical matrix" (p. 61).

Dissociative Identity Disorder

The most dramatic and currently most controversial of the dissociative disorders is dissociative identity disorder (DID), previously referred to in *DSM-III* and *DSM-III-R* as *multiple personality disorder* (MPD). *DSM-IV* diagnostic criteria for DID include (a) "[t]he presence of two or more distinct identities or personality states (each with its own relatively enduring patterns of perceiving, relating to, and thinking about the environment and self," (b) "[a]t least two of these identities or personality states recurrently take control of the person's behavior," and (c) an "[i]nability to recall important personal information that is too extensive to be explained by normal forgetfulness" (American Psychiatric Association, 1994, p. 487).

Although *DSM-IV* specifies two or more identities, it is not at all uncommon for individuals with DID to report many more personalities, as well as less coherent personality "fragments" (Bliss, 1980; Kluft, 1988; Putnam, Guroff, Silberman, Barban, & Post, 1986). Some DID patients report considerable conflict between personalities, with some personalities seeking to take control from others, although this is not inevitably the case (Kluft, 1993). It is generally believed that different personalities within a given "system" may serve different positive and negative functions, such as, for example, the expression of unacceptable thoughts and feelings (Ross, 1989). DID patients typically report an amnestic barrier between at least some personalities, such that one personality may have little or no knowledge of the existence of one or more other personalities (Putnam, 1989;

Steinberg, Rounsaville, & Cicchetti, 1990). Although *DSM-III-R* did not require the presence of amnesia, *DSM-IV* reintroduced it as a diagnostic criterion. Because different identities are thought to take control at different times, this amnestic barrier often results in any given personality (especially the primary or "host" personality) reporting blanks in memory, possession of items that they do not recall collecting or owning, and other indicators of discontinuous awareness (Loewenstein, 1993).

Of the various disorders, DID has been most frequently linked to extreme abuse during childhood, often severe sexual abuse (e.g., Coons & Milstein, 1986; Putnam, Guroff, Silberman, Barban, & Post, 1986; Ross, Norton, & Wozney, 1989). For example, Ross and his colleagues (Ross, Anderson, Heber, & Norton, 1990) examined structured interview data from 102 patients with MPD across four different sites in North America and found that 95% of them reported instances of childhood sexual or physical abuse (or both). Other childhood traumas also have been implicated in DID, including death or loss of a significant other and witnessing the intentional killing of an individual (Kluft, 1993).

As noted, the diagnosis of DID (previously MPD) is relatively controversial in mental health circles (Ross, 1989). A number of writers either question the validity of DID as a naturally occurring phenomenon, dispute the connection between DID and child abuse (especially reports of ritualistic abuse), or suggest that at least some cases are iatrogenically associated with suggestibility during treatment or exposure to mass media coverage of the issue (Aldridge, 1994; Weissberg, 1993). Although this issue is unlikely to be resolved to all parties' satisfaction, it seems likely that (a) DID can occur as a natural psychological phenomenon, although its exact incidence is unknown; (b) it frequently (but probably not inevitably) arises from extended and extreme childhood trauma; and (c) poorly conducted psychological diagnosis and treatment can result in incorrect DID diagnoses and, as a result of the heightened suggestibility found among some extreme dissociators, iatrogenically induced pseudo-DID. Some such errors can be detected in a competent diagnostic examination, however, because the basis for incorrect diagnoses can be revisited and iatrogenic or factitious symptom production may unsuccessfully mimic true DID (Coons & Milstein, 1994). As is noted in chapter 5, the use of validated structured interviews for dissociative disorders may improve diagnostic accuracy in this area.

Depersonalization Disorder

DSM-IV defined the central feature of depersonalization disorder as follows:

> [p]ersistent or recurring episodes of depersonalization characterized by a feeling of detachment or estrangement from oneself. . . . The individual may feel like an automaton or as if he or she is living in a movie. There may be a sensation of being an outside observer of one's mental processes, one's body, or parts of one's body. Various types of sensory anesthesia, lack of affective response, and a sensation of lacking control of one's actions, including speech, are often present. The individual with Depersonalization Disorder maintains adequate reality testing. (American Psychiatric Association, 1994, p. 488)

Also present may be feelings of derealization, *déja vu* experiences, and perceptual distortions, wherein objects or body parts appear to change shape or size. Sensory anesthesia often presents as feeling "dead" or "wooden." Because depersonalization is an ego dystonic, often frightening symptom, panic attacks and extreme anxiety may accompany such episodes. In other instances, panic attacks may trigger depersonalization rather than arise from it.

Feelings of depersonalization are very common in North American society, especially among psychiatric patients (Brauer, Harrow, & Tucker, 1970; Cattell & Cattell, 1974), and only reach disorder level when such symptoms are persistent and cause clinically significant distress or impairment. Actual depersonalization disorder is therefore less frequent, although various writers have suggested that it is often underdiagnosed (Edwards & Angus, 1972; Moran, 1986). Steinberg (1994a, p. 82) has suggested a number of reasons why this may occur, including (a) the relative absence of valid assessment tools that are sensitive to depersonalization phenomena, (b) the wide variety of depersonalization symptoms, (c) the overlap between depersonalization disorder symptoms and those of other disorders (e.g., schizophrenia, depression, and seizure disorders), and (d) the fact that most psychiatric patients do not refer to depersonalization symptoms in their presenting complaints.

Depersonalization and depersonalization disorder often arise from traumatic or highly stressful experiences (e.g., Noyes & Kletti, 1977; Shilony & Grossman, 1993), although other etiologies (e.g., secondary to drug use or panic attacks) are also possible. *DSM-IV*, for example, noted that brief episodes of depersonalization are often precipitated by severe stress or exposure to life-threatening danger (American Psychiatric Association, 1994, p. 489). Traumas reported to produce depersonalization symptoms or depersonalization disorder include vehicular accidents and other immediately life-threatening experiences (Noyes, Hoenk, Kuperman, & Slyman, 1977; Noyes & Kletti, 1977), child abuse (e.g., Sharpe, Tarrier, & Rotundo, 1994), hostage experiences (e.g., R. K. Siegel, 1984), natural disasters (e.g., Cardeña & Spiegel, 1993; Wilkenson, 1983), and the death of one's child (e.g., Hazzard, Weston, & Gutterres, 1992).

Dissociative Disorder Not Otherwise Specified

DDNOS is a residual diagnostic category, intended for use when an individual presents with demonstrable dissociative symptoms but does not satisfy criteria for any specific disorder. This use of residual categories is common in *DSM-III-R* and *DSM-IV*; in the dissociative area, however, it is especially invoked. The frequent use of DDNOS appears to represent at least three phenomena: (a) the wide variety of dissociative responses demonstrated by traumatized individuals, only some of which are codified in current diagnostic systems; (b) potential problems with some diagnostic criteria, such that numerous individuals with major dissociative difficulties do not quite meet the requirements of the disorder; and (c) the fact that, in the absence of specific diagnostic criteria, this label can be applied whenever a given clinician believes a dissociative disorder is present.

Whereas the first scenario may be unavoidable, given the need for reasonable limits on the number of diagnoses contained in

DSM-IV, the other two suggest the need for further adjustment in diagnostic criteria or clinical practice. The second scenario, for example, occurred in response to problems with the *DSM-III-R* definition of dissociative fugue disorder. As noted earlier, *DSM-III-R* required that the person assume a new identity upon his or her dissociated travels to a new location. In reality, however, many individuals with fugue symptoms do not take on new identities; instead, they report amnesia (or substantial confusion) regarding their current identity. As a result, many of those who would be diagnosed as having a fugue disorder in *DSM-IV* received a diagnosis of DDNOS in *DSM-III-R*.

Other, more current phenomena that increase the likelihood of a DDNOS diagnosis are (a) the absence of a derealization disorder in *DSM-IV*, such that those with derealization but not depersonalization must be diagnosed as having DDNOS (American Psychiatric Association, 1994, p. 490); and (b) the *DSM-IV* requirement that individuals with DID have two or more distinct identities "each with its own relatively enduring pattern of perceiving, relating to, and thinking about the environment and self" (p. 487). As noted by Ross (1989, p. 80), seemingly DID-like clients who present with multiple, indistinct, or fragmentary identities (none of which have sufficiently enduring patterns of perception, relationship, and thought) "are not at all atypical, and are probably common." Currently, such individuals receive the diagnosis DDNOS.[2]

Also potentially problematic is a third issue, that of the subjectivity of the DDNOS diagnosis. Because there are no formal diagnostic criteria for this category (only that the person have a "disorder" [undefined] "in which the predominant feature is a dissociative symptom" [American Psychiatric Association, 1994, p. 490]), clinical impressions become the basis for diagnosis. Although such subjectivity need not result in incorrect diagnoses, the risk of arbitrary diagnostic decision making is obviously higher for this category.

---

[2]This is not always a negative outcome, however; the use of DDNOS circumvents the premature or inappropriate use of the DID diagnosis and thus is less likely to convince the suggestible client that he or she has "multiple personalities" when, in fact, there are not multiple, distinct ego states (J. Armstrong, personal communication, February 14, 1996).

Culture-Bound Stress Responses

As indicated in chapter 1, posttraumatic presentations are influenced by a variety of individual and environmental variables. As a result, people from different cultures or subcultures may experience trauma and express posttraumatic symptoms differently than do members of mainstream North American culture. Stated in reverse, it may not always be helpful to insist on classical North American notions of posttraumatic stress and dissociation when evaluating traumatized members from other cultures (Chakraborty, 1991; Friedman & Jaranson, 1994). For example, it appears that individuals from non-North American or European societies "often fail to meet PTSD diagnostic criteria because they lack avoidant/numbing symptoms despite the presence of reexperiencing and arousal symptoms" (Marsella, Friedman, Gerrity, & Scurfield, 1996, p. 533). Furthermore, in many cultures, classic PTSD symptoms are often accompanied by more somatic and dissociative symptoms than are found in North American groups (Marsella, Friedman, & Spain, 1996).

Growing clinical awareness that not all posttraumatic stress responses are captured by the PTSD diagnosis, especially in non-North American cultures, has lead to the concept of *culture-bound stress responses*. It should be noted, however, that PTSD itself should be considered culture-bound to some extent, because it probably best applies to North Americans. This does not mean, of course, that PTSD does not occur in people from other societies (see, e.g., Durkin, 1993; Guarnaccia, Canino, Rubio-Stipec, & Bravo, 1993; Kroll et al., 1989; Mollica et al., 1987); it means only that some symptoms of posttraumatic stress may vary according to culture.

Appendix I of *DSM-IV* lists several culture-bound syndromes that appear to involve dissociation, somatization, and anxiety-related stress responses. Among these are *attaques de nervios, dhat, latah, nervios, pibloktoq, shin-byung,* and *susto,* although Kirmayer (1996) questioned whether *latah* and *pibloktoq* should be in this list. In several of these syndromes, it is not clear whether an acute stressor can produce the syndrome in question, and thus these illnesses may or may not be posttraumatic stress responses. However, three of these syndromes are generally understood to be posttraumatic, and they are briefly described below. Although each of these is found among Hispanic populations, there is little doubt that culture-bound stress syndromes occur in a variety of world locales. For example, *DSM–IV* (pp. 482, 845–849) notes a variety of culture-specific disorders from Asian, Western Pacific, Inuit, and Native American societies (e.g., *grisi siknis, zar, frenzy*, and *amok*) that appear to have significant dissociative features, although they are not necessarily seen as stress responses in their cultures of origin.

Attaques de Nervios

This disorder is most commonly described as occurring in Puerto Rico (e.g., Canino et al., 1987; Hough, Canino, Abueg, & Gusman, 1996), although it is also prevalent in other Latin American, Latin Caribbean, and Latin Mediterranean countries (American Psychiatric Association, 1994). Triggering stressors for *attaques* include automobile accidents, funerals, family arguments, natural disasters such as earthquakes or floods, or hearing of or observing the death of a family member. In Guarnaccia et al.'s (1993) study of a Puerto Rico flood and mudslide disaster, for example, 16% of their sample reported symptoms characteristic of *attaques de nervios*. Typical symptoms of this disorder are crying, trembling, heart palpitations, intense heat rising from the chest to the head (often referred to as *calor*), followed by (in some cases) shouting or physical aggression, convulsions, and loss of consciousness. Amnesia for the *attaque* is typically reported.

Nervios

Although sometimes confused with *attaques de nervios* by North American clinicians, *nervios* incorporates a much wider (and potentially less extreme) group of symptoms and sometimes is used to refer to an individual's general tendency to respond to stressors with anxiety and somatization. The stressors thought to produce *nervios* are often less acute (e.g., chronic family dysfunction) than with *attaques*, and some etiologies of this response may not be related to a stressful event at all. In other instances, however, *nervios* appears to reflect chronic anxiety, dissociation, and somatization that is less extreme than *attaques de nervios* but that nevertheless arises from an acute stressor (e.g., interpersonal victimization, earthquakes). As noted by the *DSM-IV*, *nervios*

> includes a wide range of symptoms of emotional distress, somatic disturbance, and inability to function. Common symptoms include headaches and "brain aches," irritability, stomach disturbances, sleep difficulties, nervousness, easy tearfulness, inability to concentrate, trembling, tingling sensations, and *mareos* (dizziness with occasional vertigo-like exacerbations). . . . Nervios is a very broad syndrome that spans the range from cases free of a mental disorder to presentations resembling Adjustment, Anxiety, Depressive, Dissociative, Somatoform, or Psychotic disorders. (American Psychiatric Association, 1994, p. 847)

Susto

Also referred to as *espanto, espasmo, pasmo, perdida del alma, miedo,* or *saladera,* this disorder is most typically found in Mexico, Central America, and South America. The precipitant is often a frightening or life-threatening event thought to cause the soul to leave the body (hence its frequent English translation as *soul loss*). Typical symptoms are anxiety and hyperarousal leading to appetite loss, sleep disturbance, frequent startle responses, and constant worrying, as well as depressive symptoms such as chronic sadness, decreased motivation, and decreased self-worth. Multiple somatic complaints, including headaches, muscle aches, stomachaches, and diarrhea, also may be present (American Psychiatric Association, 1994; Hough et al., 1996; Simons & Hughes, 1993).

Each of these culture-bound symptom clusters occur not only in their nations-of-origin, but also in refugees and immigrants from these countries. As a result, clinicians in North America may encounter these specific stress responses, although they may not recognize them as such.

Disorders Sometimes Associated With Traumatic Experience

In addition to the disorders and stress responses outlined in previous sections, several *DSM-IV* diagnoses are sometimes, although not inevitably, associated with traumatic experience. Three of these disorders—conversion disorder, somatization disorder, and borderline personality disorder—are outlined in this section. It should be noted, however, that other disorders (e.g, some anxiety, depressive, and psychotic disorders) may be triggered or exacerbated by traumatic or stressful experiences.

Conversion Disorder

The diagnosis *conversion disorder* is applied when an individual experiences "[o]ne or more symptoms or deficits affecting voluntary motor or sensory function that suggest a neurological or other general medical condition" but, in fact, "[p]sychological factors are judged to be associated with the symptom or deficit because the initiation or exacerbation of symptoms or deficit is preceded by conflicts or stressors" and the symptom(s) cannot be fully explained medically (American Psychiatric Association, 1994, p. 457). Examples of conversion symptoms are any of the following, if psychogenic in origin: seizures, paralysis, aphonia, difficulty swallowing, blindness, deafness, "stocking-glove" anesthesia, and hallucinations.

Until *DSM-III*, conversion symptoms were considered part of hysteria, and thus more closely aligned with dissociation. *DSM-III*, *DSM-III-R*, and *DSM-IV* consider conversion disorder to be a somatoform disorder, undoubtedly because its primary symptoms are somatic in nature. Nevertheless, dissociative disorders are listed as associated mental disorders of conversion in *DSM-IV*, and the logic of moving conversion symptoms into the somatoform arena remains controversial (e.g., Nemiah, 1993; Ross, 1989).

DSM-IV noted that conversion disorder may occur after a major stressor (e.g., combat or the recent death of a significant other), although it is also thought to arise from extreme psychological conflict (usually with associated guilt) and the availability of secondary gain. When trauma appears to be contributory, the stressors most frequently implicated in the clinical literature are child abuse (e.g., Anderson et al., 1993; Eisendrath, Way, Ostroff, & Johanson, 1986) and combat (e.g., Mansour, 1987; Neill, 1993).

As noted by Kirmayer (1996), conversion symptoms appear to vary by culture and may reflect ethnocultural models or explanations for psychological disorder. Moreover, physical distress or disability may serve as a more acceptable way of expressing posttraumatic stress in cultures where psychological symptoms have less legitimacy. Whatever their cultural functions, conversion responses are considerably more frequent in some societies than in North America (Leff, 1988) and appear to be more common among immigrants or refugees seeking medical or psychological services.

Somatization Disorder

Somatization disorder is noteworthy because it consists of a wide variety of symptoms whose only commonality is their somatic focus and the fact that they either cannot be explained medically or are more intense than would be expected from their medical etiology. According to *DSM-IV*, the diagnosis of somatization disorder requires that the individual endorse four pain symptoms (e.g., headaches, backaches), two gastrointestinal symptoms (e.g., nausea, vomiting), one non-pain-related sexual symptom (e.g., sexual dysfunction, sexual indifference), and one pseudoneurological symptom (e.g., paralysis, amnesia). The diagnosis of a related residual disorder, undifferentiated somatoform disorder, requires only one (or more) physical complaint for which no medical explanation can be found or for which the symptom(s) exceed the expected intensity. This second diagnosis, however, also requires that the symptom(s) lasts for at least 6 months. The symptoms of both somatization disorder and undifferentiated somatization disorder symptoms must be neither factitious nor feigned.

Although potentially caused by a variety of factors, somatization has been linked on multiple occasions to a history of childhood maltreatment, especially sexual abuse (Briere & Runtz,

1988; Drossman et al., 1990; Loewenstein, 1990; Morrison, 1989; Toomey, Hernandez, Gittelman, & Hulka, 1993; E. A. Walker, Katon, Roy-Byrne, Jemelka, & Russo, 1993; E. A. Walker, Katon, Hansom, Harrop-Griffiths, et al., 1992), as well as other traumatic events, such as war, disaster, or adult assault (Escobar, Canino, Rubio-Stipec, & Bravo, 1992; Hauff & Vaglum, 1994; Kimerling & Calhoun, 1994; Somasundaram & Sivayokan, 1994; Ursano et al., 1995). The reason for a link between trauma and somatization is unclear, although it may be related to the effects of sustained autonomic arousal on organ systems especially responsive to sympathetic activation and posttraumatic perceptions of vulnerability (with subsequent hypervigilance) in those areas of the body where the trauma was most salient (e.g., chronic pelvic pain in sexual abuse survivors; Briere, 1992b).

Somatic symptoms also may represent idioms of distress in some cultures, such that physical symptoms function as ways to express nonphysical concerns (Nichter, 1981). Kirmayer (1996) noted that "this idiomatic use of symptoms allows people to draw attention to and metaphorically comment on the nature of their quandaries. When reduced to symptoms of a disorder [by clinicians], this meaningful personal and social dimension of distress may be lost" (p. 133). In this regard, and similar to conversion responses, somatic symptoms may allow communication of posttraumatic distress and symptomatology within cultures where psychological symptoms either are unacceptable or are not easily expressed. In such instances, traditional Western interpretations of somatization as neurotic or conflict based may be somewhat misleading.

Borderline Personality Disorder

DSM-IV defines *borderline personality disorder* as a chronic disturbance in which there is "a pervasive pattern of instability of interpersonal relationship, self-image, and affects, and marked impulsivity beginning by early adulthood and present in a variety of contexts" (American Psychiatric Association, 1994, p. 650). It describes the primary symptoms of this disorder as follows: (a) "frantic efforts to avoid real or imagined abandonment"; (b) "a pattern of unstable and intense interpersonal relationships" (e.g., idealization, manipulation, and marked shifts in attitude);

(c) "identity disturbance: markedly and persistently unstable self image or sense of self"; (d) "impulsivity in at least two areas that are potentially self damaging," (e.g., spending, sex, substance use, reckless driving, binge eating); (e) "recurrent suicidal behavior, gestures, or threats, or self-mutilating behavior," (f) "affective instability due to a marked reactivity of mood"; (g) "chronic feelings of emptiness"; (h) "inappropriate, intense anger or difficulty in controlling anger"; and (i) "transient, stress-related paranoid ideation or severe dissociative symptoms" (p. 654).

Most traditional theories of borderline development (e.g., Kernberg, 1976; Masterson, 1976; Rinsley, 1980) trace the genesis of this disorder to dysfunctional parental (primarily maternal) behavior in the first several years of the child's life. They assert that children who become borderline are rewarded for enmeshed dependency and punished (often through abandonment) for independence. Such children (and later adults) are thought to be arrested at a pre-Oedipal level, such that they are unable to form the capacity for healthy object relations.

Although child rearing of this nature might be expected to produce significant disturbance in children, there is little empirical support for this model vis-à-vis borderline symptom development. In contrast, several studies indicate that severe childhood abuse and neglect is, in fact, associated with later borderline personality disorder (e.g., Briere & Zaidi, 1989; Bryer et al., 1987; J. L. Herman et al., 1989; Ogata et al., 1990; Paris, Zweig, & Guzder, 1994; Weaver & Clum, 1993). Thus, consistent with J. L. Herman's (1992a) formulation of complex PTSD, it is likely that the early developmental disruption associated with pervasive childhood trauma (i.e., chronic sexual or physical abuse) and parental acts of omission (e.g., neglect-related emotional deprivation) may later produce borderline personality in some people (Briere, 1996a; van der Kolk, Hostetler, Herron, & Fisler, 1994).

Summary

This chapter has outlined a number of disorders that are either intrinsically associated with traumatic events or that may arise from traumatic events or processes. Several newer trauma-related diagnoses also were presented, although these latter entities have yet to be fully accepted or codified by the general mental health community. Also considered were several stress-related disorders that are prevalent in other cultures, although not often seen in mainstream North American–European society; three of them were described.

As the role of trauma in psychological disorder becomes more widely understood by practitioners and researchers, other diagnoses may be found to relate, in some instances, to traumatic stress. In this regard, trauma can be etiologically associated with mental disorders in at least two different ways: by directly producing posttraumatic responses (e.g., as in PTSD, ASD, or the dissociative disorders) or by triggering an already latent or prepotent process into a visible disorder (e.g., acute exacerbations of schizophrenia, panic disorder, or depression secondary to a major stressor).

It is likely that as psychological understanding of stress responses becomes more sophisticated, the very notion of dichotomously present-or-absent disorders may be seen as an oversimplification in some cases. Especially with regard to PTSD-related phenomena, it is probably more accurate to refer to *posttraumatic spectrum responses* of various types: responses that—if determined to be of sufficient severity or frequency—somewhat arbitrarily meet diagnostic criteria and become a "disorder." As noted earlier, formal diagnostic status is not always a good measure of the clinical importance (or incapacitating nature) of a given posttraumatic state.

Fortunately, although the exact etiologic pathway to various diagnoses may not be fully known and the longstanding controversy between symptom continua and discrete disorders has yet to be settled, the clinician need not resolve these issues in order to assess potentially posttraumatic states. As noted in later chapters, the evaluator's responsibility is to assess the current level and configuration of symptomatology presented by the client, determine whether his or her self-reported (or otherwise determined) history appears to contain traumatic events that could contribute to or produce such symptoms, consider the relative contribution of mediating risk factors, and make hypotheses about potential links between these two phenomena. Although a

DSM-IV diagnosis may arise from this process, in some cases it will not; the symptomatology—although potentially of clinical import—may be too diverse or of insufficient intensity or frequency to justify a formal *DSM* label. Furthermore, and as discussed in the next chapter, in many cases the examiner cannot assert with absolute certainty that a given disorder or symptom pattern is directly and exclusively related to a specific traumatic event.

Nevertheless, posttraumatic states are relatively common; often arise from events that trigger judicial, clinical, or compensatory interventions from society (and thus require detailed evaluation); and yet may be overlooked by the clinical evaluator who has insufficient information on posttraumatic responses. In the remainder of this book I address the various issues that should be considered if an accurate and meaningful psychological assessment is to be made.

3

Critical Issues in Trauma-Relevant Assessment

Successful psychological assessment of posttraumatic states, whether by diagnostic interview or formal psychological testing, typically includes the following characteristics: a neutral or positive, nonintrusive evaluation environment, inquiry that extends beyond the detection of trauma symptoms alone, awareness that clients may underreport or overreport traumatic events and symptoms, and an understanding of potential constraints on the interpretation of trauma-relevant psychological assessment data. Also considered in this chapter are the effects of assessor countertransference on the client (and, thereby, the test data), the occasional need to stabilize the client who is overwhelmed by the testing stimuli or environment, and the limits of evaluator testimony in the courtroom. These issues are of considerable importance, because they affect the ultimate validity and usefulness of the assessment process.

Approach to Assessment

Because trauma victims, by definition, have been exposed to danger and intrusion, they occasionally approach the assessment process with trepidation, if not distrust. In instances of recent or especially overwhelming trauma, victims may experience psychological evaluation as yet another component of the traumatic event itself and view interviewers as additional stressors. For example, crisis workers occasionally find that their attempts to do initial mental status evaluations and triage with victims of natural disasters are perceived by some victims as intrusive, bureaucratic, or even malignant.

In fact, the assessment process is inherently stressful for some victims (e.g., Litz, Penk, Gerardi, & Keane, 1992). The request that an individual describe (and thereby recall) traumatic events can reactivate upsetting memories and painful affects, producing more distress in someone who is already traumatized. The assessment setting may also restimulate posttraumatic stress to the extent that it resembles or recapitulates the original injurious event (e.g., Vesti & Kastrup, 1995). For example, victims of political torture may sharply fear what they view as interrogation by authority figures (including medical personnel), adult survivors of childhood abuse may expect betrayal or violation rather than assistance, and rape victims may experience renewed terror if evaluated by someone in some way similar to the rapist (e.g., someone of the same sex, nationality, or ethnicity as the assailant).

In some sense, the assessor is constrained by a psychological version of the uncertainty principle. In physics, observation of an event inevitable changes that event; similarly, assessment of trauma may temporarily stress the client's internal resources and alter his or her current state. The skilled evaluator will take this reactive dimension of trauma assessment into account, so that the client is not unduly upset by the interview and the resulting assessment data are not contaminated by the client's negative reactions to assessment or the assessor.[1] In some instances, this may mean that certain psychological tests are not administered until the victim is more stable and less distressed, whereas in others

---

[1] A classic example of how this dynamic can go awry is in forensic evaluations where the examiner appears unnecessarily distant and skeptical, is excessively abrupt or intrusive with questions, or is (ironically) too invasively sympathetic regarding assumed traumatic experience. In response, the interviewee may become avoidant (e.g., nondisclosing or dissociative) or restimulated (e.g., angry or cognitively disorganized), ultimately leading to an inaccurate psychological report regarding his or her history or current psychological state.

even a trauma-based mental status exam or detailed description of the traumatic event may be delayed. Despite the sometimes pressing need to acquire assessment data from the victim, the ultimate issue is the victim's continuing well-being and the importance of avoiding any further harm.

For these reasons, the assessing clinician must strive even more than usual to provide a manifestly safe testing environment and work to develop as much rapport with the client as possible (Armstrong, 1995). Among other things, this requires that the evaluator be sensitive to the client's current situation and level of functioning, pace the interview so that the client is not overwhelmed by questions or demands for information, and briefly explain testing procedures in advance. More generally, the clinician must strive to find a psychological "place" vis-à-vis the traumatized client that is neither so distant as to be nonempathic or uncaring nor so close as to be intrusive or threatening.

It is also generally a good idea to inform the individual beforehand that assessment may be somewhat stressful—without, of course, implying that it is intrinsically injurious. In this way, the victim is able to give informed consent and is to some extent prepared for possible assessment-related distress. Additionally, the examiner may wish to consider postevaluation debriefing, wherein the victim is invited to discuss, process, and place into context the impacts of talking about distressing events.[2]

Despite the examiner's best efforts, the severely traumatized client occasionally may react negatively to the assessment process. This may occur either because (a) assessment stimuli (e.g., test materials or the examiner's physical or psychological characteristics) have restimulated posttraumatic distress in an otherwise

---

[2] Despite its potential stressfulness, even a brief or superficial discussion of prior traumatic events has been shown to decrease psychological symptoms and increase indices of physical health (Murray & Segal, 1994; Pennebaker, Kiecolt-Glaser, & Glaser, 1988; Petrie, Booth, Pennebaker, Davison, & Thomas, 1995). Brabin and Berah (1995) reported that the minority of participants in their study who found trauma questions stressful also described positive impacts of such inquiry. Thus, the potentially stressful events of trauma-focused assessment should not be seen as necessarily enduring and may be psychologically helpful in the longer term.

seemingly stable individual, or (b) especially in acute trauma settings, the client is already sufficiently destabilized that any additional psychic demands exacerbate his or her posttraumatic state. In either instance, the client may demonstrate evidence of increased stress, such as excitability, anger, tangentiality, withdrawal, flashbacks, or dissociative responses.

In such cases further assessment may be contraindicated, and the primary task becomes clinical stabilization. Clinical experience suggests that recompensation may be aided by reduced stimulation, reassurance, and grounding. First, the evaluator typically halts the assessment process and refrains from further stressful inquiries or statements. Especially important in this regard is that additional posttraumatic restimulation by trauma-relevant cues occur as little as possible. If evaluation takes place near the traumatic event (e.g., near a disaster site or in an emergency setting where other victims are visible), the clinician may choose to move the client to a less stimulating environment. If the upsetting stimulus is a Rorschach card or psychological inventory, the examiner may remove such materials so that direct restimulation is reduced and symbolic termination of the upsetting event may occur. If the examiner's characteristics (e.g., sex, ethnicity) restimulate the victim by virtue of their similarity to those of a trauma perpetrator, he or she may seek another evaluator who does not have these characteristics. If this is done, the change and the reason for the change usually should be explained to the client in a nonthreatening and nondemeaning manner.

Reassurance and grounding are also important parts of de-escalating assessment-related distress or disturbance. The client is typically reminded of the safety of the testing environment, and his or her emotional reactions are framed as reasonable given the immediate situation. During this process, the test administrator's voice and demeanor should be calming and reassuring. When necessary, the client's attention may be drawn to the concrete aspects of the immediate environment in such a way as to distract from escalating internal states. When the client has returned to a more stable state, testing may be carefully reinitiated or delayed to a later point in time.

Goals of Trauma-Relevant Assessment

Assuming that assessment can occur without overstressing the victim, a central issue concerns the actual goal of such evaluation. For example, in the assessment of a rape victim, is the ultimate intent to determine (a) whether the victim's current symptoms are directly attributable to the rape, (b) whether the victim is experiencing posttraumatic distress or disorder, or (c) the extent to which the victim is suffering from any sort of psychological disturbance, including posttraumatic stress?

Although the first option might seem important, it is often the case that a given psychological presentation cannot be absolutely linked to a prior traumatic event. Even if the victim reports definitive symptoms of ASD or acute PTSD, it is possible that some other traumatic experience produced some or all of the symptoms in question. Even more problematic are chronic PTSD, dissociative, or personality-level symptoms, because the etiology of these events may lie in the distant past. In those instances when a cause–effect relationship must be specifically evaluated (e.g., in some forensic situations), important issues include the temporal sequence (i.e., did the posttraumatic disturbance only occur after the traumatic event, in the absence of other intervening traumas) and the nature of the intrusive symptoms (e.g., does the client report flashbacks or intrusive images and memories of the specific rape experience in question). If these two conditions are met, and the validity of the test data can be assured, the clinician may be able to hypothesize that the rape, in fact, probably produced the posttraumatic symptoms exhibited by the victim.

More typically, however, the traumatic event may be long past (e.g., in childhood or at some point earlier in life), the symptoms may be less clear-cut (e.g., dissociative symptoms or depression), and other negative life events (e.g., more recent traumas or victimization experiences) may have intervened between the hypothesized stressor and the observed clinical state. In such cases, and in the absence of other relevant data, the evaluating clinician may not be able to link specific posttraumatic symptoms to a given traumatic event. Instead, many assessors are left with the conclusion that (a) his or her report of prior trauma(s) appears to be valid, (b) the client's current state is consistent with the possibility that the trauma produced the current symptom pattern, and (c) a definitive connection between these two events cannot be asserted absolutely. In other words, rarely are there psychological "litmus tests" for the existence or effects of a given trauma, especially one long past. Fortunately, a definitive trauma–response connection is more important in forensic contexts (e.g., civil litigation for psychological damages) than in clinical ones. In the latter, the clinician may determine that one likely hypothesis is that the trauma and the posttraumatic stress are related, without ruling out other potential etiologies.

The second issue, that of determining whether a posttraumatic condition exists, is typically possible in a sensitive and competent psychological evaluation. In certain instances, however, even this goal may be elusive. As noted elsewhere in this volume, many generic psychological tests are relatively insensitive to posttraumatic states, instead misclassifying such symptoms as evidence of other disorders, such as personality disorder or psychosis. Moreover, the clinician unfamiliar with (or negatively predisposed toward) posttraumatic disturbance may misinterpret or overlook existing trauma-related symptoms. Finally, as discussed later in this chapter, client avoidance responses may cause him or her to deny or mask posttraumatic symptomatology, thereby reducing the visibility of such symptoms during evaluation. Given these issues, the effective evaluator is familiar with the complexities of posttraumatic clinical presentation, includes trauma-sensitive psychological tests in his or her assessment battery (see chapter 7), and works to provide an evaluation environment that minimizes the presence of client avoidance or distortion.

Even though the assessment focus may be on posttraumatic stress and stressors, the ultimate goal of a competent evaluation is not solely to define the relationship between aversive experiences and outcomes or to identify specific posttraumatic difficulties. Instead, the client's entire symptom experience should be assessed. For example, although a 33-year-old earthquake victim's acute distress disorder is an obvious target for evaluation, his pre-existing obsessive–compulsive symptoms and current depression are also important components of the clinical picture. Similarly, individuals with psychotic disorders or certain Axis II difficulties (especially those residing in Cluster B) are thought to be especially prone to PTSD when exposed to moderate stressors, and thus a competent psychological assessment should include data on these clinical antecedents as well. Finally, some non-trauma-related symptoms (e.g., certain obsessional, psychotic, or anxiety symptoms) may mimic posttraumatic symptomatology to some extent. In such instances, failure to consider all relevant diagnostic possibilities may lead to a misidentification of posttraumatic disturbance.

As noted in chapter 2, diagnostic notions such as complex PTSD or posttraumatic depression reflect the fact that posttraumatic stress is often present in the context of other symptoms and disorders. Several studies suggest that those with PTSD may also suffer from other, coexisting disorders such as depression, anxiety disorders (especially panic disorder, phobias, and obsessive–compulsive disorder), alcohol and drug abuse, and borderline or antisocial personality disorder (Breslau & Davis, 1992; Burnam et al., 1988; Green, Lindy, Grace, & Gleser, 1989). This overlap appears to represent not only the co-occurrence of various disorders with PTSD, but also the fact that some PTSD diagnostic criteria are similar to those for depressive and anxiety disorders (Davidson & Foa, 1991; Kessler et al., 1995). Such symptom and disorder overlap emphasizes the importance of evaluating the full range of psychological disorders when assessing the traumatized client.

In summary, clinical evaluation of trauma victims must take into account the client's entire psychological experience, including the complexity of potentially etiologic or moderating events and the possibility of significant comorbidity with less trauma-related conditions. Failure to consider these broader issues may result in erroneous conclusions or unnecessarily constrained clinical data.

Avoidance and Underreporting

Because all living organisms tend to withdraw from noxious stimuli, it is not surprising that traumatic events can motivate the development and use of avoidance strategies. This may take the form of emotional or cognitive suppression, denial, dissociation, memory distortion, substance abuse, or involvement in activities that numb or distract. Combat veterans, for example, may attempt to keep from thinking about their war experiences, may avoid situations where they have to talk about the war, may enter a dissociative state when exposed to combat-relevant stimuli, or may use alcohol or drugs to reduce posttraumatic distress.

Although such avoidance strategies may be superficially adaptive, they often impede the treatment process (Briere, 1996a; Resick & Schnicke, 1993) and interfere with accurate psychological evaluation. Regarding the latter, the victim's tendency to avoid or attenuate distress may decrease his or her response to psychological assessment, in some instances leading to a significant underpresentation of trauma history or posttraumatic effects. This may occur especially if a given assessment technique requires the victim to recall or reexperience trauma-related events. More generally, as noted by Epstein (1993, p. 457), "The avoidant symptoms of PTSD can serve as a 'self-cloaking' device that may hinder or prevent timely diagnosis."

Avoidance also may present in the form of dissociative amnesia, in which case the victim may have insufficient recall of traumatic experiences and thus will not report them during the evaluation interview. As noted earlier, several studies suggest that some instances of childhood or adult trauma may be relatively unavailable to conscious memory for extended periods of time, during which, presumably, the participants of these studies would deny or underestimate historical events that did in fact occur. Although these studies have been criticized for their methodological shortcomings, the repeated replication of reduced or absent memories of childhood or adulthood traumas suggests that, in fact, individual self-reports regarding especially aversive events may be subject to a nontrivial rate of false negatives.

Avoidance also can affect clients' reports of symptomatology on assessment instruments. Dissociative numbing and defensive avoidance of painful material are prevalent in trauma survivors (e.g., Branscomb, 1991; DiTomasso & Routh, 1993), and both may suppress clients' scores on symptom measures. Shedler, Mayman, and Manis (1993, p. 1117) demonstrated in a more general context, for example, that "standard mental health scales appear unable to distinguish between genuine mental health and the facade or illusion of mental health created by psychological defenses." Apropos of this notion, Elliott and Briere (1994) reported on a subsample of children for whom there was compelling evidence of sexual abuse (e.g., unambiguous medical findings, photographs taken by the abuser, or abuser confession) but who nonetheless (a) denied that they had been abused and (b) scored significantly *lower* than controls (children without known sexual abuse histories) on the Trauma Symptom Checklist for Children (TSCC; Briere, 1996b). As we noted, it is likely that these children were using denial and other cognitive avoidance strategies to keep from confronting not only their abuse but its psychological impacts as well. In the absence of outside corroboration, these children probably would have been judged as nonabused and nondistressed on interview or by psychological evaluation.

Although symptom underreporting is potentially an important issue in the assessment of abuse survivors and other traumatized individuals, it is obviously difficult to identify in any given individual. At present, the practitioner is limited to reliance on validity scales that, for example, index defensiveness or "fake good" responses (e.g., the L and K scales of both versions of the Minnesota Multiphasic Personality Inventory [MMPI; Butcher et al., 1989; Hathaway & McKinley, 1943], the Positive Impression Management scale of the Personality Assessment Inventory [PAI; Morey, 1991], the Disclosure and Desirability indices of the three versions of the Millon Clinical Multiaxial Inventory [MCMI; Millon, 1983, 1987, 1994] or the Response Level scale of the Trauma Symptom Inventory [TSI; Briere, 1995c]). These validity indicators identify some extreme cases of underreporting, but it is likely that many other instances go unidentified unless the clinician can somehow detect defensive responding during the evaluation interview (Shedler et al., 1993).

As a result of these various processes, the clinician should not rule out the possibility of unreported traumatic events or trauma-related disturbance in a given individual's life history, whether they arise from conscious suppression of upsetting material or more unconscious defensive processes. The possibility of significant avoidance-based underreporting does not mean, however, that an individual who is symptomatic but denies a victimization history is necessarily "in denial" about or "repressing" a specific traumatic event. Unfortunately, some clinicians have attributed a variety of mental health complaints to completely repressed sexual abuse trauma in clients who steadfastly denied abuse histories, a practice not supported by current knowledge. A variety of traumatic and nontraumatic events and processes may produce most symptoms or states, such that an automatic assumption of a specific undisclosed trauma as etiologic is not tenable (Meyers, 1995). Furthermore, although complete dissociation of a trauma-related memory appears to be quite possible, such extreme avoidance responses are probably not especially common and should not be assumed unless there are specific data to support that hypothesis.

Overreporting

In addition to underreporting, some individuals overreport or misrepresent trauma histories or trauma-related symptomatology (S. A. Fairbank, McCaffrey, & Keane, 1985; Hyer, Fallon, Harrison, & Boudewyns, 1987). Occasionally, overreporting of trauma histories may occur in the context of psychosis or extreme personality disorders. On the other hand, research suggests that borderline personality disorder may also arise from severe child abuse (e.g., J. L. Herman et al., 1989; Ogata et al., 1990), among other adverse events, and recent research implicates trauma in at least some exacerbated or atypical psychotic presentations (e.g., Briere et al., in press; Goff, Brotman, Kindlon, & Waites, 1991; Ross, Anderson, & Clark, 1994). In addition, there are no data to suggest that more disturbed individuals have a lower probability of being traumatized than other people and considerable cause to expect that psychologically impaired or incapacitated people are easier prey for predatory individuals. As a result, the trauma reports of psychotic or borderline individuals should not be discounted automatically, but, instead, should be evaluated for their credibility and meaning in the same manner as any other historical statements might be considered.

With the recent concern over the likelihood of some "false memories" of childhood maltreatment (e.g., Lindsay, 1994; Loftus, 1993), the specific validity of adults' reports of childhood trauma (especially abuse) has been the subject of considerable debate. Some have contended, for example, that a given abuse allegation may be the result of psychopathology, greed, or vindictiveness, or that an evaluator or therapist has implanted "false memories" of abuse in a client who, in fact, has no history of abuse (Loftus, 1993; Wakefield & Underwager, 1992). Others suggest that adult reports of childhood abuse are often based on reality, at least in terms of their central features (e.g., Enns, McNeilly, Corkery, & Gilbert, 1995). Clinical experience, as well as the data on amnesia presented in chapter 2, tends to support the Enns et al. (1995) position regarding trauma and memory, while not discounting the possibility of confabulation. Furthermore, data from a study by Williams (1995) suggested that the content of recovered memories of sexual abuse is no less accurate than the recollections of those who have always remembered their abuse. An undetermined minority of recovered memory reports, however, are likely to be significantly distorted or entirely false. Regardless of its relative infrequency, inaccurate reporting can have major negative impacts on innocent parties, as well as distracting from the treatment focus during psychotherapy. Therefore, the possibility of distortion or confabulation must be taken into account during the assessment process.

Unfortunately, the charge that therapists can encourage the production of pseudomemories of abuse may lead some clinicians to avoid asking about abuse histories at all during evaluation or treatment (Enns et al., 1995). Such clinicians may fear that they will be sued for "implanting" false memories of abuse or that the mere asking about abuse will lead to a confabulated history. However, Lindsay (1995), a leading proponent of the false memory perspective, noted:

> Criticisms of memory work in psychotherapy are not directed at survivors of CSA [child sexual abuse] who have always remembered their abuse or at those who spontaneously remember previously forgotten abuse. Furthermore, most critics of memory work in psychotherapy do not claim that all memories of CSA recovered in therapy are false. Finally, most

critics do not suggest that practitioners should never broach the subject of CSA, nor do they claim that a few probing questions about CSA are likely to lead clients to create illusory memories. (p. 281)

Although Lindsay's position may not be supported by all of his colleagues, his statement may be helpful to those who fear that any work with abuse-related memories is likely to produce intrinsically false memories. As Enns et al. (1995, p. 230) noted, "when inquiries are embedded within a thorough assessment about various aspects of a person's psychological status, it is highly unlikely that these questions will pressure the client to falsely believe they were abused."

Given the reliable correlation between child abuse and later psychological difficulties, it is recommended that clinicians inquire about childhood abuse experiences (as well as adult traumas) as a routine part of all those clinical evaluations where such questions can be tolerated and are likely to be valid. These questions should be posed as a regular part of history taking, as opposed to being given special attention or emphasis in such a way as to suggest that a specific answer is desired (see chapter 4 for more on taking a trauma history). It is also strongly recommended that such questions not occur during hypnosis, drug-assisted interviews, or within any other context that might capitalize on suggestibility or lead the client to report more than he or she actually recalls. As Courtois (1995) outlined in the specific instance of sexual abuse:

> Paraphrasing Judith Herman [1992b] on this matter, the therapist must be technically neutral while being morally cognizant of the prevalence and possibility of an abuse history. But technical neutrality does not mean not asking and cognizance does not mean that the therapist assumes sexual abuse to the exclusion of other issues. The therapist should be open to the possibility of other childhood events and trauma that might account for the symptom picture and should not prematurely foreclose these other possibilities. (p. 21)

Beyond trauma and memory concerns, the client may suffer from a factitious disorder, wherein he or she is driven to report nonexistent traumatic events as a result of psychological disorder. Although factition is typically associated with attempts to appear as if one has a physical disorder, trauma specialists occasionally come across individuals whose presenting description of traumatic events and posttraumatic stress appears to serve a neurotic need for psychological or medical attention and intervention. For example, an individual without military experience may present to a crisis center or outpatient clinic with reports of traumatic combat experiences and resultant posttraumatic stress. Although factitious trauma presentations are probably uncommon, they are not unheard of and should be considered in instances where the presenting problem seems overstated or in some other way suspect.

Because our legal system entitles individuals to file suits against their alleged perpetrators and some institutions appropriately provide financial support or compensation to those who have been traumatized (e.g., the Veteran's Administration and Victim Compensation boards), there also may be a financial motivation for some trauma reports and trauma symptom endorsements (Litz et al., 1992). Thus, a competent forensic assessment during (for example) a psychological damages suit should consider the possibility of malingering. Similarly, a more treatment-focused evaluation should not overlook the possibility of intentional misrepresentation because such phenomena obviously require different sorts of intervention strategies. This possibility should be a normal "rule out" issue, however, as opposed to a way to act out undue skepticism or countertransference regarding actual traumatic events and posttraumatic states. Clinical experience suggests that false reports of trauma or trauma-related symptomatology are more rare than common in nonforensic clinical settings and should not be automatically assumed, just as other reports should not be automatically accepted in their entirety.

Unfortunately, it is sometimes difficult to identify cases of overreporting through the use of psychological tests (e.g., Lyons, Caddell, Pittman, Rawls, & Perrin, 1994). Some overreporting of symptomatology may be detected through validity scale scores, such as elevations on the F and Ds (Dissimulation) scales (along with F-K) of the MMPI and MMPI-2, the Debasement scale of the

MCMI, or the Atypical Response scale of the TSI. However, those who have experienced interpersonal victimization tend to score more deviantly on validity scales, thereby decreasing the usefulness of such scales with traumatized individuals. Several studies, for example, suggest that Vietnam combat veterans and child abuse survivors may have elevated F-scale scores as a result of chronic posttraumatic difficulties or comorbid affective symptoms, as opposed to motivated symptom overendorsement (Elliott, 1993; Hyer, Woods, Harrison, Boudewyns, & O'Leary, 1989; Jordan, Nunley, & Cook, 1992; Smith & Frueh, 1996). As a result, the clinician or forensic evaluator is faced with a difficult trade-off: Does one strictly apply validity cutoffs, thereby catching some cases of overreporting but also potentially eliminating valid protocols of especially traumatized individuals? Or does one use more liberal cutoffs in order to retain valid trauma protocols, yet run the risk of incorrectly interpreting overreported or false test responses?

Fortunately, several MMPI-2 validity indicators that are elevated for trauma survivors are even more elevated for those who intentionally overreport. Consistent with the general trauma literature, Wetter, Baer, Berry, Robinson, and Sumpter (1993) found that 20 patients with PTSD had an average F (T score) of 79.8 (SD = 23.7). As high as this score was, 22 nonclinical individuals instructed to fake PTSD (after being given information on the disorder and being promised a monetary reward for success) had a substantially higher F score (M = 111.3, SD = 17.1). Wetter et al. (1993) found that the Ds and F-K indices were even better at detecting "motivated faking:" Raw Ds scores for the PTSD group averaged 24.4 (SD = 9.7), whereas the mean score for the faking group was 42.3 (SD = 11.1), and raw F-K for the PTSD group was 4.4 (SD = 12.0) as compared to 27.4 (SD = 15.8) for the motivated fakers. The Variable Response Inconsistency Scale (VRIN) did not differ between PTSD and motivated faking groups—a finding that replicates previous data (Wetter, Baer, Berry, Smith, & Larson, 1992). Similarly, a later study by Wetter, Baer, Berry, and Reynolds (1994) found that an F-K value of 14 or higher discriminated motivated fakers of borderline personality disorder from nonfakers. Finally, Smith and Frueh (1996) reported that an F-K of 14 or higher was a reasonable index of "apparent exaggerators" of PTSD. By way of caution, however, it should be noted that the sample sizes in these studies were relatively small and the standard deviations for the relevant validity indicators relatively large. As a result, it may not be appropriate to use the means of these studies as absolutely definitive cutoffs for malingering or overreporting in any given client.

In addition to validity scale data, elevated psychosis scores on standardized instruments, if found to represent true psychotic symptoms, may suggest that the client is too cognitively disorganized or delusional to respond in valid ways to psychological tests of trauma. The use of independent malingering scales or interviews (e.g., the Structured Interview of Reported Symptoms; Rogers, Bagby, & Dickens, 1992) also may be indicated when there is a significant possibility of intentional misrepresentation (e.g., in some forensic domains). Finally, the client whose historical reports or symptom presentation appear especially unlikely (e.g., descriptions of technically impossible scenarios or especially florid or nonsensical symptomatology) obviously may be overreporting, although even such individuals may have experienced other, actual victimization events and may nevertheless report at least some events or symptomatology accurately.

Misidentification and Distortion Effects

Because most standard psychological tests (e.g., the MMPI or Rorschach) were not developed at a time when psychological trauma was well recognized, such tests may underidentify or distort trauma effects. As described in chapter 6, examiners using older instruments may confuse intrusive posttraumatic symptomatology with hallucinations, obsessions, primary process, or "fake bad" responses; misinterpret dissociative avoidance as fragmented thinking, chaotic internal states, or the negative signs of schizophrenia; and misidentify trauma-based cognitive phenomena (e.g., hypervigilance or generalized distrust) as evidence of paranoia or other delusional processes. Furthermore, the effects of childhood trauma may be misinterpreted as personality disorders to the extent that they involve interpersonal difficulties, chaotic internal states, and tension-reduction or other affect-avoidance activities.

This tendency for traditional measures to misrepresent post-traumatic symptoms as psychosis or personality disorder might seemingly preclude their use in trauma assessment. However, the issue may be less that of intrinsically bad data (i.e., the test items themselves) as erroneous interpretation (i.e., how the items and scales are understood). For example, as described in chapter 6, although many sexual abuse survivors have elevations on scales 4 and 8 of the MMPI or MMPI-2, it is often inappropriate to view them as potentially schizophrenic (scale 8), psychopathic (scale 4), or borderline (e.g., a 4–8 profile). Instead, examination of specific items and available subscale scores may indicate the presence of nonpsychotic reexperiencing symptoms, interpersonal distrust or social alienation, and dissociative responses, as well as accurate reporting of familial discord during childhood. Thus, to the extent that more trauma-relevant interpretations can be made, standard psychological tests can be a helpful part of the trauma assessment process. This is important, because there are tremendous databases available on clients' responses to the MMPI, MMCI, Rorschach, and other tests that can be well-used when applied with care.

The following four issues are important to consider when using traditional psychological test data:

1. The test itself should be generally understood, in terms of how it was developed and normed; its relevant psychometric qualities, including its reliability, sensitivity (the percentage of instances that it detects people with the disorder in question), and specificity (the percentage of instances that it correctly detects people who do not have the disorder); and the underlying theory on which interpretation of scores is based. For example, a test normed on a relatively homogeneous sample of midwestern adults may not have much applicability to an African American combat veteran with severe and chronic posttraumatic stress disorder. Similarly, a projective test interpretation system that regularly relies on traditional psychodynamic theory may be of limited validity in the assessment of an individual who was repeatedly incestuously assaulted as a child.

2. The item domain of the instrument should be evaluated: Do the items tap the labeled construct well, or can they misinterpret other phenomena (i.e., posttraumatic states) as evidence of the construct? To the extent that the items within a given scale reflect multiple phenomena, some of which are more relevant to trauma than others, are there interpretable subscales available? For example, scale 8 (Sc) of the MMPI contains the following Harris–Lingoes subscales (Harris & Lingoes, 1968): Social Alienation; Emotional Alienation; Lack of Ego Mastery, Cognitive; Lack of Ego Mastery, Conative; Lack of Ego Mastery, Defective Inhibition; and Bizarre Sensory Experiences. Because such subscales are typically more unidimensional than summary scale scores, their meaning with regard to the client's current state may be more transparent and therefore more helpful.

3. The presence of more specific trauma scales within the instrument should be taken into account. For example, the MMPI-2 and the third edition of the MCMI (MCMI-III; Millon, 1994) each have PTSD scales. Although each has less than perfect content domain coverage (both underestimate certain posttraumatic symptoms and each contains a number of symptoms less relevant to trauma, such as depression), these scales may alert the examiner to the possibility of significant posttraumatic stress and thus to alternate explanations for other scale elevations. Furthermore, ad hoc, trauma-specific scoring rules for a given instrument are available (e.g., Keane, Malloy, & Fairbank's, 1984, F-2-8 cutoffs for identifying PTSD in the MMPI or Armstrong and Loewenstein's, 1990, Traumatic Content Index for the Rorschach), thereby adding more information for interpretation.

4. Standard psychological tests should be augmented with additional, more trauma-specific instruments. Because the notion of posttraumatic stress is a relatively new one, however, only a limited number of standardized instruments are available in this area thus far. Trauma-focused tests should be normed on large, sociodemo-

graphically diverse samples; have demonstrated reliability and validity; and, if possible, measure a number of areas of posttraumatic disturbance. A scale that yields a single summary measure of PTSD may be inherently problematic because PTSD minimally involves three separate components—reexperiencing, avoidance, and hyperarousal—each of which may vary in magnitude in any specific instance. As a result, the most helpful measures examine clients' scores on each component, so that a more detailed assessment of posttraumatic stress can be made. For example, whereas a summary measure of PTSD (e.g., as found in the MMPI or MCMI) might indicate that a female assault victim has moderately high posttraumatic stress, a more detailed instrument might suggest that her levels of intrusion and arousal are high but that her avoidance is within normal limits.

Trauma-Related Testimony in Court

Although this is not a book on forensic psychology, a few points should be made with regard to expert testimony in trauma cases. There are at least two ways in which trauma evaluators or clinicians may become involved in the courts. Clinicians who treat or evaluate trauma survivors may easily find themselves testifying with regard to one of their clients, either in a criminal case or in a civil suit. Second, forensic evaluators may be called on to render expert opinions regarding the presence of posttraumatic distress or disorder in someone who is involved in a criminal or civil proceeding.

In my opinion, nontreating evaluators are best qualified to offer expert testimony regarding the effects of trauma and the potential validity of a specific allegation. To the extent that the treating clinician has formed a therapeutic relationship with the client, he or she is less likely to be objective regarding the facts of the case. Moreover, in some cases objective testimony regarding the client's history and its meaning may result in dual relationship issues that might negatively affect ongoing therapy (American Academy of Psychiatry and the Law, 1995). Of course, this does not preclude treating clinicians from testifying about the process or content of a given course of therapy.

During trial or deposition, the examiner should adhere to four principles of expert testimony, sometimes expressed as the acronym HELP: honesty, evenhandedness, limits of expertise, and preparation (Meyers, 1995). Honesty with regard to trauma testimony typically means acknowledging an unavoidable set of realities: (a) in the absence of external corroboration, it may be difficult to determine with complete certainty whether a traumatic event has occurred; (b) it is not always possible to rule out the existence of symptom underreporting, overreporting, or malingering; and (c) when a pattern of symptoms has been established, it is rarely possible to assert with complete confidence that the symptoms in question arose entirely from a specific past traumatic event.

That these limitations exist does not, however, mean that the evaluator has no role in the courtroom. First of all, the judge and jury may need to be appraised of the limits of "medical certainty" with regard to potential posttraumatic states. Second, although the expert witness may not be able to provide definitive testimony regarding trauma or effect, he or she can assist the court in considering the various possibilities and the general likelihood of each.

In this regard, evenhandedness and an acknowledgment of the limits of potential expertise means that the evaluator should consider all reasonable explanations for the client's reports of trauma and posttraumatic difficulty, and, to the extent that data are available, offer a carefully constrained opinion regarding the likelihood of each. For example, the interviewer may believe that, on balance, the alleged victim's reports have merit, but he or she should also be prepared to discuss the possibility of misrepresentation or malingering. Similarly, although an expert may have been hired by the plaintiff's attorney to support the argument that a given traumatic event caused short- or long-term damages, the evaluator must remain objective and consider the possibility that other antecedent or intervening negative experiences produced at least some of the symptoms in question or that the plaintiff's reports are distorted by financial considerations. Finally, an interviewer who believes that a given allegation of trauma or posttraumatic stress is false must also consider the possibility that his or her expectations, demeanor, or even choice of assessment procedures precluded access to information that would contradicted that belief. He or she must also accept the fact that an absence of evidence does not mean that an event did not take place. In this regard, psychological testimony that a traumatic event did not occur may be as inappropriate as unsupported testimony that it did.

Forensic experience suggests that expert witnesses who come to significant grief in the courtroom are often those who are not well prepared regarding the actual needs of the court. Such individuals may argue one "side" without considering the other, not evaluating competing hypotheses for the complainant's allegations, symptoms, and presentation. For example, the examiner who categorically states that event A occurred and absolutely produced posttraumatic response B is less likely to be viewed as an objective expert by judge or jury—and is much more easily discredited on cross-examination—than the examiner who offers several potential hypotheses regarding what may have occurred. By applying relevant test and interview data to these hypotheses, along with an understanding of the relevant literature, the expert may then offer a considered, but explicitly probabilistic conclusion regarding A and B. Such testimony not only honors the ethical responsibilities incumbent on psychologists and other mental health professionals, it carries with it greater professionalism and probity and, ultimately, greater credibility.

Summary

Posttraumatic states are in some sense unique in the clinical field because of their tendency to become reactivated during assessment of their presence. This reactivation, in turn, may distort psychological test or interview data. This problem is compounded by the fact that most evaluation approaches used in this area were developed without specific reference to posttraumatic phenomena and thus may misinterpret trauma responses as evidence of other clinical states. Because psychologists and others have only recently considered these issues in psychological assessment, no definitive information is available regarding the exact meaning of posttraumatic stress responses tapped by traditional assessment methodologies. As a result, some trauma victims are likely to be seen as suffering from non-trauma-related psychopathology, and some nontraumatized individuals who seek to present themselves as posttraumatic are likely to go undetected. Thus, the examiner may be on shaky ground to the extent that he or she absolutely concludes, on the basis of test or interview data, that a given incident of trauma and subsequent stress have occurred and are related.

Fortunately, research on the assessment and diagnosis of posttraumatic states is proceeding at a rapid pace, and new, more trauma-specific tests are being developed on an ongoing basis. The remainder of this book outlines what we have learned thus far and highlights new approaches to posttrauma assessment that substantially increase the sensitivity and specificity of trauma-specific clinical evaluation.

Structured Assessment of Traumatic Events

As noted in chapters 1 and 2, traumatic events are not un-common in people's lives and often lead to subsequent psychological distress and impairment. For this reason, when conditions allow—that is, in the absence of florid psychosis, emotional instability, or substantial cognitive impairment—the interviewer should inquire about childhood and adulthood trauma history in those seeking psychological assistance. To some extent, how this is done is up to the interviewer but should include general questions about major negative experiences throughout the life span. As described later in this chapter, such questions should be behaviorally anchored, as opposed to asking solely about "child abuse," "rape," or exposure to "disasters."

Taking a routine trauma history may result in considerable information about important traumatic events (e.g., Briere & Zaidi, 1989; Lanktree, Briere, & Zaidi, 1991; Pope, 1994; B. E. Saunders et al., 1992), and the process need not be experienced as overly intrusive if handled in a sensitive manner. For example, Briere and Zaidi (1989) surveyed the charts of 50 psychiatric emergency room patients for references to a childhood history of sexual abuse and found that only 6% documented such events. In a second phase of the study, clinicians were requested routinely to ask emergency room patients about any history of childhood sexual victimization. When 50 charts written during this phase were examined, reference to a positive sexual abuse history increased more than tenfold, to 70%. Furthermore, phase two abuse history was associated with a wide variety of presenting problems, ranging from suicidality and substance abuse to multiple Axis I diagnoses and an increased rate of borderline personality disorder diagnoses. As we noted:

> Diagnostic work-ups and evaluations are of necessity constrained in the emergency room and appropriately focus most on acute concerns. In such a context, issues relating to childhood history are easily seen as irrelevant to the patient's immediate or presenting problem.... The current data clearly suggest, however, that sexual abuse histories are both frequent and predictive in emergency room populations and that questions regarding childhood maltreatment are a useful component of psychiatric emergency protocols. (Briere & Zaidi, 1989, p. 1605)

When the client reports a significant trauma history on interview, or whenever a more precise assessment is required, the clinician may use one of the structured clinical interviews or inventories for traumatic events presented in the next section. Time or logistic constraints may preclude this option, of course, in which case the clinician may choose to use a version of the customized trauma interview presented later in this chapter.

Trauma (Criterion A) Interviews and Measures

A number of structured clinical interviews survey clients' adult trauma histories; the five best known are presented in the following sections. Each of these interviews evaluates a range of traumatic experience. Most may either be used to prompt interviewer questions or be given to the client to fill out. Other Criterion A instruments address specific traumatic events and are not reported here. These include measures that evaluate combat experiences (e.g., Keane et al., 1989; Wolfe, Brown, Furey, & Levin, 1993), adult sexual assault (e.g., Koss & Gidycz, 1985), and adult spouse abuse (e.g., Shepard & Campbell, 1992; Straus, 1979; Tolman, 1989). For a detailed review of Criterion A measures, the reader may consult the chapter by Norris and Riad in Wilson and Keane's (1996) excellent volume on PTSD assessment.

It should be noted that although these instruments are designated Criterion A measures, few do, in fact, evaluate all of *DSM-IV* Criterion A. As discussed previously, *DSM-IV* has added a second component to Criterion A for adults: the requirement that the stressor induce intense fear, horror, or helplessness in the victim. Because the structured interviews outlined below tend to focus on events rather than on subjective reactions to them, they typically provide insufficient information regarding whether the event in question satisfies *DSM-IV*'s requirements for an ASD- or PTSD-level stressor. Although future versions of these measures probably will tap the required subjective responses, at the present time the clinician should ask explicitly about intense fear, horror, or helplessness regarding any stressor identified by these interviews.

It is important that the evaluator attend to the victim's reaction to the structured interview as it unfolds, so that it can be modified or even terminated if necessary. These interviews tend to move from one traumatic event to the next, typically without any formalized acknowledgment of the emotional impact of such questions or of the rapport and sensitivity required in such contexts. As a result, the client may become overwhelmed or retraumatized by the process, thereby both defeating the purpose of the interview (ultimately, to help the client) and decreasing the quality of the interview data (i.e., by motivating avoidance or producing confusion). Although structured interviews allow for the acquisition of information in a reliable and focused manner, the clinician should see the interview items as a series of helpful prompts, rather than as a script that must be followed regardless of the respondent's distress or psychological state.

Another issue to be discussed prior to reviewing specific Criterion A measures is that of trauma description. Although most of the measures reviewed in the following sections provide a seemingly exhaustive list of potential stressors, many do not offer behavioral descriptions of these events. Instead, they may ask respondents to report whether they have ever been raped, physically assaulted, sexually abused as a child, and so on. Although some stressors may not require much elaboration (e.g., earthquakes, hurricanes, or floods), others—especially acts of interpersonal victimization—often must be described behaviorally before accurate assessment can occur. Hanson, Kilpatrick, Falsetti, and Resnick (1995) discussed the specific problems inherent in screening for a sexual assault history:

> Studies have documented that the use of behaviorally specific questions to detect trauma history produce significantly higher prevalence rates (and presumably more accurate) than single-item screening questions. For sexual assault, studies find that asking respondents if they have been "raped" elicits much lower prevalence rates than if behaviorally specific structured questions are used to define sexual assault (Koss, 1983, 1993). One reason for this is that people do not always perceive a sexual assault incident to be a rape. If the assailant was a family member, a friend, or a dating partner, some individuals may not label the incident as a rape. If the assault did not involve vaginal penetration, but did involve some other type of sexual penetration (i.e., oral or anal), individuals may not categorize the event as a rape. (p. 135)

Similar to Hanson et al.'s (1995) concerns regarding rape, it is not at all uncommon for a respondent to deny a history of childhood "sexual abuse" or "physical abuse" because of differing interpretations of these words. For example, some individuals may not consider their sexual intercourse at age 14 with a 24-year-old "boyfriend" to be sexual abuse, and some respondents are known to interpret relatively extreme examples of physical maltreatment as being appropriate parental discipline (Briere, 1992a). Similarly, some battered women may reframe their experiences as merely "fighting" or "not getting along" with their partner, or they may not consider it abuse if they believe that they deserved to be beaten. In some instances this confusion appears to represent a lack of definitional understanding, whereas in others it is more likely to arise from psychological defenses against acknowledging traumatic events.

Given this variability in response to screening items, the clinician is advised to avoid merely presenting a list of potentially traumatic events during trauma assessment. Instead, acts of interpersonal violence should be described in such a way that their definitions are unambiguous. Furthermore, brief pre-assessment comments regarding victimization may be helpful to the extent that they normalize or destigmatize the reporting of interpersonal violence experiences (Falsetti & Resnick, 1995; Resnick, Kilpatrick, & Lipovsky, 1991). They should not, however, take the form of pressuring or prescribing trauma disclosures, such that the respondent believes he or she *should* have something traumatic to report.

Traumatic Events Questionnaire (TEQ)

The TEQ (Vrana & Lauterbach, 1994) taps 11 stressors relevant to Criterion A: combat; large fires or explosions; serious industrial or farm accidents; sexual assault or rape; natural disasters; violent crimes; adult abusive relationships; physical or sexual child abuse; witnessing someone being mutilated, seriously injured, or violently killed; other life-threatening experiences; and violent or unexpected death of a loved one. Two additional items ask about (a) any other traumatic event and (b) an "event can't tell" (an event so traumatic that the respondent can't describe it). Little additional information is assessed in the TEQ, such as detailed behavioral characteristics of the trauma or the client's subjective response to it. The major advantage of an interview such as the TEQ is its relative brevity and its systematic examination of a wide variety of traumatic events. However, the relative lack of codable detail on the TEQ may discourage its use when detailed trauma information is needed. Moreover, some traumas listed in this questionnaire require further elaboration before responses to them can be considered fully valid.

Traumatic Stress Schedule (TSS)

The TSS was published by Norris in 1990 and was revised soon thereafter (Norris, 1992). The revised version, available in both English and Spanish versions, inquires about 10 potentially traumatic events: combat; robbery or theft involving force; physical assault; sexual assault (forced or unwanted sexual activity); loss of a loved one through accident, homicide, or suicide; personal injury or property loss as a result or fire; personal injury or property loss as a result of severe weather or a disaster; forced evacuation or otherwise learning of an imminent danger or hazard in the environment; a motor vehicle accident causing injury to one or more passengers; and any other event that is terrifying or shocking.

The TSS also allows each identified trauma to be further probed according to the extent of loss it produced (i.e., people, property), its scope (number of people involved), threat to life and physical integrity, whether the individual was blamed, and familiarity of the trauma. Like most other measures in this area, the TSS uses single questions to tap each content area, an approach that may cause some traumatic experiences to be overlooked (Krinsley & Weathers, 1995).

Potential Stressful Events Interview (PSEI)

The PSEI (Kilpatrick, Resnick, & Freedy, 1991a, 1991b, described in Falsetti, Resnick, Kilpatrick, & Freedy, 1994) is best known for its use in the *DSM-IV* PTSD field trials. This interview serves as an important example of how a research measure can be a useful clinical tool.

Components of the PSEI relevant to this section are modules tapping stressor type (divided into low- and high-magnitude stressors), objective–behavioral characteristics of the stressor, and subjective reactions to the stressor. High-magnitude stressors evaluated are war zone or combat experiences; serious accidents associated with motor vehicles, work, or elsewhere; natural disasters; serious illnesses; childhood sexual abuse; childhood sexual assaults; other forced sexual contact; aggravated physical assaults (i.e., involving a weapon); simple physical assaults; other situations involving serious injury; other situations involving fear of injury or death; witnessing serious injury or death; and other extraordinarily stressful events. The low-magnitude stressors module evaluates events that may contribute to stress, but would not qualify as *DSM-IV* stressors themselves.

Following the stressor modules, the PSEI inquires about various qualities of the stressor and subjective reactions to it. These items are used to characterize responses to the first, most recent, and worst event, although the clinician might want to apply them to any stressor thought to be a significant traumatic event. The module examining characteristics of the high-magnitude stressor evaluates injury to self and others; perceived cause of the event; perception of the perpetrator's intent to harm (if relevant); the suddenness of the event; its expectedness; and the presence or absence of a warning regarding the event. Finally, the subjective reaction module consists of 15 items tapping feelings of surprise, detachment, panic, embarrassment, shame, and disgust. Not all subjective reactions required by *DSM-IV* stressors are included, however.

The Trauma Assessment for Adults (TAA; Resnick, Kilpatrick, Dansky, Saunders, & Best, 1993) is a shorter version of the PSEI, containing 13 specific event questions with 4 follow-up questions per event (Resnick, 1996). It goes into less detail, but its greater brevity probably makes it more clinically useful in some cases.

Traumatic Events Scale (TES)

The TES (Elliott, 1992) is a comprehensive measure that assesses a wide range of childhood and adult traumas. Both childhood and adult stressors are operationalized in detail, so that subjective interpretations of what constitutes a traumatic event are less likely. Of the 30 interpersonal and environmental traumas examined by the TES, 20 evaluate adult events and 10 are devoted to childhood events. Adult traumas evaluated by the TES include natural disasters, sexual and physical assault, torture, war, auto accidents, and witness of a murder. Among the characteristics evaluated for each trauma are frequency of occurrence over the life span; age at the time of the first, last, and worst incident; and level of distress both at the time of the event and at present. A version of the TES was used in part of the Trauma Symptom Inventory standardization project, where it predicted a wide variety of symptoms on multiple measures (e.g., Briere et al., 1995; Elliott & Briere, 1995).

Harvard Trauma Questionnaire (HTQ)

The HTQ (Mollica et al., 1992; Mollica et al., 1995) was developed specifically for the assessment of refugees, primarily those from

Indochina. It has been translated into Khmer, Lao, and Vietnamese. In addition to the stressor section reviewed here, the HTQ has a symptom section that evaluates *DSM-IV* PTSD and other stress symptoms relevant to the Indochinese culture (see chapter 7). The stressor section has 17 items, tapping common refugee-related traumas, including torture, rape, starvation, and exposure to the murder of others. Unfortunately, like most other trauma questionnaires, the HTQ does not describe or define most stressors in detail, and thus confusion and underreporting are possible. The questionnaire includes an open-ended question that inquires about the most terrifying events that have happened.

Research on 91 refugees (Mollica et al., 1992) indicated that the stressor section is reliable, both in terms of internal consistency ($\alpha = .90$) and stability over 1 week (test–retest $= .89$). The HTQ is a frequently cited measure of refugee traumatic experiences, both because of its structural quality and because there are few other established measures of refugee experiences (especially torture) available.

Childhood History Interviews and Measures

Unfortunately, most instruments that evaluate traumatic events in adulthood either overlook childhood abuse or merely include it—typically without operational definition—as one of many traumas that the respondent can endorse. Described here are five scales that specifically examine childhood maltreatment history. These scales vary considerably in terms of the number of forms of abuse or neglect they assess and the amount of abuse-specific detail they offer. An additional measure, the Psychological Maltreatment Scales (Brassard, Hart, & Hardy, 1993) is not reviewed here because it involves clinician ratings of actual parent–child interactions—a methodology not relevant to the topic of this volume.

Assessing Environments III, Form SD (AEIII-Form SD)

The AEIII-Form SD (Rausch & Knutson, 1991) is a revision of the AEIII, first introduced by Berger, Knutson, Mehm, and Perkins in 1988. It consists of 170 items that form the following scales:

Physical Punishment Scale, Sibling Physical Punishment Scale, Perception of Discipline Scale, Sibling Perception of Punishment Scale, Deserving Punishment Scale, and Sibling Deserving Punishment Scale. The reliability of scales comprising the current (Form SD) version of the AEIII was evaluated in a sample of 421 university students, yielding KR-20 coefficients ranging from .68 to .74 (Rausch & Knutson, 1991). No test–retest data were presented. In a study using the AEIII, DiTomasso and Routh (1993) found that the Physical Abuse Scale (presumably equivalent to the Physical Punishment Scale of the AEIII-Form SD) correlated with several measures of dissociation—relationships that support the potential construct validity of at least the earlier version of the AEIII.

Childhood Trauma Questionnaire (CTQ)

The CTQ (D. P. Bernstein et al., 1994) is a 70-item measure that assesses childhood trauma in six areas: physical, sexual, and emotional abuse physical and emotional neglect "and related areas of family dysfunction (e.g., substance abuse)" (p. 1133). This measure reportedly requires 10–15 minutes to administer. Items in the CTQ begin with the phrase "When I was growing up" and are rated on 5-point Likert-type scales ranging from *never true* to *very often true*. Principle components analysis of the CTQ in a sample of 286 substance-dependent patients yielded four factors that subsequently comprised the scales of this measure: physical and emotional abuse, emotional neglect, sexual abuse, and physical neglect. Internal consistency of these factor subscales were moderately high (alphas ranged from .79 to .94) and, in a subsample of 40 patients, test–retest correlations ranged from .80 to .83 for an average intertest interval of 3.6 months (D. P. Bernstein et al., 1994).

Traumatic Events Scale (TES)

As noted above for adult traumas, the TES evaluates a number of childhood traumas. Among these are exposure to disasters, peer sexual and physical assault, witnessing school and neighborhood violence, physical abuse, psychological abuse, sexual abuse, and witnessing spouse abuse. Considerable detail is obtained vis-à-vis characteristics of the various reported traumas. For example, in the case of child abuse, the client is asked about age at first and last incident, relationship to perpetrator, and level of distress about the abuse—both at the time it occurred and at present. Additional details are ascertained for sexual abuse in particular, such as whether the abuser used threats or force to gain sexual access and whether oral, anal, or vaginal penetration occurred.

Child Maltreatment Interview Schedule (CMIS)

The CMIS (Briere, 1992a) is a 46-item measure, with some items containing a number of subquestions that yield greater detail on a given abuse or neglect experience. The CMIS evaluates the following areas of maltreatment, each limited to events that occurred before age 17: level of parental physical availability (including number and time-range of parents, stepparents, and foster parents and instances of institutional care), parental disorder (i.e., history of inpatient or outpatient psychological treatment, alcoholism or drug abuse, and domestic violence), parental psychological availability, psychological abuse, physical abuse, emotional abuse, sexual abuse, ritualistic abuse, and perception of physical and sexual abuse status. For each area, specific questions probe the age of onset, the relationship to the abuser, and the severity of the maltreatment. The Psychological Abuse component of the CMIS is a seven-item scale taken from Briere and Runtz (1988, 1990b), where it has demonstrated moderate internal consistency (alphas ranging from .75 to .87) and has been shown to predict various symptom scales (e.g., Rorty, Yager, & Rossotto, 1994). The CMIS is also available in a short form (CMIS-SF; Briere, 1992a) that contains most of the material of the original measure, but without quite as much detail.

Childhood Maltreatment Questionnaire (CMQ)

The CMQ (Demaré, 1993) focuses extensively on psychological abuse and neglect; it also includes scales for sexual and physical maltreatment. The questionnaire contains three components: the Psychological Maltreatment Questionnaire (PMQ), the Physical Abuse Questionnaire (PAQ), and the Sexual Abuse Questionnaire (SAQ). The PMQ has 12 scales, each tapping a form of child maltreatment identified in the psychological abuse literature as significant: Rejecting, Degrading, Isolating, Corrupting, Denying Emotional Responsiveness, Exploiting (Nonsexual), Verbal Terrorism, Physical Terrorism, Witness to Violence, Unreliable and Inconsistent Care, Controlling and Stifling Independence, and Physical Neglect. The PAQ has a single scale, whereas the SAQ consists of Parental and Nonparental versions. Each CMQ scale item is scored on a 5-point Likert-like scale (anchored at *never* and *very often*) and assesses the frequency of maltreatment behaviors on or before age 17. Demaré and Briere (1994) examined the psychometric characteristics of these scales in a sample of 1,179 university students and found them relatively reliable (alphas ranged from .67 to .95) and predictive of symptomatology on the Trauma Symptom Checklist-40 (Briere & Runtz, 1989) for both men and women. Similar results have been found for the CMQ with reference to the Trauma Symptom Inventory (TSI; Briere, 1995c; Demaré & Briere, 1996).

What becomes clear when reviewing most trauma interviews and inventories in the field is their inherent research focus, as opposed to being specific clinical tools. Some provide insufficient information on a given stressor, including its behavioral definition, whereas others access far more information than would be clinically indicated. For this reason, the clinician may wish to choose among the specific items of these interview measures and to add any additional items that might be relevant. A customized, comprehensive trauma interview should ideally inquire about the following, some of which borrows from the PSEI, TSS, and TES. A less detailed version of this interview, or a subset of its items, is obviously appropriate when there are time constraints or the respondent is unable to tolerate extended questions.

A Customized Traumatic Events Interview

I. Inquire about a history of traumatic events:

- ☐ Childhood noninterpersonal traumas (e.g., disasters, fires, automobile accidents, loss of a parent)
- ☐ Childhood interpersonal traumas (e.g., childhood sexual and physical abuse, physical and sexual assaults by peers)

- ☐ Witnessing injury to others as a child (e.g., spouse abuse, murder of a parent or sibling)
- ☐ Adult noninterpersonal traumas (e.g., disasters, fires, automobile accidents, loss of a child)
- ☐ Adult interpersonal traumas (e.g., sexual and physical assault, spouse abuse, robbery, combat)
- ☐ Witnessing injury to others in adulthood (e.g., murder of a spouse or friend, death or disfigurement of a comrade during combat)

Any potential trauma categories that are not self-evident should be described in behavioral detail. The following are (nonexhaustive) examples of how the interviewer might present various interpersonal traumas.

[For adult physical assault]: "Have you ever been physically hit, attacked, beat up, or assaulted as an adult (age 18 or older)?" [If yes]: "Has this ever happened in marriage or a sexual relationship?"

[For adult rape or sexual assault]: "Has anyone ever done anything sexual to you against your will since you've been an adult (age 18 or older)?" [If yes]: "Has this ever happened in marriage or a sexual relationship?"

[For childhood sexual assault or abuse]: "Did anyone ever do something sexual to you against your will when you were under age 18?"

[For possible childhood sexual abuse]: "Did someone older than you ever do anything sexual to you or with you (with or without your permission) when you were under age 18?" [If yes]: "How old was this person?"

[For childhood sexual experiences and possible abuse]: How old were you when you had your first sexual experience? How old was the other person? How old were you the first time you had sexual intercourse? How old was the other person?"

[For possible childhood physical assault or abuse]: "Did anyone ever physically hit or assault you, or beat you up, when you were under age 18?" [If yes]: "What did they do to you?"

[For possible childhood physical abuse]: "What was the worst physical punishment you ever got from your parents or another adult when you were under 18?"

II. Inquire about characteristics of the trauma (for each trauma endorsed above, or for those identified as having a significant effect):

- □ When the event occurred (victim's age), its duration, number of incidents, number of people involved (both as victims and, if relevant, as perpetrators), perpetrator's relationship to the victim (if relevant), presence of vaginal/oral/anal penetration (if sexual), presence of threats (if relevant)
- □ Suddenness/expectedness/presence of warning
- □ Perceived self-responsibility for the event or its impacts
- □ Presence of physical injury
- □ Response of others (e.g., family, friends, neighbors, professionals)
- □ Medical and psychological treatment received
- □ Perpetrator's intent to harm (if relevant)
- □ Grotesqueness of the event
- □ Bizarreness of the event

III. Inquire about subjective experience (for each trauma endorsed above):

- □ Level of horror, fear, revulsion, shame, disgust, anger
- □ Perceived helplessness at the time of the event
- □ Level of guilt or self-blame
- □ Immediate posttraumatic response (e.g., withdrawal, numbing, denial/disbelief, detachment, screaming, crying, raging, aggression, self-injury, assisting others)

Summary

This chapter has outlined structured interviews and measures available for the assessment of traumatic events. Most of these interviews cannot assess all *DSM-IV* Criterion A at present, at least short of some modification by the interviewer, and many do not include behavioral definitions for interpersonal traumas. Furthermore, because of their schematic (if not rote) interrogatory style and potential to decrease interviewer–interviewee rapport, these interviews may not be immediately acceptable to the general clinical interviewer. On the other hand, these protocols tend to insure that relevant clinical and diagnostic issues are addressed, and they can decrease the subjectivity of the diagnostic process.

Because of their focus and attention to detail, structured instruments may be especially useful in instances where the clinical picture is complex or in forensic situations where the client's history may be subject to special scrutiny. In less exacting situations, the clinician might consider adapting one or more of these interviews to create a more customized, "user friendly" assessment protocol for regular personal use.

5

Diagnostic Interviews

Most trauma-focused assessment in North America occurs in a diagnostic interview or opening psychotherapy session, as opposed to through formal psychological testing. In fact, the occasional suggestion that emergency room or crisis center personnel consider using "pencil-and-paper" trauma measures is usually greeted, at best, with amusement. This reaction is contextually appropriate, in the sense that (a) trauma work often occurs in a rapid, relatively intense environment where clinical impressions are quickly formed; (b) trauma victims are often too distraught or distracted to attend fully to reading and writing; and (c) many mental health emergency staff are psychiatrists or social workers, that is, members of disciplines that typically have little training in psychological test administration and interpretation.

Although a central tenet of this book is that psychological testing can substantially assist the assessment of posttraumatic states, it is also true that no psychological test can replace the focused attention, visible empathy, and extensive clinical experience of a well-trained and seasoned trauma clinician. As a result, it is likely that both interview-based and (when timely and appropriate) formal psychological assessments are intrinsic to a complete trauma work-up. For this reason, this chapter focuses on issues and methodologies relevant to the face-to-face diagnostic interview. Because informal interview-based assessments are potentially less organized and focused, however, two assessment approaches are presented here: the trauma-relevant psychological interview and the structured diagnostic interview. As is noted in the next chapter, these procedures can help the clinician to identify symptoms and make a *DSM–IV* diagnosis; they cannot provide the more in-depth and normative–comparative information generated from comprehensive psychological testing. Thus, it is recommended that structured, interview-based assessment be seen as an important tool but not as a procedure that necessarily obviates the (often later) need for psychological test data.

Finally, the description of structured interviews in this chapter is not meant to suggest that such instruments are necessary in all instances or for all interviewers. Some clinical settings and situations do not require the detailed assessment provided by structured interviews, and some trauma-specialized clinicians consider themselves sufficiently conversant with the relevant criteria and issues that they do not require the prompts of a structured procedure. Even experienced trauma clinicians, however, are likely to use structured interviews on occasion, such as in certain forensic contexts or research settings or when diagnostic issues are especially complex.

The Trauma-Relevant Psychological Interview

In most mental health clinics and psychiatric emergency rooms, the assessment of psychological disturbance occurs during the diagnostic interview. In the interview session, the client is typically evaluated for (a) altered mental status (i.e., for evidence of dementia, confusion, disorientation, delirium, retardation, or other cognitive–organic disturbance); (b) psychotic symptoms (e.g., hallucinations, delusions, formal thought disorder, negative signs); (c) evidence of self-injurious or suicidal thoughts and behaviors; (d) potential danger to others; (e) mood disturbance (i.e., depression, anxiety); (f) substance abuse or addiction; and (g) personality dysfunction. In combination with other information (e.g., from the client, significant others, and outside agencies), this interview data provides the basis for diagnosis and an intervention plan.

Because the previously mentioned clinical issues are frequently of immediate importance, assessment for other disorders or dysfunctional states may be postponed or deferred entirely. However, if the presenting problem is a posttraumatic reaction, these standard clinical screens may miss important information. When there is a possibility of trauma-related disturbance, the interview should consider investigating the following additional components, if time allows and the client is sufficiently stable:

Symptoms of posttraumatic stress

- □ Intrusive symptoms such as flashbacks, nightmares, intrusive thoughts and memories, reliving experiences, distress or physiological reaction to trauma-reminiscent cues
- □ Avoidant symptoms such as behavioral or cognitive attempts to avoid trauma-reminiscent stimuli, or psychic numbing
- □ Hyperarousal symptoms such as decreased or restless sleep, muscle tension, irritability, jumpiness, or attention–concentration difficulties

Dissociative responses

- □ Depersonalization or derealization
- □ Fugue states
- □ "Spacing out" or cognitive disengagement
- □ Trance states
- □ Amnesia or missing time
- □ Identity alteration or confusion

Somatic disturbance

- □ Conversion reactions (e.g., paralysis, anesthesia, blindness, deafness)
- □ Somatization
- □ Psychogenic pain (e.g., pelvic pain, chronic pain)

Sexual disturbance

- □ Sexual distress (including sexual dysfunction)
- □ Sexual fears and conflicts

Trauma-related cognitive disturbance

- ☐ Low self-esteem
- ☐ Helplessness
- ☐ Hopelessness
- ☐ Overvalued ideas regarding the level of danger in the environment
- ☐ Idealization of perpetrators

Tension-reduction activities (Briere, 1992a)

- ☐ Self-mutilation
- ☐ Bingeing–purging
- ☐ Dyfunctional sexual behavior (including sex "addiction")
- ☐ Compulsive stealing
- ☐ Impulsive violent behavior

Transient posttraumatic psychotic reactions

- ☐ Stress-induced cognitive slippage, loosened associations
- ☐ Stress-induced hallucinations (often trauma congruent)
- ☐ Stress-induced delusions (often trauma congruent, especially paranoia)

Structured Diagnostic Interviews

Structured diagnostic interviews are used to generate objectively determined *DSM* diagnoses. By providing the examiner with a list of diagnostic criteria and, in some cases, specific questions to tap those criteria, such interviews ideally decrease the chance of diagnostic error and increase the likelihood of covering all relevant symptoms. In the area of posttraumatic stress, several structured interviews for diagnosing PTSD and dissociative disorders are available. At the time of this writing, however, only the Structured Clinical Interview for DSM–IV Dissociative Disorders (SCID-D; Steinberg, 1994a, 1994b), described below, suggests a diagnosis of ASD.

This book was written soon after the transition from *DSM-III-R* to *DSM-IV*; nevertheless, almost all of the interview measures reviewed here use *DSM-III-R* criteria for posttraumatic disorders. As a result, these measures cannot support *DSM-IV* diagnoses without some modification. The subjective response component (Criterion A2) is missed, and one PTSD item (physiological reactivity to reminiscent stimuli) is coded as an arousal symptom (a D criterion) by *DSM-III-R* structured interviews whereas it is considered a reexperiencing symptom (a B criterion) in *DSM-IV*. Thus, the examiner who uses currently available structured interviews must attend to these A, B, and D criteria changes in order to make a valid *DSM-IV* diagnosis. It is very likely, however, that the authors of these instruments will update them to reflect *DSM-IV* criteria.

It also should be noted that not all interview measures link specific traumatic events to specific posttraumatic symptoms. For example, an interview may inquire about the presence of a Criterion A stressor and then, if one is found, go on to ask about the presence of various reexperiencing, avoidance, and hyperarousal symptoms. However, for an accurate *DSM-IV* (or *DSM-III-R*) diagnosis to be made, it must be established that at least one trauma was specifically associated with *all* required diagnostic symptoms. In other words, it is not technically accurate to refer to the presence of PTSD if some required symptoms arise from one trauma and others arise from another.

There is considerable discussion in the trauma field regarding the appropriateness of this criterion (see Carlson, in press). Some would suggest, for example, that the presence of sufficient reliving, avoidant, and hyperarousal symptoms is indicative of PTSD, regardless of whether these symptoms arose from a single event or several. Apropos of this notion, it is not clear that "sexual abuse" or "combat" even represent single events in many cases. Instead, such stressors can occur over an extended period of time during which, presumably, different parts of these experiences might produce different PTSD symptoms. Furthermore, a complete assessment of history– symptomatology links can be quite involved, especially if one examines the client's complete lifetime. As noted by Kessler et al. (1995), "more than 10% of men and 6% of women in the [National Comorbidity Survey sample] reported four or more types of lifetime traumas, some of which involved multiple occurrences. . . . In some cases, a complete assessment of trauma history would involve an assessment of 20 or more traumas" (p. 1058).

Given the number of traumas potentially experienced by the

average client, as well as the need to link these traumas with specific PTSD or ASD symptoms, clinicians often either (a) diagnose PTSD or ASD if one or more Criterion A events can be found and the client presents with symptomatic diagnostic criteria for the disorder, or (b) determine which stressors the client views as most traumatic and then evaluate the link between this smaller set and specific PTSD–ASD symptoms. Of these two options, the latter strategy often is preferable, because (unlike the former approach) it does not produce what *DSM–IV* would consider to be false positives.

SCID—PTSD Module (SCID–PTSD)

The SCID (Spitzer, Williams, Gibbon, & First, 1990) is one of the most widely used of diagnostic interview systems. Unfortunately, the PTSD module of the SCID is not included in the published *DSM-III-R* version and must be acquired separately. A *DSM-IV* edition of the SCID is in progress, but it is not known whether the PTSD module will be included for general distribution.

The 19 items of the SCID–PTSD inquire about the presence or absence of each PTSD diagnostic criteria, along with two items tapping guilt. The client's responses are coded as "absent," "present," or "subthreshold." PTSD status can be determined for the present (in the past month) or for the individual's lifetime (worst month ever). The reader is referred to Weiss (1993, 1996) for detailed descriptions of each SCID–PTSD symptom–item and examples of criterion and noncriterion responses. This is a helpful addition, because the SCID–PTSD does not provide explicit rating descriptors.

Although formal, large-sample psychometric studies have not been performed on the SCID–PTSD module, a number of studies on specific groups of individuals suggest that it has good reliability and validity (Keane, Kolb, & Thomas, 1990; Kulka et al., 1990; McFall, Smith, Roszell, Tarver, & Malas, 1990; Weiss, 1996). The SCID has the advantage of screening for a variety of disorders in addition to PTSD, but it does not assess for the dissociative disorders. Its broad diagnostic range thus provides a more comprehensive clinical picture than is available with most trauma-specific measures.

Diagnostic Interview Schedule— PTSD Module (DIS–PTSD)

The DIS–PTSD represents a relatively new addition to the standard DIS (Robins & Heltzer, 1985). This module asks about life experiences that might be traumatic and then inquires whether any of these events led to each of 17 *DSM-III-R* PTSD symptoms. The DIS–PTSD is generally less accepted by trauma researchers and clinicians than the SCID–PTSD, however, for at least two reasons. First, the DIS, in general, has not proven to be especially sensitive to psychiatric disorders (Anthony et al., 1985; Weiss, 1996). Second, data on the performance of the DIS–PTSD module in the National Vietnam Veterans Readjustment Study was less than stellar (Kulka et al., 1988). Although the DIS–PTSD had fair sensitivity (.87), specificity (.73), and reliability ($\kappa = .64$) in the initial validation study, it had a sensitivity of only .22, a specificity of .98, and a kappa of .26 in the community sample component. However, Watson et al. (1994) found that the DIS–PTSD had high sensitivity and low specificity with reference to several other PTSD instruments.

The original DIS–PTSD module has been revised twice in recent research projects to assess more accurately *DSM-III-R* PTSD (Breslau et al., 1991; Kessler et al., 1995). These changes include, for example, considerably greater attention to stressor specification. These revisions to the DIS–PTSD module probably improve its psychometric validity considerably. However, until more data are available on these changes (along with new ones required by *DSM-IV*), it is recommended that the SCID–PTSD or some other interview be used instead of the DIS–PTSD, or at least that it not be considered in isolation from other PTSD measures (see reviews by Lating, Zeichner, & Keane, 1995, and Litz et al., 1992, for similar conclusions).

Anxiety Disorders Interview— Revised PTSD Module (ADIS–R PTSD)

The ADIS–R (DiNardo & Barlow, 1988) is a revision of the original ADIS (DiNardo, O'Brien, Barlow, Waddell, & Blanchard, 1983), which did not have a PTSD module. The PTSD module consists of 17 dichotomously scored items. Unfortunately, it does not include the prompt questions for individual symptoms found in some other structured PTSD interviews and may lead to some confusion regarding frequency-versus-intensity issues (S. D. Solomon, Keane, Newman, & Kaloupek, 1996).

At least one study (Blanchard, Gerardi, Kolb, & Barlow, 1986) suggested that the ADIS–R PTSD module is relatively reliable and valid. In that study, the ADIS–R PTSD module agreed with a clinical diagnosis of PTSD in 93% of 40 Veteran's Administration patients, yielding a kappa of .86. Weiss (1996) suggested that the ADIS–R may not be the best choice for a PTSD interview, but that it can be helpful for a differential diagnosis of PTSD versus other anxiety disorders.

Structured Interview for PTSD (SI–PTSD)

The SI–PTSD (Davidson, Smith, & Kudler, 1989) consists of 13 items designed to tap *DSM-III* PTSD criteria. A *DSM-III-R* version (with 17 items) is also available, although data on this newer version are more sparse (Davidson, Kudler, & Smith, 1990). Items are rated on a 5-point scale (0 = *absent*, 4 = *extremely severe*) and are endorsed for both current and lifetime ("worst ever") status. Symptoms must be rated as a 2 or higher to meet PTSD criteria. There are no descriptors for symptom items.

In a study of 116 veterans, the SI–PTSD had very good internal consistency (α = .94) and, in a subsample of 41 patients, good sensitivity and specificity with regard to the SCID–PTSD (.96 and .80, respectively, yielding a kappa of .79). No data are available for groups other than this sample of veterans or with traumas other than combat experience.

PTSD Symptom Scale—Interviewer Version (PSS-I)

The PSS-I (Foa, Riggs, Dancu, & Rothbaum, 1993) is a 17-item instrument that taps *DSM-III-R* symptoms of PTSD. Initially developed for sexual assault victims, the PSS-I can be easily modified for use with other traumas. Items are rated on a 0 (*not at all*) to 3 (*very much*) scale for symptoms experienced during the month preceding the interview. A symptom is considered to be present (for diagnostic purposes) if it is rated a 1 or higher. Lifetime PTSD status is not assessed.

In a sample of female physical or sexual assault victims, the PSS-I had good internal consistency (α = .85) and excellent interrater reliability for PTSD determination (κ = .91). Using the SCID as a criterion, the PSS-I had good sensitivity (.88) and excellent specificity (.96). Because the study by Foa and colleagues (1993) introducing the PSS-I examined symptoms over a 2-week period, instead of 4 weeks as required by *DSM-IV*, the reader might assume that a formal *DSM* diagnosis cannot be made with this measure. The normal PSS-I symptom interval is 4 weeks, however (E. Foa, personal communication, August 30, 1996), as required by *DSM-IV*.

Clinician-Administered PTSD Scale (CAPS-1)

The CAPS-1 (Blake et al., 1995; Blake et al., 1990) is considered one of the most promising structured interviews for PTSD. This measure was based on *DSM-III-R* criteria and was developed to address a variety of methodological problems with other trauma measures. As a result, the CAPS-1 has several helpful features, including standard prompt questions and explicit, behaviorally anchored rating scales, and it assesses both frequency and intensity of symptoms. The CAPS-1 generates both dichotomous and continuous scores for current (1 month) and lifetime ("worst ever") PTSD. In addition to the standard 17 PTSD items, the CAPS-1 also contains (a) five items tapping posttraumatic impacts on social and occupational functioning, improvement in PTSD symptoms since a previous CAPS-1 assessment, overall response validity, and overall PTSD severity; and (b) eight items addressing guilt, homicidality, disillusionment with authority, hopelessness, memory impairment, depression, and feelings of being overwhelmed.

Items of the CAPS-1 are rated on two scales that range from 0 to 4, one for frequency (*never* to *daily or almost daily*) and one for intensity (*none* to *extreme, overwhelming,* or *incapacitating*). The specific anchors for individual items vary from item to item. The interviewer has the option to indicate that any given client response is of "questionable validity." For diagnostic purposes, a symptom is considered endorsed if it is rated a 1 or greater in frequency (i.e., that it has occurred at least once in the previous month) and also rated a 2 or more in intensity (i.e., at least moderate in intensity). The authors also offer a more conservative scoring approach, considering a symptom endorsed only if the sum of frequency and intensity scales is 4 or higher. One complaint of the CAPS is that its detail and length can extend administration time up to 90 minutes (S. D. Solomon et al., 1996).

Psychometric data on the CAPS-1 is quite encouraging at this point. In a study of 60 combat veterans (Weathers, Blake, & Litz, 1991; Weathers et al., 1992), the CAPS-1 has a 2–3 day test–retest reliability of .90 to .98 for the total score and very good internal consistency (α = .94) for the composite severity score (frequency + intensity). Using the SCID as a criterion, a CAPS-1 score of 65 has a sensitivity of .84, a specificity .95, and a kappa of .78.[1] Its correlation with the Mississippi Scale for Combat-related PTSD was .91. In addition, research by the authors of the CAPS-1 suggests that scores on this measure do not differ for Whites and Blacks and therefore may be appropriate for members of both racial groups (Blake et al., 1995; Blake et al., 1990). This interview also appears to predict PTSD in older combat veterans (i.e., from World War II and the Korean war) as well as it does in younger ones (e.g., from the Vietnam war; Hyer, Summers, Boyd, Litaker, & Boudewyns, 1996).

Dissociative Disorders Interview Schedule (DDIS)

The DDIS (Ross, Heber, Norton, Anderson, & Barchat, 1989; Ross, Joshi, & Currie, 1990) consists of 131 items, each of which is coded as "yes," "no," or "unsure." This inventory provides *DSM-III* diagnoses for major depressive episode, borderline personality disorder, psychogenic amnesia, psychogenic fugue, depersonalization disorder, multiple personality disorder, and atypical dissociative disorder. Other questions include somatic

---

[1] It should be noted that a lack of complete concordance between the CAPS-1 and SCID may arise from problems with either measure, or both, as opposed to solely error variance in the CAPS-1.

complaints, substance abuse, history of psychiatric disorders and psychiatric treatment, Schneiderian First Rank symptoms, reports of paranormal experiences, and child abuse history.

Interrater reliability ranges from .68 to .76 (Ross, 1989; Ross, Anderson, et al., 1990), and Ross, Miller, et al. (1990) reported high sensitivity and specificity (.90 and 1.0, respectively) for the MPD module in a sample of 80 patients. Although this interview schedule yields only *DSM-III* diagnoses in most cases, it is a well-organized, easily administered instrument.

Office Mental Status Examination for Complex Dissociative Symptoms and Multiple Personality Disorder

The Loewenstein office mental status examination (Loewenstein, 1991) is not a structured interview in the usual sense, but rather an outline of important issues relevant to the diagnosis of dissociative disorders. This examination provides questions that can be asked to determine dissociative symptoms and examples of client responses that illustrate dissociative responses. Phenomena tapped by this examination include affective, somatoform, amnestic, autohypnotic, and process symptoms. Because this interview is not structured and does not yield quantitative results, it does not generate definitive *DSM* diagnoses. As a result, the Loewenstein does not lend itself to reliability and validity studies. Despite the lack of objective diagnostic output from this interview, however, it provides organization that can be of considerable assistance to the trained clinician.

Structured Clinical Interview for DSM–IV Dissociative Disorders (SCID-D)

The SCID-D (Steinberg, 1994a, 1994b) was developed in 1985, later undergoing revisions for *DSM-III-R* and *DSM-IV* dissociative disorders criteria. The SCID-D has more than 250 items, many of which are open-ended questions, although the use of branching options means the number of questions asked per individual is variable. It evaluates the existence and severity of five "core" dissociative symptoms (amnesia, depersonalization, derealization, identity confusion, and identity alteration) on scales ranging from 0 (*none*) to 4 (*extremely*). These ratings are based on symptom frequency, duration, distress, and level of impairment or dysfunction. The SCID-D provides diagnoses for five *DSM-IV* dissociative disorders: dissociative amnesia, dissociative fugue, depersonalization disorder, dissociative identity disorder, and dissociative disorder not otherwise specified (DDNOS). ASD and the experimental (*DSM-IV* Appendix) dissociative trance disorder can also be assessed. The SCID-D also provides very helpful intra-interview dissociative cues, such as alterations in demeanor, spontaneous age regression, and trance-like appearance, which are coded in a postinterview section.

The reliability and validity of the SCID-D have been assessed in several studies (Steinberg, Cicchetti, Buchanan, Hall, & Rounsaville, 1989–1993; Steinberg et al., 1990), although the instrument's relative recency means that very few published psychometric analyses are available to date. Unlike PTSD measures (which are generally evaluated in terms of the SCID-PTSD), there is no widely recognized "gold standard" instrument that can be used as a criterion measure of dissociative disorder diagnoses. For this reason, little data are available on the sensitivity or specificity of the SCID-D.[2]

Despite these difficulties, Steinberg et al. (1990) found the *DSM-III-R* version of the SCID-D to have very high interrater reliability (intraclass correlation coefficients and kappas were in the .90s for presence of any dissociative disorder, and they ranged from .65 to .90 for the presence of a specific dissociative disorder). Although Steinberg et al. (1990) did not report on the sensitivity and specificity of the SCID-D with reference to clinician diagnoses of dissociative disorder, they did show that patients with dissociative disorders ($n = 18$) scored significantly higher ($p < .0001$) than patients with a nondissociative disorder ($n = 23$) or a control group of nonclinical volunteers ($n = 7$).

---

[2]It is likely that as the SCID-D becomes better known, it will become the standard for diagnoses of dissociative disorder that are interview based.

Summary

As indicated in this chapter, a number of interviews are available to assist the clinician in the diagnosis of PTSD and dissociative disorders. Some of these yield *DSM–IV* diagnoses, whereas some are more relevant to *DSM–III–R* or *DSM–III*. Even in the latter cases, however, adjustments often can be made so that these interviews can suggest a *DSM–IV* diagnosis. Of the PTSD interviews, the CAPS-1 is probably most helpful, whereas the SCID-D appears to be the most comprehensive interview for dissociative disorders. Some clinicians may find these interviews too extensive or time consuming, however, and they may desire more brief or limited diagnostic support. In such cases, other interviews described in this chapter (e.g., the PSS-I for PTSD) may be sufficient. Moreover, some clinicians may eschew any structured interview for posttraumatic states, instead choosing to cover more informally the various symptoms and disorders associated with trauma, perhaps using a format similar to the trauma-relevant psychological interview presented here.

In any given instance, each of these interview approaches may be appropriate. In this regard, the "correct" interview usually is a function of the amount of time available, the extent to which the client can tolerate detailed face-to-face assessment, the goals of assessment, and the interviewer's level of expertise. When an accurate and defensible *DSM–IV* diagnosis is most important (e.g., in some forensic and research contexts), more structured interviews are usually (although not inevitably) best. When the assessment occurs in more general clinical contexts, however, the evaluator is advised to use whatever best fits the demands of the clinical situation. In some cases this too will mean use of instruments such as the CAPS-1 or SCID-D, whereas in others (e.g., when the client is especially distressed or time is of the essence) only a cursory diagnostic evaluation may be possible. When the level of evaluation is significantly reduced, however, the clinician should indicate in the assessment report any decreased confidence he or she might have in the reliability of the final assessment product.

6

General Objective and Projective Measures

In contrast to interview-based measures, objective and projective tests rely on individuals' responses to stimuli that do not arise from the clinical interview per se. In this chapter, several major objective tests and one projective instrument (the Rorschach) are described in terms of their sensitivity to posttraumatic states. In some instances, these tests contain no trauma-specific items or scales. In others, special items or scoring approaches have been added, typically within the last several years. Detailed information on the psychometric assessment of posttraumatic states can also be found in Wilson and Keane (1996), Stamm (1996), and Carlson (in press) and in chapters by Lating et al. (1995); Litz et al. (1992); and Newman, Kaloupek, and Keane (1996).

The First and Second Editions of the Minnesota Multiphasic Personality Inventory (MMPI and MMPI-2)

The MMPI (Hathaway & McKinley, 1943) and the more recent MMPI-2 (Butcher et al., 1989) have been used in a number of studies to assess posttraumatic states and dysfunction. Generally, the same trauma-related scale elevations found in the MMPI seem to occur in the MMPI-2 (Litz et al., 1991; Munley, Bains,

Bloem, & Busby, 1995). This is a preliminary impression, however, and further work is indicated before previous MMPI findings regarding specific scale elevations or multipoint profiles in traumatized groups can be applied with certainty to the MMPI-2.

Overall, individuals with PTSD often have an 8–2 profile on the MMPI and MMPI-2, as well as an elevated F scale (J. A. Fairbank, Keane, & Malloy, 1983; Keane et al., 1984; Munley et al., 1995; Wilson & Walker, 1990). Other clinical scales are often elevated above 65T or 70T as well, typically generating a variety of 3-point profiles (Munley et al., 1995).

The inevitability of an F-8-2 PTSD profile is in no way guaranteed, however. Because of the complexity of many traumatic events and the mediation by individual and environmental variables described in chapter 1, posttraumatic MMPI profiles may vary considerably. Munley et al. (1995) noted in this regard that their findings

> highlight the complexity and variability of individual profile configurations in terms of a single scale high point and high 2-point code types within a group of PTSD patients. Although Scales 2 and 8 may frequently be elevated . . . , often they may not be found as the highest clinical scale or as one of the highest two clinical elevations in the profile, and may frequently occur in combinations with other clinical scale elevations. (p. 176)

It is not surprising that a combination of standard MMPI scales—none of which were developed with reference to traumatic stress—would be less than definitive regarding the presence of posttraumatic states. Fortunately, the MMPI-2 has two scorable PTSD scales: the PS (Schlenger et al., 1989) and the PK (Keane et al., 1984). Although the PS has good internal consistency and discriminates PTSD-positive from PTSD-negative individuals, the PK is used more often, may be somewhat more predictive of PTSD (e.g., Munley et al., 1995), and has been recently revised and normed on the MMPI-2 sample (Lyons & Keane, 1992). In addition, scores on the PK appear to be generally equivalent for Blacks versus Whites (J. A. Fairbank, Caddell, & Keane, 1985), a phenomenon that has yet to be demonstrated for the PS.

The PK scale, developed by Keane and colleagues in 1984 for the MMPI, has been revised slightly for the MMPI-2. The MMPI version was validated on a sample of 200 veterans, wherein 49 items were found to discriminate PTSD status maximally. On the basis of visual inspection of the distribution of scores on this new scale, it was determined that a raw score of 30 was the best cutoff for discriminating PTSD from other psychiatric diagnoses. This cutoff yielded a hit rate of 82% in the original validation sample. Other studies have since verified the predictive validity of the original PK scale (e.g., Canon, Bell, Andrews, & Finkelstein, 1987; Gayton, Burchstead, & Matthews, 1986; Koretzky & Peck, 1990; Litz et al., 1991; Orr et al., 1990; Watson et al., 1994), although cutoffs as low as 19 to 23 have been recommended (D. Herman, Weathers, Litz, Joaquim, & Keane, 1993; Koretsky & Peck, 1990; Norris & Riad, 1996). The PK scale appears to be valid even when administered as a stand-alone measure (D. Herman et al., 1993; Scotti, Sturges, & Lyons, 1996). It is probably most helpful, however, in the context of other MMPI scores.

The MMPI-2 version of the PK scale has 46 items, rather than the 49 contained in the MMPI version. This version has less research supporting it, but there is little reason to expect that the new PK version would have lesser psychometric properties. This PK version was standardized on the MMPI-2 normative sample and thus generates T scores based on 2,600 individuals from the general population (Lyons & Keane, 1992). In the normative sample analysis, the PK had alpha reliabilities of .86 and .89 for men and women, respectively. More recently, D. Herman and colleagues (1993) reported that the internal consistency of the MMPI-2 PK scale was even higher ($\alpha = .95$). Because the MMPI-2 PK scale has 3 fewer items, Lyons and Keane suggested a cutoff of 28. Using this new cutoff score, Munley et al. (1995) found the PK to have a 76% hit rate for PTSD in a sample of 54 Veteran's Administration patients.

The MMPI and MMPI-2 PK scales have been criticized, however. Among the concerns are (a) its development and validation in primarily veteran samples (including the notion that it may be more sensitive to war-related PTSD than to that arising from civilian events), (b) the possibility that the 30- or 28-point cutoff (MMPI and MMPI-2, respectively) is too high (see Norris &

Riad, 1996, for a review, and their suggestion that 23 may be the optimal cutpoint for the MMPI-2 version), and (c) the wide variety of non-PTSD-like symptom items (as opposed to the small number of PTSD-specific items) contained in the scale. Regarding the last point, consider Graham's (1990) description of the PK scale:

> The content of the PK scale items suggests great emotional turmoil. Some items deal with anxiety, worry, and sleep disturbance. Others suggest guilt and depression. In some items subjects are reporting the presence of unwanted and disturbing thoughts, and in others they are describing lack of emotional control. Feeling misunderstood and mistreated is also present in some item content. (p. 165)

Despite these and other potential issues, there is little question that this scale is a welcome addition to the MMPI-2 in terms of assessing posttraumatic stress.

Less developed than MMPI-2 PTSD scales are those attempting to measure dissociation. Although several MMPI or MMPI-2 dissociation scales have been devised (e.g., Mann, 1995; Phillips, 1994; S. Sanders, 1986; Tellegen & Atkinson, 1974), none have sufficient psychometric data to justify their general clinical use at this point in time. Part of the problem in this area is that the writers of the MMPI and MMPI-2 items did not focus on dissociation, and thus few items may tap the construct sufficiently to warrant their inclusion in a dissociation scale. Nevertheless, several of these scales (e.g., Mann's, 1995, North Carolina Dissociation Index) look promising and should be further tested.

Beyond their relation to PTSD and dissociation, the MMPI and MMPI-2 have been used to evaluate the long-term psychological effects of childhood maltreatment. The MMPI scores of sexual abuse survivors, for example, often produce a profile characterized by elevations in scales 4 (Pd) and 8 (Sc), frequently followed by lesser elevations on 2 (D), 7 (Pt), or 6 (Pa; e.g., Belkin, Greene, Rodrigue, & Boggs, 1994; Engles, Moisan, & Harris, 1994; Goldwater & Duffy, 1990; Hunter, 1991; Lundberg-Love, Marmion, Ford, Geffner, & Peacock, 1992; Scott & Stone, 1986; Tsai, Feldman-Summers, & Edgar, 1979). The relationship between this 2-point profile and a history of childhood sexual abuse has been documented for some time—for example, Caldwell and O'Hare (1975) noted two decades ago that women with elevated 4–8 profiles often reported "a seductive and ambivalent father" and "a high frequency of incest" (p. 94).

Although a body of evidence suggests that sexual abuse survivors in therapy tend to present with a 4–8 MMPI profile (see, however, Carlin & Ward, 1992, for other scale clusters), it is not clear whether this configuration should be interpreted in the manner suggested by standard interpretive texts. Consider, for example, the following description by Graham (1990), a well-known MMPI authority:

> 48/84 individuals do not seem to fit into their environment. They are seen by others as odd, peculiar, and queer. They are nonconforming and resentful of authority, and they often espouse radical religious or political views. Their behavior is erratic and unpredictable, and they have marked problems with impulse control. They tend to be angry, irritable, and resentful, and they act out in asocial or antisocial ways. (p. 99)

Although there is some overlap between what is known about clinically presenting abuse survivors and standard 4–8 interpretations, traditional approaches to MMPI interpretation may be misleading in the evaluation of abuse-related disturbance. Lundberg-Love et al. (1992) noted:

> Historically, clinically significant elevations on the Pd and Sc scales have been interpreted as evidence of sociopathy and schizophrenia, respectively. Indeed, Scott and Stone (1986) concluded that the results of their testing indicated that incest survivors possessed a general deviancy from societal standards and a tendency to act out in antisocial, immature, and egocentric ways. (p. 98)

Lundberg-Love et al. indicated that the sexual abuse survivors in their sample accomplished a 4–8 profile through the differential endorsement of certain Pd and Sc items (as measured by Harris & Lingoes, 1968, subscales) over others. Specifically, abuse survivors' scale 4 elevations were due primarily to endorsement of familial discord and current feelings of alienation, rather than the authority and social imperturbability Pd items often endorsed by more antisocial individuals. Similarly, their sexual abuse sample scored highest on the social alienation and reduced ego-mastery items of scale 8, as opposed to the clinical levels of bizarre sensory experiences and emotional alienation endorsements often found in individuals with schizophrenia.

It is not only clinical scale interpretation of the MMPI that may suffer when applied to abuse survivors. Also problematic is the F scale of this measure, which, as often found in trauma victims, tends to be endorsed to a greater extent by former child abuse victims. Elliott (1993), for example, reported that psychiatric inpatients with victimization histories had twice the likelihood of invalid MMPI profiles than their nonvictimized cohorts (30% vs. 15%). As noted in previous chapters, this may reflect the tendency for posttraumatic dissociative and intrusive symptomatology to produce unusual experiences and chaotic, disorganized internal states (Armstrong, 1995). Under such conditions, an elevated F scale does not represent a fake bad response or invalid protocol as much as an accurate portrayal of atypical experiences and extreme stress.

Most of the problems inherent in traditional interpretations of abuse survivors' MMPI responses have also been found for victims of domestic violence. In a study specifically examining the scale 4 (Pd) endorsements of battered women, for example, Rhodes (1992) found that although battered women scored significantly higher on 4 than did nonbattered women, the most elevated Harris and Lingoes (1968) subscale was Family Discord (T 69). Like Lundberg-Love, Rhodes drew on such findings to highlight the importance of content subscales in the interpretation of victims' MMPI scale scores. Similarly, Khan, Welch, and Zillmer (1993) found that battered women typically presented with an F-4-6-8 profile, but that traditional interpretations of this configuration could lead to misdiagnosis. This sample also had elevated PS and PK scale scores, suggesting the potential posttraumatic basis of at least some of their MMPI-2 responses.

MCMI

The MCMI (Millon, 1983), MCMI-II (Millon, 1987), and MCMI-III (Millon, 1994) are among the most popular of personality tests (Choca, Shanley, & Van Denburg, 1992; Piotrowski & Lubin, 1990), yet only recently have they been applied to survivors of adult traumas. By contrast, there are a number of studies on the MCMI profiles of child abuse survivors, as noted later in this section. This differential attention probably is due to the frequent use of the MCMI to detect dysfunctional personality traits or frank personality disorders—outcomes now understood to arise, in many cases, from extended child abuse and neglect. The classic understanding of adult-onset PTSD, on the other hand, has stressed more acute, anxiety-related responses to overwhelming traumatic events, thereby potentially overlooking the more relational aspects of severe posttraumatic disturbance.

Another reason that the MCMI has been underapplied to trauma victims is the absence of a PTSD scale in the MCMI and MCMI-II. Lacking such a scale, PTSD symptoms are easily misinterpreted as evidence of personality dysfunction (e.g., borderline personality or, prior to the MCMI-III, the ill-conceived construct of "self-defeating" personality). Choca et al. (1992), for example, noted that individuals satisfying diagnostic criteria for PTSD often score in the clinical range on a variety of MCMI scales. They further noted that these scale elevations "do not exclusively identify individuals with PTSD because there may be individuals with other diagnoses who also fit the same pattern of scale elevations" (p. 128). Stated in the reverse, individuals with PTSD are likely to appear to have other psychiatric disorders on the MCMI by virtue of the relevance of other scale items to posttraumatic symptomatology.

The absence of specific posttraumatic indicators on the MCMI and MCMI-II has been partially remedied with the advent of the MCMI-III. The MCMI-III contains a PTSD scale (the R scale within the "clinical syndromes" group) that is loosely tied to some *DSM-IV* criteria. However, the content domain of this scale is somewhat problematic. Review of the R scale reveals a majority of items not directly associated with *DSM-IV* diagnostic criteria for PTSD. These include items that examine sadness, feelings of worthlessness, having "strange" thoughts, rapid mood changes, inability to experience pleasure, repeated thoughts (content unstated), fears about the future, emptiness, and suicidality. In fact, only 6 of 16 R scale items actually tap current PTSD criteria: four address reexperiencing symptoms, two tap hyperarousal, and none tap avoidance.[1] Thus, this scale seemingly overvalues reexperiencing phenomena and substantially underestimates avoidance and hyperarousal.

As also occurs for other MCMI-III scales, the R scale gives twice the weight to certain items. The values of 4 specific reexperiencing items and 1 hyperarousal item are doubled, as opposed to 1 other true PTSD item (involving past experiences "haunting" one's thoughts and dreams) and the 10 more general distress items, each of which are scored at face value. This differential weighing procedure is unique among trauma scales, and the psychometric effects of specifically doubling the value of some items but not others are unknown.

The Base Rate (BR) standardization method used by the MCMI-III may be affected by the contamination of the R scale with nontrauma-related (primarily depressive) items and its over-representation of reexperiencing symptoms. To the extent that these items do not represent the entire (or specific) content domain of PTSD, the use of cutting scores to define the "presence" (BR ≥ 75) or "prominence" (BR ≥ 85) of PTSD is of questionable merit. Until the sensitivity and specificity of these cutting scores can be assessed (ideally against a standard like CAPS-1), and in the absence of supporting interview data, it is not appropriate to state that an individual "has" PTSD by virtue of his or her MCMI-III R score, regardless of its BR elevation.

These various concerns do not mean that this scale is necessarily of lesser quality than that of the MMPI PK, a scale that also includes many depression and other nontrauma-related items. In fact, the MCMI-III scale may perform better than the PK as a continuous measure of posttraumatic stress. Rather, the fact that this scale was developed specifically to tap PTSD symptoms (as opposed to the PK, which used existing MMPI items) raises expectations that are only partially met. Moreover, unlike T-score standardization approaches, the BR method implies that a certain range of scores represents the presence of PTSD—a presump-

---

[1] Some may consider the inability to have pleasurable feelings item of the MCMI-III a summary index of the "restricted range of affect" avoidance criterion for PTSD. If so, then the PTSD scale has one avoidance item.

tion that cannot be supported without additional data. Ultimately, it may be that the R and PK scales are to some extent measures of complex PTSD (or PTSD with associated features, especially depression) than pure PTSD.

Because the MCMI-III R scale is relatively new, little data are available on its reliability or validity. The MCMI-III test manual reports that the R scale had an alpha of .89 in 398 individuals used for cross-validation purposes and a test–retest coefficient of .94 in 87 individuals tested over a 5–14 day interval (Millon, 1994). The manual indicates that the R's BR score correlates at approximately the same levels (around .5 to .6) with the depression scales of the MMPI-2 and Symptom Checklist–90–R (SCL-90-R) and the Beck Depression Inventory (BDI; Beck, Ward, Mandelson, Mock, & Erbaugh, 1961) as it does with a measure of traumatic stress (the Impacts of Event Scale; IES; Horowitz, Wilner, & Alvarez, 1979). Such data suggest that the R scale may have less than optimal discriminant validity, although this is a common problem for PTSD scales vis-à-vis depression.

As noted earlier, no data are available on the PTSD scale's sensitivity or specificity with regard to a structured interview (e.g., CAPS-1) diagnosis of PTSD. Millon (1994) did present data, however, on the relationship between two dichotomous variables: a variable indicating whether the PTSD scale was the highest or second highest BR score on an MCMI-III profile, and another reflecting whether the clinician rated PTSD as the most prominent or second most prominent characteristic. Using this relatively broad criterion for diagnostic agreement, Millon found R to have a sensitivity of only .37 and a specificity of .84 in a sample of 1,079 individuals evaluated by "several hundred" clinicians (p. 19). Millon noted, however, that "most clinical judges in our rating study saw the subject only once and usually without the benefit of clinical interviews or extensive readings of their histories" (p. 34).

The few studies available on possible MCMI adult trauma profiles are limited to the MCMI and MCMI-II and deal almost exclusively with Vietnam veterans. They suggest that those suffering posttraumatic stress may have elevations on some combination of the Avoidant, Schizoid, Passive–Aggressive, and Borderline scales, along with (in many cases) Anxiety and Dysthymia clinical syndrome scales (Hyer, Woods, Boudewyns, Bruno, & O'Leary, 1988; Hyer, Woods, Boudewyns, Harrison, & Tamkin, 1990; McDermott, 1987). Two studies in this area also report elevated scores on the Self-defeating Personality scale of the MCMI-II (Hyer, Davis, Albrecht, Boudewyns, & Woods, 1994; Hyer, Davis, Woods, Albrecht, & Boudewyns, 1992), a scale that tends to interpret suicidality and other detrimental behaviors as evidence of an unconscious desire to seek out negative outcomes and self-punishment. Perhaps apropos of its absence in the MCMI-III, however, this scale (and its underlying assumption) appears to be misleading, if not victim blaming, rather than clinically helpful. It is likely that as the new MCMI-III is applied to trauma survivors, some version of the MCMI pattern outlined above (minus Self-defeating personality) may continue to appear, probably with especially elevated R as well.

As noted earlier in this chapter, the MCMI has been used to evaluate the lasting effects of child abuse on adults. At least three studies (Bryer et al., 1987; Busby, Glenn, Steggell, & Adamson, 1993; Fisher, Winne, & Ley, 1993) indicated that physical or sexual abuse survivors score in the clinical range on a variety of MCMI-I and MCMI-II scales, most typically on the Avoidant, Dependent, Passive–Aggressive, and Borderline Personality scales, along with elevated Anxiety, Somatoform, Thought Disorder, Major Depression, and Delusional Disorder scales.

As with other traumatized individuals, a potential problem associated with interpreting child abuse survivors' responses to the MCMI is whether high scores on a given scale indicate that the survivor, in fact, "has" the relevant disorder or personality style. For example, although yet to be tested empirically, clinical experience suggests that most abuse survivors who have elevated scores on the MCMI Thought Disorder or Delusional Disorder scales do not have psychotic symptoms, nor do all of those with a clinically elevated Borderline scale score necessarily have borderline personality disorder. Instead, the MCMI psychotic scales (like the Rorschach in various trauma contexts) are likely to tap the posttraumatic symptoms (especially intrusion and avoidance) and chaotic internal experience of severe abuse survivors, whereas the Borderline scale may be affected by the greater tension-reduction activities and interpersonal difficulties of the severely abused.

With the advent of the MCMI-III R scale, some of the issues associated with misidentification of child abuse survivors may be reduced. To the extent that the R scale operates as advertised, it may facilitate the interpretation of abuse survivors' MCMI scores by indicating the presence of at least some instances of posttraumatic stress. In such cases, although other less relevant scales might also be elevated (e.g., Thought Disorder), the presence of a high PTSD score would alert the examiner to the possibility of alternate explanations for such scale elevations.

Despite its several limitations, the MCMI-III's broad coverage of Axis I and II, plus its inclusion of a PTSD-related scale, support its specific application with trauma survivors. Its use may be especially warranted in instances where posttraumatic states coexist with personality disorders or where complex PTSD is a probable diagnostic issue.

Psychological Assessment Inventory (PAI)

The PAI (Morey, 1991) is a 344-item inventory consisting of 4 validity scales and 18 nonoverlapping clinical scales, many of which have scorable subscales. Because it is relatively new, the PAI has not been well studied in terms of its association with traumatic stress. However, it contains a PTSD subscale, evaluates both Axis I and Axis II disorders, and—as one of the latest generation of psychological tests—has superior psychometric characteristics.

One of three components of the full Anxiety-Related Disorders (ARD) scale is the PTSD subscale (ARD-T) of the PAI. Five items of ARD-T tap reexperiencing phenomena, and three are concerned with guilt, loss of interest, and avoidance of memory-triggering stimuli. In the beta stage of test development, ARD-T had an alpha of .89 in 325 individuals. In follow-up reliability studies, alphas ranged from .81 to .89 in community, college student, and clinical samples. The ARD-T subscale correlated significantly ($r = .59$) with the Mississippi Scale for Combat-related PTSD (Keane, Caddell, & Taylor, 1988) in 21 Veterans Administration patients, 11 of whom had diagnoses of PTSD (Morey, 1991). No concurrent validity with respect to the SCID-R, CAPS-1, or other structured interview was reported in the PAI manual. In a study of the PAI profiles of 53 individuals with clinical diagnoses of PTSD (diagnostic method not reported), Morey (1991) noted:

> the posttraumatic stress group had a more elevated profile [than those with other anxiety disorders], with mean scores above 70T on DEP [depression] and ARD [anxiety-related disorder]. The subscale configuration for the PTSD group was particularly interesting; marked ARD-T (traumatic stress), accompanied by indicators of confusion (SCZ-T), social estrangement (SCZ-S and BOR-N), and poor control over anger and aggression (BOR-A and AGG-P). (p. 104)

Although the ARD-T tends to prize posttraumatic reexperiencing over avoidance or hyperarousal, its moderate correlation with the Mississippi Scale for Combat-related PTSD and its specific elevation among PTSD sufferers suggests its potential usefulness when the PAI is applied to traumatized individuals. Because its sensitivity and specificity with reference to PTSD and other posttraumatic disorders are unknown, however, it should not be used in isolation to make a posttraumatic stress diagnosis. The PAI, itself, has wide content coverage (i.e., covering both Axis I and II disorders) and very good psychometric characteristics—qualities that may justify its frequent use in standard trauma assessment batteries.

Symptom Checklist-90—Revised (SCL-90-R)

The SCL-90-R (Derogatis, 1977, 1983), a widely used symptom checklist measure, is based on the earlier Hopkins Symptom Checklist (HSCL; Derogatis, Lipman, Rickels, Ulenhuth, & Covi, 1974). Derogatis has since developed the Brief Symptom Inventory (BSI; Derogatis & Spencer, 1982), a shorter version of the SCL-90-R. The SCL-90-R consists of nine subscales and an index of global distress. The various subscales of the SCL-90-R appear to predict trauma-related disturbance in a wide variety of individuals, including survivors of the Holocaust (e.g., Yehuda et al., 1994), women subjected to marital rape (e.g., Riggs, Kilpatrick,

& Resnick, 1992), war veterans (e.g., Davidson, Kudler, Saunders, & Smith, 1990; Wolfe, Brown, & Bucsela, 1992), and adults abused as children (e.g., Murphy et al., 1988; Surrey, Swett, Michaels, & Levin, 1990). The SCL-90-R does not have a specific scale to assess posttraumatic disturbance, however, and several scales have items that may interpret trauma effects as, for example, obsessive–compulsive or psychotic symptomatology, or as interpersonal sensitivity. As noted by Elliott (1994a):

> Although this instrument provides valuable information related to psychological distress, its development without specific reference to victimization may limit its usefulness in this regard. For example, some of the items thought to be indicative of psychosis are consistent with long-term sexual abuse or battering relationships (such as feeling lonely even when you are with people and never feeling close to another person). Thus, as with other measures, item analysis is recommended when clinical elevations are reached on various scales. (p. 11)

The SCL-90-R does not have a specific posttraumatic stress scale, but two SCL-PTSD scales have been developed—one by Saunders and colleagues (B. E. Saunders, Arata, & Kilpatrick, 1990) and one by Ursano, Fullerton, Kao, Bhartiya, and Dinneen (1992). The Saunders et al. scale consists of the 28 SCL-90-R items that best discriminated PTSD status in a sample of 355 individuals from the general population. The authors noted that this subscale represents an additional way to score the SCL-90-R but should not be considered a separate, stand-alone symptom measure. B. E. Saunders and colleagues found that the resultant subscale was internally consistent ($\alpha = .93$) and could discriminate crime-related PTSD (CR-PTSD) in 89% of cases. Further analysis of this subscale was performed with a subsample of 266 female crime victims (Arata, Saunders, & Kilpatrick, 1991). The SCL-PTSD subscale was found to have incremental validity with respect to the IES and was able to discriminate individuals with CR-PTSD from those without crime-related PTSD. Using the DIS as the PTSD criterion, the SCL-PTSD had a sensitivity of .75 and a specificity of .91. Because this subscale was validated in the same sample in which it was created, the authors correctly noted that the generalizability of these results is unknown. Furthermore, the applicability of this subscale to noncrime-related PTSD is unclear, and no normative data are available for this measure, as opposed to the full SCL-90-R. Nevertheless, if further tested and standardized, this scoring approach could provide clinicians with the opportunity to assess posttraumatic stress with the SCL-90-R, generally in a manner similar to the trauma scales of the MMPI-2, MCMI-III, and PAI.

A second SCL-90-R PTSD scale, created by Ursano et al. (1992), uses those 30 items from the SCL-90-R judged by a panel of experts to best represent the symptoms of PTSD, along with 12 new reexperiencing, avoidance, and hyperarousal items written in the SCL-90-R format. The resultant 42-item measure had a mean sensitivity of .67 and a specificity of .91 in four samples (total $N = 1{,}273$) of individuals exposed to disasters when compared to a cutoff score of 19 on the PK scale (Ursano et al., 1992; also described in Ursano et al., 1995). Like the CR-PTSD, no normative data are available for this scale.

Because both the B. E. Saunders et al. (1990) and Ursano et al. (1992) measures represent nonstandard scoring of the SCL-90-R, and the Ursano et al. scale involves the addition of new items, clinical use of either scale should be predicated on permission from the test publisher (reportedly absent thus far). It is especially doubtful that permission would be given for either scale to be used separate from the SCL-90-R.

Rorschach

As is true of the other standard measures reviewed here, the Rorschach (Rorschach, 1921/1981) has both positive and negative qualities with regard to the assessment of posttraumatic states. On one hand, this test provides an opportunity to avoid the constraints of objective testing, wherein the client typically is forced to respond to a specific test item and therefore to a specific minihypothesis regarding the structure of psychological disturbance. Instead, the Rorschach and other projectives offer a set of relatively free-form stimuli, to which the client may respond in any manner he or she chooses. As a result, the productions of the client are less predetermined and therefore more free to reflect whatever trauma effects might be discoverable by such a method.

On the other hand, the interpretation systems used to classify Rorschach responses (especially non-Exnerian systems) are not entirely free of theoretical assumptions and are subject to whatever level of misinterpretation of posttraumatic states the underlying assessment perspective may entail. For example, some PTSD sufferers seemingly revealed signs of thought disorder or impaired reality testing in one Rorschach study of war veterans (van der Kolk & Ducey, 1984, 1989), even though these indicators "coexisted with an absence of psychotic thinking in clinical interviews, suggesting that the subjects possessed a basically intact reality orientation that was only overwhelmed by intrusive traumatic material in the context of unstructured tests" (E. A. Saunders, 1991, p. 50). Similar problems arise with reference to misdiagnosis of personality disorder in some trauma protocols (e.g., Levin & Reis, 1996; E. A. Saunders, 1991). The potential overlap between psychotic, personality disordered, and posttraumatic Rorschach presentations requires the clinician to be familiar with all three diagnostic scenarios and their Rorschach representations when evaluating posttraumatic dysfunction or disorder.

A number of studies have reported a specific cluster of Rorschach indicators that appear to tap various aspects of posttraumatic stress (see Levin & Reis, 1996, for a review). Although such indicators frequently make intuitive sense, the methodology of these studies often involved the mere comparison of a group of posttraumatic Rorschach scores to Exner's (1986) normative data. Such a procedure is not only potentially confounded by differences in background variables between the posttraumatic subjects and Exner's normative sample, but it also does not allow much discrimination between types of posttraumatic disturbance. For example, although a given study may find that clients with a dissociative disorder score higher on unstructured color or morbid content relative to norms, it is not clear whether this difference represents dissociation per se, differences in clinical acuity between samples, comorbid posttraumatic stress, or perhaps the generalized effects of a trauma history on affect regulation capacities. As a result, the reader is advised to use caution in making especially specific interpretations regarding what otherwise might be more general posttraumatic Rorschach responses.

Given these caveats, several studies outline potential Rorschach indicators of the reexperiencing, avoidant, and hypervigilant symptoms of acute distress disorder, PTSD, and other posttraumatic states. For example, protocols with unusually extratensive Erlebnistypus (Experience Balance; EB), low human movement (M), and extensive unstructured color responses (CF and pure C > FC) have been interpreted as reflecting posttraumatic intrusion and reliving (e.g., van der Kolk & Ducey, 1984, 1989). Posttraumatic avoidance and psychic numbing, on the other hand, often covary with low affective ratios (Afr) and high Lambdas (Hartman et al., 1990; Kaser-Boyd, 1993). Hypervigilance in response to trauma often presents, as expected, as HVI (Levin, 1993, 1994 [described in Levin & Reis, 1996]). Also present in such protocols may be evidence of feelings of helpless and powerlessness, such as inanimate movement responses (m) and diffuse shading determinants (Y; Levin, 1993, 1994, in Levin & Reis, 1996; Salley & Teiling, 1984; van der Kolk & Ducey, 1984, 1989).

Rorschach correlates of dissociation appear to parallel those of posttraumatic avoidance, along with potentially elevated form dimension responses (FD) and introversive–superintroversive EB styles (Armstrong, 1991; Lovitt & Lefkoff, 1985). Drawing on the work of Labott, Leavitt, Braun, and Sachs (1992) and E. A. Saunders (1991), Leavitt and Labott (1996) also considered three Rorschach responses to be potential indicators of dissociation:

> (1) Reference to forms seen through obscuring media, such as veils, fog, or mist so that people or objects look unclear or blurry; (2) reference to unusual responses in which distance appears exaggerated such that objects or figures appear vague and far away from other specified objects; (3) reference to a sense of disorientation in which Rorschach stimuli are experienced as unstable, shifting, moving, or rapidly changing. (p. 488)

It should be noted, however, that this list has yet to be established as, in fact, definitive evidence of dissociation.

As is noted later in this chapter, Armstrong and Loewenstein (1990) also documented especially frequent sex, blood, anatomy, and aggression content scores among those with dissociative identity disorder. However, this relationship may have more to do with the traumatic etiology of dissociation than to dissociative symptomatology per se.

Survivors of chronic trauma, especially those experiencing the long-term effects of child abuse, tend to produce the unstructured color responses, poor form quality, and frequent morbid, blood, sexual, and anatomy content described above; greater aggression; both more active and more passive movement; more atypical movement responses (per the Rappaport, Gil, & Schafer, 1945–1946, system, modified by E. A. Saunders, 1991); and greater bodily concerns (e.g., Meyers, 1988; Nash et al., 1993; Owens, 1984; E. A. Saunders, 1991). Also present may be elevated thought disorder and confabulation indicators (Cerney, 1990; Hartman et al., 1990; Hofmann-Patsalides, 1994; Levin, 1993; E. A. Saunders, 1991; van der Kolk & Ducey, 1984, 1989). Together, these responses traditionally are considered to be evidence of personality disorder, perhaps especially of the borderline type (e.g., Kwawer, Lerner, Lerner, & Sugarman, 1980). Trauma-specialized clinicians (e.g., Briere, 1989; Levin & Reis, 1996; E. A. Saunders, 1991; van der Kolk & Ducey, 1989), on the other hand, noted that these same responses are provided by severely traumatized individuals and suggested that they need not represent characterologic difficulties as much as posttraumatic stress.

The presence of a history of trauma does not rule out the possibility of personality disorder, however. Although severe trauma can destabilize, affectively overwhelm, produce flashbacks, and lead to preoccupation with violent and sexual themes, it is also true that early traumas such as child abuse are risk factors for true personality-level symptoms and dysfunctions (e.g., Briere & Zaidi, 1989; J. L. Herman et al., 1989). As a result, although unstructured color responses in a trauma victim may reflect the intrusion of flashbacks or other reliving experiences, they also may arise from more borderlinelike difficulties in affect regulation that ultimately lead to externalizing tension-reduction activities (i.e., "acting out"). Similarly, the presence of thought disorder or confabulation responses may signal a disorganized internal state arising from an acute and overwhelming trauma or may represent the more diffuse impairment in self functions found in some individuals with borderline personality disorder. As noted at various points in this book, this concatenation of posttraumatic stress and characterologic disturbance is especially salient in adult survivors of severe childhood abuse, where traditional distinctions between these two symptom clusters or axes may be difficult to make or even counterproductive in some instances (Briere, 1992a; J. L. Herman, 1992b; Kroll, 1993). Perhaps the "bottom line" with regard to this issue is one of interpretive balance: It is as wrong to misinterpret PTSD responses as psychosis or borderline personality disorder as it is to rule out the latter disorders solely because the individual has a history of trauma.

Traditional interpretive approaches to the Rorschach are particularly likely to misinterpret posttraumatic symptomatology in one area: that of ideographic (i.e., morbid, aggressive, blood, sex, and anatomy) content responses (e.g., Armstrong, 1991; Briere, 1989; Leavitt & Labott, 1996; Levin, 1993; van der Kolk & Ducey, 1984, 1989). These responses, if excessive in frequency, are often seen as signs of thought disorder, primary process breakthrough, or primitive personality organization (e.g., Kissen, 1986; Kwawer et al., 1980). Yet, as noted by various authors (e.g., Armstrong, 1991; van der Kolk & Ducey, 1984, 1989), such responses often do not seem to relate to psychosis or personality disorder in traumatized individuals as much as to the intrusion of actual historical themes into perception. Apropos of this, Armstrong and Loewenstein (1990) created a special *Traumatic Content Index* (TC/R) for identifying potentially traumatized individuals, defined as "the sum of the sex, blood, and anatomy content scores plus the morbid and aggressive special scores divided by the total number of responses" and expressed as a percentage (p. 450). In a sample of 14 individuals, the authors found those with multiple personality disorder (dissociative identity disorder) had very high TC/R scores (a mean of 50%, with a range of 30% to 80%), which they attributed to "disruption by posttraumatic intrusions" (p. 453). Armstrong has since added considerably more individuals to this study and reports that this Index continues to be a strong indicator of trauma (J. Armstrong, personal communication, January 25, 1996).

In an attempt to define Rorschach indicators of sexual abuse in particular, Leavitt and Labott (1996) compared the Rorschach responses of 29 psychiatric inpatient women with sexual abuse histories to 85 similar inpatients who reported no sexual abuse history. The authors found eight content indicators that were (a) significantly more common among the sexual abuse group than the nonabuse group, and (b) occurred in the nonabused group infrequently (i.e., 5% or less of the time). These were sexual activity, sexual anxiety, sexual violence, damage to the body, imagery of adults as victims, imagery of children as victims, imagery of fearful adults, and imagery of fearful children. Using a "sexual abuse index" consisting of the number of signs present (ranging from zero to eight), the authors found that a cutoff score of two or more signs correctly classified 93% of the abused inpatients and 98% of the nonabused inpatients. This index also identified as abused 88% of a separate sample of women ($N = 26$) reporting recovered memories of sexual abuse who evidenced dissociative symptoms on the Rorschach.

Given the frequent relationship between trauma and certain content indicators, the sex, aggression, victimization, and anatomy responses of a rape victim or sexual abuse survivor may reflect projection of victimization-related content onto the Rorschach (Briere, 1989), just as a Vietnam veteran's frequent blood, violence, or morbid responses may arise from real wartime experiences. As first noted by Exner in 1979 (p. 304), "[a]ny excess of content should be regarded as a form of preoccupation, after which, the impact of that preoccupation should be judged." In the case of posttraumatic intrusion, the preoccupation often appears to arise from unresolved traumatic memories that are easily elicited or cued by Rorschach stimuli. Carlson and Armstrong (1995) argued that "for traumatized patients, tests like the Rorschach can cease to be a projective measure, and become instead a traumatic trigger. Unless the assessor is conversant with the PTSD literature . . . , traumatic reactions are likely to be misdiagnosed as indicators of psychotic or characterologically primitive function" (p. 169).

Summary

As indicated in this chapter, traditional objective and projective psychological tests can be an important part of the trauma-focused assessment battery. Generic tests provide important information on less trauma-specific phenomena, such as the presence of anxiety, depression, personality disorder, or psychosis. When trauma-specific scales or scoring procedures are available within generic tests, elevated scores on these measures may signal the possibility of one or more posttraumatic states. In most cases these scales are normed on general population samples, allowing the clinician to interpret specific scores in terms of their extremity, if not severity.

Unfortunately, almost none of the currently available generic measures, with or without trauma-specific features, are especially sensitive to posttraumatic stress. They typically include a variety of items that are not directly related to posttraumatic symptomatology, do not represent the three components of PTSD very well, and do not assess symptoms within the 1-month range required by *DSM-IV*. Equally important, almost none of these measures test for acute stress disorder or dissociative disorders. As a result, it is recommended that generic tests be administered with—or followed up by—more specialized trauma measures whenever possible, rather than being used in isolation to index posttraumatic disturbance.

Chapter 7

Trauma-Specific
Self-Report Measures

In addition to the generic psychological tests outlined in chapter 6, a number of more trauma-specific self-report measures are available to clinicians. Two kinds of measures are used to assess posttraumatic difficulties: diagnostic criterion-based measures that tend to focus on *DSM-III-R* or *DSM-IV* diagnoses (although some also measure symptom intensity) and longer instruments that are more concerned with assessing the relevant *extent* of posttraumatic symptoms, such as reexperiencing, avoidant, or dissociative responses. Both types of tests are discussed in this chapter.

Trauma-specific self-report measures have strengths and weaknesses. The primary advantages of such instruments are (a) their avoidance of the subjectivity associated with some trauma-based diagnostic interviews; (b) the greater reliability they potentially offer because multiple items address the same phenomena; (c) the reduced need for qualified clinicians to be physically present during parts of the evaluation; and (d) the ease with which such tests can be administered, both in terms of the amount of time involved per test and the possibility of assessing multiple persons simultaneously.

The growing availability of trauma-specific measures has been of critical importance in the development of effective research and treatment approaches to posttraumatic states. However, problems remain because of the relative youth of the field (especially in terms of assessing and treating non-combat-related traumatic stress) and the continuing changes in our understanding and categorization of posttraumatic states (e.g., the transition from *DSM-III-R* to *DSM-IV* stress categories). First, research clinicians have tended to produce slightly different versions of essentially the same trauma measure. As is discussed in this chapter, a number of investigators have written measures that consist of 17 items reflecting the 17 diagnostic indicators of *DSM-III-R* posttraumatic stress disorder. These measures differ primarily in terms of how these criteria are worded in lay language, with differences in reliability and validity arising from the various levels of success associated with this endeavor and the sample used to test each measure. Not only is this approach somewhat redundant, it creates inherent limitations in the resultant instruments. Most importantly, such measures by definition only provide one item per criterion of PTSD. If the individual misinterprets or avoids that item, the underlying construct goes unassessed or is distorted. Furthermore, in accordance with standard measurement theory, a single item is a far less reliable estimate of a construct than are several related items and leads to error variation in the assessment of, for example, flashbacks or psychic numbing.

Second, most current trauma measures examine only three symptom clusters: posttraumatic reexperiencing, avoidance, and hyperarousal. Yet, as outlined in chapter 2 and elsewhere, there are a variety of other posttraumatic states or responses, ranging from acute stress disorder (yet to be assessed by most current instruments) to dissociation, somatization, and posttraumatic personality dysfunction. A comprehensive trauma assessment also should evaluate these symptom clusters, perhaps especially the confluence of dissociation and more classic notions of posttraumatic stress.

Third, objective trauma measures that use a total score to reflect posttraumatic stress (i.e., in terms of a cutting score for the presence or absence of PTSD) inappropriately collapse the three dimensions of posttraumatic stress into a single score. As a result, there may be several different ways for individuals to achieve the same total PTSD score: some primarily through reexperiencing, some through extensive avoidance, some mostly through hyperarousal, and some through moderate endorsement of all symptom items. Clearly, these different responses represent different clinical scenarios, each of which ideally should be measured through separate scales.

Another problem for authors of trauma measures is determining whether to anchor the items in a specific, identified event; to leave the trauma unspecified; or to avoid any reference to a trauma altogether. Because acute stress disorder and PTSD are, by definition, linked to a specific traumatic experience, it would seem that measures of these disorders would have to include the specific stressor directly. However, this approach is difficult to accomplish in a measure that may be used to address different traumas for different people, as well as those who have experienced multiple traumas. Some test authors have therefore included reference to a stressor but left it unspecified. This is often an improvement but can still easily confuse the victim of multiple traumas, who may not be sure whether flashback X is associated with stressor Y or Z, or whose dissociative numbing or hyperarousal is not easily tied to any specific traumatic event. Because of this potential confusion, a few test developers (e.g., Briere, 1995c; Foy et al., 1984) sought to measure the general level of intrusive reexperiencing or cognitive avoidance, without reference to any specific stressor at all (e.g., "Upsetting thoughts about the past keep popping into my mind"). This approach has merit but produces a new problem: Does a person have PTSD if he or she has flashbacks from event A, avoidance associated with events B and C, and hyperarousal related to event D? Clearly, *DSM-IV* would not support this position; it requires a specific etiologic event for all symptoms. However, the clinician has a few other ways to assess the total amount of posttraumatic stress a given client is experiencing, short of asking him or her to indicate for each symptom the specific trauma(s) on which it is based.

Finally, although a number of trauma-specific measures demonstrate reliability and validity in research contexts, their use in clinical settings is dependent on additional psychometric issues. Most importantly, with a few exceptions, none of these instruments are accompanied by appropriate normative data. As a result, the clinician has little way to determine to what extent (if at all) the respondent's level of symptom endorsement is above what most people would endorse. In contrast, standardized measures allow the evaluator to compare the client's score with that of the general population and determine how deviant (i.e., clinically significant) it is.

In the case of solely diagnostic screening instruments, the absence of normative data is generally not a problem, because the only issue is whether a given set of symptoms is present. For continuous measures of a clinical construct, however, the evaluator is left without knowing whether a score of X is normal or symptomatic. On occasion, this problem is partially addressed by cutting scores, wherein a given score (or higher) is reported to be associated with a given diagnosis with a certain level of probability. However, the cutoff for a given diagnosis may vary from sample to sample, and this approach does not allow for interpretation of the entire range of scores below and above the cutoff point.

In light of these normative concerns, the clinician is advised to qualify his or her interpretation of scores on nonstandardized trauma-specific measures. In some cases, the examiner may be able to say that approximately X% of individuals with Y disorder scored higher or lower than the respondent (based on available means and standard deviations) in a given sample in a given published study. If this is done, the examiner should also describe the extent to which the respondent matches the demographics and clinical status of that sample.

Despite these various issues, the trauma field has produced a number of trauma-specific instruments that provide a general assessment of posttraumatic stress and dissociative disturbance, at least in research contexts. The following measures are presented here because they have been tested in at least one relevant sample and achieve some reasonable level of reliability and validity. Because the field is progressing rapidly, it is quite possible that other useful measures have been overlooked in this review.

Impact of Event Scale
(IES) and IES–Revised (IES-R)

The IES (Horowitz, Wilner, & Alvarez, 1979) is one of the earliest self-report measures of posttraumatic disturbance. This instrument specifically evaluates trauma-related intrusion and avoidance in terms of Horowitz's (1976) theory of stress response syndromes. Respondents are asked to rate IES symptom items on a 4-point scale according to how often each has occurred in the last 7 days, on a scale marked 0 (*not at all*), 1 (*rarely*), 3 (*sometimes*), and 5 (*often*). Seven items evaluate intrusion and eight items tap avoidance, yielding two subscale scores. All items of the IES are anchored to a specific stressor (e.g., "Pictures about __ popped into my mind"). Horowitz et al. (1979) reported acceptable reliability for both the Intrusion and Avoidance scales (alphas of .79 and .82, respectively) in a sample of 66 "stress response syndrome" outpatients. The IES has been shown to discriminate a variety of traumatized groups from their nontraumatized cohorts, including combat veterans, emergency services personnel, natural disaster survivors, victims of crimes, and adults sexually abused as children (e.g., Alexander, 1993; Arata et al., 1991; Briere & Elliott, 1996a; Bryant & Harvey, 1996; Elliott & Briere, 1995; Hendrix, Jurich, & Schumm, 1994; Lundin & Bodegard, 1993; McFarlane, 1988; Runtz, 1990).

Although the IES taps intrusive and avoidant symptomatology, it has no scale for the PTSD cluster of hyperarousal symptoms. In response, researchers have developed a revised version of the IES (IES-R; Weiss, Marmar, Metzler, & Ronfeldt, 1995; Marmar, Weiss, Metzler, & Delucchi, 1996). The IES-R contains six new hyperarousal items and an additional item to parallel *DSM-IV* criteria. In their summary of this revision, Weiss and Marmar (1996) noted that the additional hyperarousal scale has good internal consistency (alphas ranging from .79 to .90 in different samples) and predictive validity with regard to trauma.

Unfortunately, the IES and IES-R were developed as research measures and generally lack the requisite normative data associated with modern clinical tests. With regard to the latter issue, however, data are now available on this measure (but not the IES-R) for 505 individuals from the general population (Briere & Elliott, 1996a). Although such data may allow statistical interpretation of Intrusion and Avoidance scores in terms of their relative elevations above "normal" levels, the nonclinical focus, potentially limited content domain, and brevity of the IES suggests that it should not be used as more than a screen for the presence of (non-arousal-related) posttraumatic stress. This caution is especially true if the IES is used in isolation from other, more fully validated instruments.

An important caveat for use of the IES in clinical or research settings is its considerable variability as a function of race. In our general population study, Briere and Elliott (1996a) found that Blacks scored substantially higher than Whites on the IES total score. This race difference decreased (but did not disappear) when the relative amount of violence experienced by Whites versus Blacks was controlled for. As a result, interpretations based on IES score differences should always take race into account.

Los Angeles Symptom Checklist (LASC)

The LASC (Foy et al., 1984) is a 43-item measure of posttraumatic stress, 17 items of which measure the reexperiencing, avoidance, and hyperarousal components of *DSM-III-R* PTSD. These items can be scored to yield a suggested *DSM-IV* PTSD diagnosis, although this revised scoring has yet to be fully tested for sensitivity and specificity (D. Foy, personal communication, September 10, 1996). Other items of the LASC tap physical status (e.g., appetite), social competence, general psychological distress, and suicidality (King, King, Leskin, & Foy, 1995). Individuals rate symptoms according to how much they are "a problem," ranging from 0 (*no problem*) to 4 (*extreme problem*). The LASC may be used to suggest a PTSD diagnosis if the relevant symptoms are endorsed at a "2" or higher, although the absence of a symptom duration time frame for this measure precludes a technical PTSD designation. In addition to a dichotomous PTSD indication, the LASC provides continuous measures of (a) general PTSD severity (sum of the 17 items); (b) three PTSD subscales (separate sums of the items representing reexperiencing, avoidance, and arousal, e.g., Briere, 1995c; Elliott & Briere, 1995); and (c) general distress and adjustment problems (sum of all 43 items).

Originally named the Symptom Checklist (SCL; Foy et al., 1984), the LASC has been validated in studies across a broad range of traumas (e.g., Astin et al., 1993; Butler, Foy, Snodgrass, Lea-Hurwicz, & Goldfarb, 1988; Elliott & Briere, 1995; Foy et al., 1984; Houskamp & Foy, 1991; Lawrence, Cozolino, & Foy, 1995;

Rowan et al., 1994). On the basis of a review of these studies and a new analysis of 874 individuals with mixed trauma, L. A. King et al. (1995) concluded that the LASC has high internal and test–retest reliability and acceptable convergent validity with respect to the Structured Clinical Interview for DSM–III–R (SCID-R). In the 874 sample, alphas for the 17 and 43 items were .94 and .95 respectively, with very good 2-week test–retest reliabilities (.94 and .90, respectively) in a subset of 19 Vietnam veterans. Using the 17 items as a continuous variable, sensitivity of the LASC with reference to SCID-identified PTSD was .74 and specificity was .77. When the 17 LASC items were scored to generate a *DSM-III-R* diagnosis (i.e., dichotomously), its sensitivity and specificity vis-à-vis the SCID-R was .78 and .82, respectively.

Like most other trauma measures described in this chapter, the LASC does not have published general population norms. However, general population data are available on the 17 PTSD items of the LASC (Briere & Elliott, 1996b). These data may allow technical interpretation of the LASC reexperiencing, avoidance, and arousal subscale scores with reference to their deviation from normal levels, although not of the full 43-item scale. Such data support the use of the LASC as a screening instrument, which then may be followed up with a clinical interview or further psychological testing.

Mississippi Scale for Combat-Related PTSD

The Mississippi Scale for Combat-related PTSD (Keane et al., 1988) is a 35-item instrument developed to measure PTSD in veterans of war. All items are anchored in war experiences, and respondents rate symptomatology that has occurred "since I was in the military" on 5-point Likert-like scales. This instrument is the most commonly used PTSD measure for veteran populations. It has been shown to have excellent reliability (i.e., test–retest and internal consistency coefficients in the .90s; Keane et al., 1988; McFall, Smith, McKay, & Tarver, 1990; Kulka et al., 1990) and is generally felt to have among the highest hit rates for diagnosed PTSD among similar measures (McFall, Smith, McKay, et al., 1990; McFall, Smith, Roszell, et al., 1990; Watson,

1990). For these reasons, the Mississippi Scale was chosen for use in the national survey component of the National Vietnam Veterans Readjustment Study (NVVRS). However, recent research on 80 help-seeking Vietnam veterans by Watson et al. (1994) suggested that the Mississippi may be approximately equivalent to other measures in terms of its ability to identify PTSD-positive individuals (i.e., hit rates in the low .80s).

Analyses of potential race differences in the Mississippi Scale suggest that scores on this measure are generally equivalent for Whites and Blacks (Keane et al., 1988). If replicated in other studies, this finding suggests that the Mississippi may be applicable to African Americans, although its performance with other racial groups has yet to be demonstrated.

There is also a 39-item Hostage Version of the combat Mississippi (Keane et al., 1988), as well as a 39-item version[1] for Persian Gulf war zone personnel (Keane et al., 1988). Both of these measures are quite similar to the combat version, except that they are more relevant to hostage and Persian Gulf experiences, respectively.

Civilian Mississippi Scale (CMS) and Revised Mississippi Scale (RCMS)

The CMS, developed by Keane and colleagues, was used as an experimental scale in the NVVRS study as a way to evaluate the rate of PTSD in nonveterans (Vreven, Gudanowski, King, & King, 1995). The CMS contains 11 reexperiencing and situational avoidance items, 11 withdrawal and numbing items, 8 arousal items, and 5 guilt and suicidality items. Like the Mississippi Scale, this instrument does not yield subscale scores. All items of the CMS are rated on 5-point scales that ask about "the past," but the response anchors vary from item to item (e.g., *never true* to

---

[1] The Persian Gulf version has been characterized erroneously as a 38-item measure in other texts because of a misprint in the original instrument (T. Keane, personal communication, September 3, 1996).

always true, never to *very frequently* or *not at all true* to *almost always true*). Because there are no subscales for the CMS, reliability is reported only for the total score ($\alpha = .86$). The CMS appears to correlate reasonably well with a measure of lifetime traumatic stressors ($r^2 = .33$), but its convergent validity vis-à-vis the Diagnostic Interview Schedule (DIS) was poor ($r^2 = .09$)—a finding that the authors attributed to the DIS rather than the CMS. Vreven et al. (1995) concluded that the CMS "emerges from the various analyses as an instrument with potential but in need of further study and perhaps refinement" (p. 104).

In response to some of the problems associated with the CMS, Norris and Perilla (1996) developed the Revised Civilian Mississippi Scale (RCMS). This measure consists of 28 items from the original CMS and two items from Norris's (1990) Traumatic Stress Schedule. In most cases, the RCMS is anchored in undefined past trauma, referred to as *the event* (e.g., "Since the event, unexpected noises make me jump"), although it can be used to evaluate a specific trauma (e.g., "since the hurricane ... "). When the stressor is undefined, the authors of the RCMS nevertheless recommend asking the respondent to think of a specific traumatic event (often identified in a previous trauma screener) when responding to questions (F. Norris, personal communication, September 9, 1996). In contrast to the CMS, all items are rated on the same 5-point scale (1 = *not at all true*, 5 = *extremely true*). Available in both English and Spanish versions, the total RCMS has alphas of .86 and .88, respectively. As opposed to the CMS, this measure has the expected three subscales (Reexperiencing, Avoidance, and Arousal), all of which are reasonably reliable.

PTSD Symptom Scale—Self-Report (PSS-SR) and Modified PTSD Symptom Scale— Self-Report (MPSS-SR)

As noted earlier, the rater version of the PSS was developed by Foa et al. (1993) to assess PTSD symptoms in rape victims. Similarly, all of the 17 PSS-SR items are anchored in rape experiences, although a revised version (described below) is usable for assessing the impacts of other traumatic events. Respondents rate each item in terms of its severity in the past month. (See page 101 for a discussion of 2-week vs. 1-month time spans on Foa et al.'s, 1993, measures.) Responses are made on 4-point scales ranging from 0 (*not at all*) to 3 (*very much*). A rating of 1 or higher is required for the symptom to be considered present. In a sample of 44 rape victims, the three subscales of the PSS-SR (Reexperiencing, Avoidant, and Arousal) were reasonably reliable, with alphas ranging from .78 to .82 and 4-week test–retest coefficients ranging from .56 to .71. The PSS-SR demonstrated good concurrent validity with other measures and some convergent validity with the SCID (sensitivity of .62 and specificity of 1.0).

The PSS-SR has been modified by Falsetti, Resnick, Resick, and Kilpatrick (1993) for use with other trauma populations. This version, the *Modified PTSD Symptom Scale—Self-Report (MPSS-SR)*, contains two rating scales per item: one for the frequency of each symptom over the last 2 (or 4) weeks and one for how distressing it was.

Posttraumatic Stress Diagnostic Scale (PDS)

The PDS was developed by Foa (1995), apparently in an attempt to adapt the PSS-SR for general clinical use. By all indications, this endeavor was successful. This instrument consists of four parts: Part 1 surveys exposure to 11 traumatic events, as well as a 12th unspecified (fill in the blank) event; Part 2 examines characteristics of what the respondent believes was the most traumatic event (from Part 1), including time of occurrence, presence of injury, life endangerment, and whether the respondent felt helpless or terrified at the time of the event; Part 3 lists 17 symptom items corresponding to the *DSM–IV* symptomatic criteria for PTSD, rated on a scale of 0 (*not at all or only one time*) to 3 (*5 or more times a week/almost always*) over the preceding month, as well as two items tapping duration of symptoms and time from traumatic event to the onset of symptoms; and Part 4 asks whether these symptoms "have interfered with any of the following areas of your life during the past month" (p. 3), with areas including work, household chores and duties, schoolwork, sex life, and general satisfaction with life. The PDS yields a potential diagnosis of PTSD, as well as a symptom severity rating and an estimate of level of impairment in functioning.

According to the PDS manual, this instrument has well above-average psychometrics. In a normative sample of 248 individuals with histories of trauma exposure, the PDS has good test–retest reliability (κ = .74 for PTSD diagnosis over a 10- to 22-day period), high internal consistency (α = .92 for the 17 symptom items), and good sensitivity (.82) and specificity (.77) for SCID diagnoses of PTSD.

As the only published psychological test that specifically evaluates *DSM–IV* PTSD, the PDS appears to be an excellent choice as a PTSD screener. For unknown reasons, however, the PDS examines only the fear and helplessness components of the PTSD A2 criteria, and thus does not tap self-reported experiences of horror. Although this omission is unlikely to have much impact, the examiner may wish to inquire about this last component so as to evaluate completely *DSM–IV* PTSD diagnostic criteria.

Purdue PTSD Questionnaire (PPTSD) and PPTSD—Revised (PPTSD-R)

The PPTSD was developed by Hartsough (1986) at Purdue University. This 15-item measure of combat-related PTSD was designed to tap *DSM-III* criteria, and thus it is less relevant to *DSM-III-R* and *DSM-IV* diagnostic requirements. Eleven items relate to symptoms experienced within the last 7 days, and 4 assess symptoms that have occurred since the respondents' war experience. Symptoms are rated on scales ranging from 1 (*not at all*) to 4 (*extremely*). In a sample of 133 Vietnam veterans, Hendrix, Anelli, Gibbs, and Fournier (1994) found the PPTSD to be quite reliable (α = .94) and to correlate with the IES at r = .78.

Given the lack of concordance with recent PTSD criteria and its explicit focus on combat veterans, the PPTSD was revised by Lauterbach and Vrana (1996) and named the PPTSD-R. This new version has been expanded to 17 items in order to tap *DSM-III-R* (and potentially *DSM-IV*) criteria in general trauma populations.

Moreover, the scales now uniformly examine symptoms over a 4-week period and use a 5-point scale ranging from *not at all* to *often*. Lauterbach and Vrana's (1996) report that the total score and three subscales of the PPTSD-R (Reexperiencing, Avoidance, and Arousal) are reliable (αs = .91, .84, .79, and .81, respectively) and correlate moderately well with the IES and CMS (rs = .66 and .50, respectively) in samples of university students.

Penn Inventory for PTSD

The Penn Inventory for PTSD (Hammarberg, 1992) is a 26-item scale that diverges somewhat from the approach used by most other PTSD scale developers. Items consist of four statements about a feeling or thought that represent increasing levels of symptom intensity. The respondent chooses the statement that best describes him or her, and the corresponding value of the statement (ranging from 0 to 3) is the item score. The scale generates a total PTSD score, without subscales. In two samples of Vietnam veterans and one mixed sample, Hammarberg (1992) found the Penn to have excellent reliability (α = .94) and stability over a 5-day period (r = .96). Unusually high hit rates with respect to PTSD diagnoses were found for this scale: Sensitivities ranged from .90 to .98 across the three samples, and specificities were 1.0, 0.94, and 0.61, respectively.

A potential problem for the Penn Inventory is its moderately high correlation with depression (Hammarberg, 1992). However, the relatively broad range of symptoms it taps (i.e., beyond the standard 17 PTSD items examined by most measures) and the natural comorbidity of PTSD and depression explains this relationship to some extent.

Harvard Trauma Questionnaire (HTQ)

The trauma section of the HTQ was described in chapter 4. This measure also has a symptom section, consisting of both PTSD and non-PTSD items. The PTSD component consists of 17 items that can be scored to suggest a *DSM-IV* diagnosis of PTSD. Fourteen items evaluate other stress symptoms frequently experienced by Indochinese refugees. In a sample of 91 Cambodian, Laotian, and Vietnamese refugees, the HTQ had a sensitivity of .78 and a specificity of .65 with reference to independent diagnoses of PTSD.

If appropriately translated, the HTQ may be applicable to cultures beyond those of the Indochinese. In such instances, however, only the PTSD items would be directly applicable without significant further adaptation because the remaining items of the HTQ are intended to be specific to the culture in which it is applied.

Dissociative Experiences Scale (DES)

The DES (E. M. Bernstein & Putnam, 1986) is a 28-item self-report measure of dissociation. Items of the DES tap "disturbance in identity, memory, awareness, and cognitions and feelings of derealization or depersonalization or associated phenomena such as deja vu and absorption" (E. M. Bernstein & Putnam, 1986, p. 729). Factor analyses have suggested that the DES consists of three factors (Amnesia, Depersonalization and Derealization, and Absorption and Imaginative Involvement; e.g., Carlson et al., 1991), although further investigation indicated that this seeming multidimensionality may be due, at least in part, to differences in item skewedness (Carlson & Armstrong, 1995; Waller, in press).

Two versions of the DES are available, the only difference being the way in which individual items are rated. In the original version, respondents were asked to mark on a continuous line (anchored at 0 and 100) what percentage of the time they experienced each symptom. This scoring approach required the examiner to hand measure the client's responses to each item. A second, more easily scored version has the individual score each response by circling a number from 0 to 100 in increments of 10.

The DES has been shown to have good internal consistency (typically in the mid-.80s to mid-.90s; e.g., E. M. Bernstein & Putnam, 1986; Frischholz et al., 1990) and test–retest reliabilities in the .8–.9 range (E. M. Bernstein & Putnam, 1986; Carlson &

Rosser-Hogan, 1991; Dubester & Braun, 1995; Frischholz et al., 1990). Furthermore, DES scores discriminate trauma victims and those with dissociative disorders in a wide variety of studies (see Carlson & Armstrong, 1995, and van IJzendoorn & Schuengel, in press, for reviews). In a study of 1,051 psychiatric patients (Carlson et al., 1993), a score of 30 or higher on the DES correctly identified 74% of those with multiple personality disorder (now dissociative identity disorder [DID]) and 80% of those without it. In a comprehensive meta-analysis of DES studies, van IJzendoorn and Schuengel (in press) concluded that the DES has good to excellent reliability, convergent validity, and predictive validity, but that its discriminant validity is lessened by virtue of the DES's moderate correlation with measures of general distress (e.g., Walker, Katon, Neraas, Jemelka, & Massoth, 1992). This concern may be overstated to the extent that dissociative symptoms do, in fact, occur in the context of at least some distress and dysphoria.

Because the DES is the best known of the dissociation measures, trauma clinicians often administer it in the context of a psychological test battery. If the inclusion of the DES is to determine the existence of DID, using the 30-point cutoff, the clinician should report only moderate sensitivity and specificity of that cutoff. Armstrong (1995) noted that it is not at all unusual for a person without DID to achieve a DES score of well over 30, and concludes that "no matter how high the [DES] score, we should never conclude that this score confirms that the patient has DID. We can only say that we have cause to suspect that the patient may have a dissociative disorder and that we need to investigate our hypothesis further" (p. 20).

The lack of normative data on the DES precludes definitive clinical interpretation of a given DES score in terms of relative level of dissociative symptomatology. Fortunately, the Carlson et al. (1993) data are of some assistance, because they outline the distribution of DES scores for a large clinical sample. Thus, although the examiner may not be able to estimate the severity of a given DES score with regard to "normal" levels of dissociation, he or she can provide information regarding how extreme the respondent's score is relative to those of other mental health patients.

Peritraumatic Dissociative Experiences Questionnaire (PDEQ)

Unlike the DES, the PDEQ (Marmar, Weiss, Metzler, & Delucchi, 1996) examines individuals' self-reports of dissociation that occurred *during* a traumatic event. In support of the need for such a measure, Marmar, Weiss, and Metzler (1996) noted that many victims report derealization, depersonalization, time distortion, reduced pain perception, and other dissociative responses when experiencing trauma. They cited the research of Holen (1993); Koopman, Classen, and Spiegel (1994); and others indicating that dissociative response during trauma is a risk factor for later PTSD. As a result, the authors suggested that assessment of peritraumatic dissociative phenomena provides important information regarding longer term psychological response to traumatic events.

The PDEQ was initially developed as a 9-item measure, with both rater and self-report formats. Marmar, Weiss, and Metzler (1996) has also developed an 8-item "subject version" that, because of its research focus, is not reviewed here. Individuals are asked on the PDEQ to recall how they felt and what they experienced during a specific traumatic event. The self-report version has respondents rate each item on a 4-point scale (ranging from *not at all* to *extremely*), whereas in the rater version responses are coded as *don't know*, *absent or false*, *subthreshold*, and *threshold*. A 10-item version of the PDEQ is still in the development process, and detailed psychometric data are not available at this time. Recent research with 9- and 10-item self-report and rater versions, however, suggests that this instrument has good reliability, is associated with other measures of dissociation and posttraumatic stress, and increases with greater levels of exposure to traumatic events (Marmar, 1996). Because it was only recently introduced, no normative data are available on this scale, and thus its clinical use is currently limited to screening functions.

Stanford Acute Stress Reaction Questionnaire (SASRQ)

The SASRQ (Cardeña, Koopman, Classen, & Spiegel, 1996) is one of the only objective measures available for the assessment of acute stress disorder. The current version of the SASRQ consists of an open-ended question about the characteristics of the traumatic event, a 5-point item asking "How disturbing was this event to you," 30 items tapping the *DSM-IV* diagnostic criteria for acute stress disorder with response options ranging from 0 (*not experienced*) to 5 (*very often experienced*), and an item regarding the duration of "the worst symptoms of distress." There are both English and Spanish versions of this measure.

The current version of the SASRQ is undergoing psychometric evaluation. Preliminary analyses suggest that it is internally consistent ($\alpha = .92$) and relatively stable across time when no traumas intervene (test–retest $r = .78$; Cardeña, Koopman, et al., 1996). The various versions of the SASRQ demonstrate predictive validity with respect to a variety of traumas, including earthquakes (Cardeña & Spiegel, 1993), fires (Cardeña, Classen, & Spiegel, 1991; Koopman, Classen, & Spiegel, 1996), and witnessing an execution (Freinkel, Koopman, & Spiegel, 1994). Normative data on the SASRQ are not available at present but are planned for the near future (Koopman et al., 1995).

Trauma Symptom Checklist–40 (TSC-40)

The TSC-40 (Briere & Runtz, 1989; Elliott & Briere, 1992) is a 40-item self-report research measure that evaluates symptomatology in adults arising from childhood and adult traumatic experiences. It is briefly described here only for its clinical research applications. The TSC-40 is an expanded version of the Trauma Symptom Checklist–33 (TSC-33; Briere & Runtz, 1989). It consists of six subscales (e.g., Anxiety, Dissociation, and Sleep Disturbance) and a total score. Each TSC symptom item is rated according to frequency over the preceding 2 months, using a 4-point scale ranging from 0 (*never*) to 3 (*often*). Studies using the

TSC-33 and TSC-40 indicate that they are moderately reliable measures that have reasonable predictive validity with reference to a wide variety of traumatic experiences (e.g., Demaré & Briere, 1995; D. G. Dutton & Painter, 1993; Elliott & Briere, 1992; Follette et al., 1996; Gold, Milan, Mayall, & Johnson, 1994; Roesler & McKenzie, 1994). Because it is intended solely as a research measure, and given its only moderate psychometrics and the absence of standardization data, the TSC-40 should not be used as a clinical test of posttraumatic states.

Trauma Symptom Inventory (TSI)

The TSI (Briere, 1995c) contains 100 items and taps acute and chronic posttraumatic symptomatology. Each symptom item is rated according to its frequency of occurrence over the preceding 6 months on a 4-point scale ranging from 0 (*never*) to 3 (*often*). Because of the length of this time frame, the TSI identifies traumatic responses that may have occurred in the more distant past and thus cannot generate a *DSM-IV* PTSD diagnosis.

The TSI has 3 validity scales and 10 clinical scales, all of which yield normative (*T*) scores. The validity scales of the TSI are Response Level, measuring a general underendorsement response style or a need to appear unusually symptom free; Atypical Response, evaluating extreme distress or an attempt to appear especially disturbed or dysfunctional; and Inconsistent Response, measuring unusually inconsistent responses to TSI item pairs. These validity scales correlate as expected with similar scales from other measures (Briere, 1995c). The 10 clinical scales of the TSI are Anxious Arousal, Depression, Anger/Irritability, Intrusive Experiences, Defensive Avoidance, Dissociation, Sexual Concerns, Dysfunctional Sexual Behavior, Impaired Self-Reference, and Tension Reduction Behavior.

The TSI was standardized on a sample of 828 adults whose demographics generally represent the United States general population. There are also normative data for military personnel, derived from a sample of 3,659 Navy recruits. Norms are available for four combinations of sex and age (men and women ages 18–54 and 55 or older). TSI scores vary slightly as a function of race (accounting for 2%–3% of the variance in most scales), and minor adjustments for validity scale cutoffs are suggested for certain racial groups.

The clinical scales of the TSI are relatively consistent internally (mean alphas ranging from .84 to .87 in general population, clinical, university, and military samples) and exhibit reasonable convergent, predictive, and incremental validity (Briere, 1995c). In a standardization subsample, TSI scales demonstrated convergent validity with independently assessed PTSD status (using Astin et al.'s, 1993, joint scoring of the IES and LASC), with a specificity of .92 and a sensitivity of .91. In a psychiatric inpatient sample, TSI scales identified 89% of those independently diagnosed with borderline personality disorder. Studies indicate that specific TSI scale elevations and configurations are associated with a wide variety of childhood and adult traumatic experiences (e.g., Briere, 1995c; Briere et al., 1995; Demaré & Briere, 1996; Runtz, Roche, & Embree, 1996).

Traumatic Stress Institute Belief Scale

The Traumatic Stress Institute Belief Scale, Form L (Pearlman, 1996) is a revised version of the McPearl Belief Scale (McCann & Pearlman, 1990). The Belief Scale is based on constructivist self-development theory (CSDT; McCann & Pearlman, 1990; Pearlman & Saakvitne, 1995) and consists of 80 items that measure disrupted cognitive schemas associated with traumatic stress. CSDT posits that trauma survivors experience disruptions in five psychological need areas: safety, trust, esteem, intimacy, and control. The Belief Scale has subscales for each of these schema, rated both for "self" and "other," with each item endorsed on a 6-point scale ranging from 1 (*disagree strongly*) to 6 (*agree strongly*). A typical item of the Belief Scale is "You can't trust anyone" (Pearlman & Mac Ian, 1995, p. 559). In a sample of 188 mental health professionals and graduate students, Pearlman and Mac Ian (1995) reported subscale alphas ranging from .65 (Other-Esteem) to .84 (Self-Esteem) and a total scale score alpha of .93. A previous version of the Belief Scale, tested in 102 outpatients, yielded similar reliability estimates (Pearlman, MacIan, Johnson, & Mas, 1992).

The Belief scale and its previous version (the McPearl Belief Scale) have been shown to predict trauma history in both client and therapist groups, as well as *secondary* or *vicarious traumatization*, the development of trauma-related signs and symptoms in clinicians as a result of working with traumatized clients (e.g., Mas, 1992; Pearlman, 1996; Pearlman & Mac Ian, 1995). No data are available, however, on the sensitivity or specificity of that prediction. The Belief Scale correlates significantly with the IES and Symptom Checklist–90–Revised, suggesting that disrupted cognitive schemas do, in fact, covary with traumatic stress and dysfunction (Pearlman & Mac Ian, 1995). Although the validation and standardization of this scale are only now under way, its preliminary psychometrics and the importance of the information it conveys suggest its potential future usefulness in therapy-focused trauma assessment.

Summary

A number of trauma-specific instruments have been reviewed in this chapter. Many of these tests are relatively new and thus have relatively short track records. Others are older, but tend to use *DSM-III* PTSD criteria or are limited to combat veterans. Two (the IES and TSC-40) are more research measures than actual clinical tests. Even given these limitations, however, most of the instruments described in this chapter appear to be reliable and to have reasonably high sensitivity and specificity with regard to posttraumatic disturbance.

Despite the proliferation of objective measures designed to yield a psychiatric diagnosis, a *DSM-IV* diagnosis of PTSD, acute stress disorder, or dissociative disorder should never be based on paper-and-pencil measures alone. Instead, the diagnostic tests described in this chapter should be used to suggest the probability of PTSD, after which a diagnostic interview should be conducted to confirm or reject this finding.

Although the screening functions of the classic 17-item PTSD measures should not be discounted, especially in research contexts, a better use of trauma-specific tests ultimately may be to determine the relative type and level of posttraumatic stress or dissociation present for a given client. When the disorder of interest is PTSD, for example, the most helpful instruments might yield standardized, continuous scores on at least three different subscales: reexperiencing, avoidance, and hyperarousal. Such scales might also tap the associated features of PTSD, expressing them as separate subscale scores rather than combining them with posttraumatic stress symptoms. An important contribution to the trauma field at this point in time would be for test authors or trauma researchers to develop normative data for the best of the currently available instruments and to insure that future trauma-specific tests include normative data.

8

Putting It All Together

The chapters of this book outline a variety of assessment domains and measures that are helpful in understanding posttraumatic states. The intent of this chapter is to integrate this information into a practical form that can be applied to a comprehensive trauma assessment protocol. During this process, certain instruments are highlighted as especially useful, but other measures also may be acceptable.

Based on the literature reviewed in this volume, the primary targets of assessment may be divided into six areas: (a) pretrauma functioning, (b) trauma exposure, (c) social supports, (d) comorbidity, (e) potential malingering or secondary gain, and (f) posttraumatic response. Whether each of these areas is addressed in any given instance depends in part on the referral or assessment question, the amount of time or resources available to the assessor, and the extent to which the respondent can or will participate in evaluation. As a result, although each area is reviewed in this chapter, it should not be assumed that all useful assessment reports necessarily cover each of these areas in depth or at all.

Pretrauma Psychological Functioning

As noted in this volume, it is often helpful to evaluate the client's pretrauma functioning to determine whether the client's current difficulties antedate the trauma or potentially arise from it. Furthermore, knowledge of pretrauma psychological difficulties can provide insight into predisposing or exacerbating factors associated with a current posttraumatic state. For example, information that a given client has a history of generalized anxiety disorder or prior PTSD may help to explain why he or she develops seemingly "excessive" posttraumatic anxiety and hyperarousal in response to a moderately stressful event. Similarly, it may be helpful to know whether an individual who presents with a posttraumatic depression has had a previous depressive episode, grief reaction, or a history of alcoholism.

When practical, the assessing clinician should consider as many of the following potential indicators of prior functioning as is reasonably possible given the constraints of the specific assessment situation:

- previous psychological symptoms and disorders;
- previous psychiatric or psychological treatment;
- alcohol and drug abuse history;
- prior occupational functioning;
- criminal and incarceration history;
- premorbid social adjustment;
- evidence of pretrauma personality disturbance; and
- relevant medical history (e.g., history of brain injury or disorder)

Unfortunately, assessment of pretrauma functioning may not be easy. Individuals with current psychological disturbance are sometimes poor historians regarding prior disturbance—either underestimating previous symptoms so as to appear less chronically dysfunctional, or overstating previous disturbance in response to the distorting effects of current dysphoria. Furthermore, especially debilitating psychological states (e.g., psychosis, severe posttraumatic depression, extreme dissociative withdrawal, or cognitive impairment) may impede the client's ability to communicate with the evaluator regarding his or her previous level of functioning.

Because information gathered from the traumatized individual may be distorted or unreliable, collateral sources of information also should be considered when appropriate (Newman et al.,

1996). These may include spouses or cohabiting partners, family members, friends, and treating medical and psychological practitioners. When available, premorbid history may also be inferred from medical and psychotherapy files, police and prison records, and other institutional databases. However, clinicians should always be aware of confidentiality issues when consulting individuals other than their clients regarding the clients' psychological state, history, treatment status, and other relevant domains. Evaluators are advised to consult their professional ethics code and both state and federal laws regarding their responsibilities in this area.

Trauma Exposure

As has been discussed in detail in this book, it is often not sufficient to know that an individual has been traumatized by an event. The clinician should also ascertain the specific details of the stressor, such as its type, duration, frequency, and severity, as well as any significant prior traumatic events that the individual may have experienced.

Any of the Criterion A measures described in chapter 4 may assist the evaluator in assessing trauma exposure, as long as he or she insures that behavioral definitions are available for the various traumas listed by these instruments. In addition, most of these interviews do not assess for the specific PTSD A2 criteria of intense fear, horror, or helplessness, so the interviewer often has to inquire independently about these subjective responses before a PTSD diagnosis can be made.

Given these provisos, the most inclusive trauma exposure measures currently available appear to be the Potential Stressful Events Interview (PSEI; Falsetti et al., 1994) and the Traumatic Events Scale (TES; Elliott, 1992), each of which provides an extensive review of traumatic events and their specific characteristics. These measures also provide more definitional information than other similar instruments. When a shorter measure is needed, the clinician may wish to use the Trauma Assessment for Adults (TAA; Resnick et al., 1993) or the revised version of the Traumatic Stress Schedule (TSS; Norris, 1992). If torture is thought to have occurred and the client is an Indochinese immigrant, the Harvard Trauma Questionnaire (Mollica et al., 1992) can be especially useful. If previous combat experiences are relevant, use of one of the several combat exposure scales (see Meichenbaum, 1994, for a review) is recommended.

When a detailed evaluation of childhood trauma is indicated, the most helpful measures appear to be the TES, the Childhood Trauma Questionnaire (CTQ), and the Child Maltreatment Interview Schedule (CMIS). If psychological abuse is a significant concern, the clinician should consider the Childhood Maltreatment Questionnaire (CMQ). Unfortunately, existing norms are not yet sufficient to allow specific interpretation of CTQ or CMQ scale scores, and thus the evaluator is forced to examine each item qualitatively to determine the level of maltreatment. Moreover, the CMIS and most other maltreatment scales evaluate only childhood experiences of abuse and neglect and thus cannot screen for non-abuse-related childhood traumas (e.g., neighborhood violence). For this reason, the TES may be preferable for rapid screening of general childhood trauma.

For those clinicians who would rather use their own set of traumatic experience questions, the customized traumatic events interview presented on pages 89–91 may provide a useful evaluative schema. If this entire interview outline is used, it generates information not only on traumatic events, but also on their various characteristics and the client's subjective response to them. On other occasions, however, the clinician may choose a subset of these questions that are most relevant to the assessment question at hand.

Social Supports

As noted in chapter 1, social support after a stressful event is often associated with a more positive outcome. As a result, the level of social supports in the trauma victim's personal environment can provide important assessment information. Although instruments are available to measure social support, both in general and in the context of stress (see Meichenbaum, 1994, for a review), many clinicians choose to evaluate this phenomenon more informally. For example, they may ask clients about the number and quality of friendships and family connections, their posttrauma availability, and their perceived supportiveness.

Regarding the latter, it is useful to know whether clients are undergoing a loss spiral (Hobfoll, 1988), wherein their sustained need for support is draining social resources and producing further neediness and a growing sense of loss. The evaluator should keep in mind that seemingly supportive individuals may, especially over time, communicate unhelpful messages to clients, for example, that they should "just get over it" and not express strong emotions associated with grief, despair, rage, or terror. As a result, the absolute number of potential social supports may be less important to trauma recovery than the quality and reliability of the clients' immediate interpersonal environment.

Comorbidity

Because posttraumatic states often occur in the context of other psychological symptoms and disorders, comprehensive assessment of traumatized individuals also should include evaluation of less trauma-specific dysfunction (Davidson & Fairbank, 1993). For this reason, it is recommended that generic, multiscale measures of psychological disturbance be co-administered with more trauma-specific ones and that test data be followed up with one or more clinical–diagnostic interviews.

Although many tests yield important information on a broad range of psychological disturbance, clinical experience with trauma victims suggests the special validity of four: the second edition of the Minnesota Multiphasic Personality Inventory (MMPI-2), the Personality Assessment Inventory (PAI), the third version of the Millon Clinical Multiaxial Inventory (MCMI-III), and the Rorschach. The first two provide information on a variety of psychological disorders or symptom clusters, whereas the MCMI-III allows especially detailed assessment of Axis II disturbance. The Rorschach, on the other hand, can yield data on more subtle and dynamic psychological processes that are unlikely to be accessed by objective tests. All four have scales or special scores that address trauma-related symptomatology.

Which of these tests should be used in a given circumstance is dependent on the resources and the amount of time that are available, clinician training and test preferences, and the client's overall level of tolerance for psychological testing. If only a single generic test can be used, the MMPI-2 or PAI may be the best choice. If two tests can be administered, the MMPI or PAI can be augmented with the MCMI-III. If three generic tests are possible, the Rorschach may be added. Specific clinical situations may require different combination of these (or other) tests, however. For example, clients with symptoms of bulimia or anorexia nervosa may benefit from evaluation with the Eating Disorder Inventory (Garner, Olmstead, & Polivney, 1983; Garner, 1991) or similar measure, whereas those presenting with multiple trauma-related fears or phobias may be assessed with an instrument such as the Modified Fear Survey (Veronen & Kilpatrick, 1980).

Three additional comorbidity concerns relevant to posttraumatic states are suicidality, substance abuse, and medical–neurologic disorders. Although they are not formal disorders per se, the first two are nevertheless important coexisting problems for many of those experiencing significant posttraumatic disturbance. The third concern, medical disorder, is sometimes overlooked in trauma assessments despite its ocasionally critical importance.

Suicidal thoughts and behaviors are relatively common among traumatized individuals, frequently arising from the depressive symptoms, low self-esteem, loss, hopelessness, and overwhelming internal distress often associated with posttraumatic states. Elevated levels of suicidality have been documented in combat veterans (e.g., Bremner et al., 1993; Centers for Disease Control, 1987), prisoners of war (e.g., J. L. Herman, 1992a, 1992b; Segal, Hunter, & Segal, 1976), torture survivors (e.g., Hougen, Kelstrup, Petersen, & Rasmussen, 1988; Solkoff, 1992), and victims of various forms of interpersonal violence (e.g., Briere & Runtz, 1986; Briere & Zaidi, 1989; Gayford, 1975; Gidycz & Koss, 1990; Kilpatrick et al., 1985).

Although a number of instruments tap suicidal ideation, intent, and behavior (e.g., the Adult Suicidal Ideation Questionnaire, Reynolds, 1991; and the Suicide Intent Scale, Beck et al., 1979), the low base rate of actual suicidal behavior makes its psychometric prediction difficult at best (Bongar, 1991). In addition to the use of screening instruments, when indicated, the clinician should always conduct a face-to-face suicide assessment interview with those suspected of suicidal intent. Excellent coverage of the various issues inherent in conducting such an interview is provided in Bongar (1991), chapter 15 of Linehan's (1993) volume on treating borderline personality disorder, and Section III of Meichenbaum's (1994) trauma handbook.

Drug and alcohol abuse is a well-known sequel of posttraumatic stress, as documented in studies of combat veterans (e.g., Branchey, Davis, & Lieber, 1984; Reifman & Windle, 1996), prisoners of war (Engdahl, Speed, Eberly, & Schwartz, 1991), and crime victims (Kilpatrick, Edmunds, & Seymour, 1992). Victims of childhood maltreatment also appear to have elevated rates of substance abuse (e.g., Briere & Runtz, 1987; Dembo et al., 1989; Singer, Petchers, & Hussey, 1989). As a result, a detailed assessment of trauma victims usually includes evaluation of drug and alcohol use, either informally or through a structured interview or pencil-and-paper measure.

The advantage of structured substance abuse evaluation, whether interview or inventory based, is that it provides comprehensive coverage of a wide variety of substances and typically quantifies the amount and frequency of use for each. This attention to detail is especially helpful because many substance abusers underestimate their consumption when asked global questions or have their own interpretations of what constitute psychoactive substances and their abuse. As a result, the clinician who only asks about alcohol and one or two drugs or who inquires solely about "substance abuse," "alcoholism," or "addiction," may inadvertently facilitate client nondisclosure.

Fortunately for those using standardized diagnostic interviews, both the Structured Clinical Interview for DSM–III–R and the Diagnostic Interview Schedule assess for substance use disorders. More detailed assessment is possible through the use of measures such as the Michigan Alcoholism Screening Test (Selzer, 1971), Drug Abuse Screening Test (Skinner, 1992), or the

Addiction Severity Index (Cacciola, Griffith, & McLellan, 1987). One of the most detailed measures of substance abuse is a structured interview entitled "A Structured Addictions Assessment Interview for Selecting Treatment" (ASIST; Addiction Research Foundation, 1985), which reportedly takes as long as 2 hours to administer. Because it was written in Canada and is based on the Canadian health system, however, this interview may be somewhat less relevant to U.S. residents. For MMPI and MMPI-2 users, there is also the MacAndrew Scale (MacAndrew, 1965), which, although it contains no specific items regarding alcoholism or drug abuse, has reasonable sensitivity (but questionable specificity) in the detection of alcoholism (Jacobson, 1989). Unfortunately, scores on this measure may be confounded by race (Graham, 1987), criminality, and legal substance use such as coffee or heavy cigarette smoking (Jacobson, 1989).

A final comorbidity issue is that of medical or neurological disorder. Although not performed by nonmedical practitioners (or, in some settings, psychiatrists), physical and laboratory examination of individuals presenting with significant posttraumatic disturbance is often indicated. As noted by Kudler and Davidson (1995), "a number of physical disorders can mimic or exacerbate posttraumatic pathology. These include reactions to drugs (prescribed or abused), endocrine disorder (including hypothalamic, pituitary, thyroid, adrenal, and diabetic dysfunction), neurologic disorders (including acute or chronic brain injury endured in the trauma), cardiac, hepatic, and respiratory problems" (p. 76).

Especially relevant to posttraumatic presentations is potential central nervous system pathology, such as seizure disorders (e.g., complex partial seizures producing an epileptic fugue or depersonalization); dementia caused by head trauma or systemic disease; delirium; substance-induced mental disorders; and organic amnestic disorders caused by brain injury, a general medical condition, or psychoactive substance use. Because these conditions may mimic some posttraumatic or dissociative symptoms and can reflect critically important (if not potentially fatal) pathophysiological processes, referral for a medical assessment should occur whenever there is a significant possibility of a physical etiology.

Malingering or Secondary Gain

As described in chapter 3, malingering and potential secondary gain for appearing traumatized can complicate the assessment of posttraumatic states. Although such behavior may be relatively rare in certain clinical contexts, the probability of malingering obviously increases in certain situations:

□ forensic settings where posttraumatic disturbance is being used as a defense against criminal prosecution;

□ in civil litigation, where a suit for psychological damages includes allegations of posttraumatic disturbance or dysfunction;

□ instances where a finding of posttraumatic stress may result in financial compensation or wanted services (e.g., in Veterans Administration settings, victims' compensation hearings, supplemental social security or disability applications); or

□ where symptoms of posttraumatic stress or disorder would result in increased attention or support from the social milieu (e.g., in certain families or relationships).

It should be emphasized, however, that malingering is only something to be ruled out in the above contexts, not an assured fact. For example, individuals claiming posttraumatic stress at disability hearings or in civil litigation often *do* suffer from posttraumatic difficulties. Although a person presenting with posttraumatic stress is as likely as anyone else to be misrepresenting, malingering, or seeking secondary gain, it should not be assumed beforehand that he or she is in fact doing so.

When malingering is possible, the clinician should consider the client's general demeanor during the evaluation, the extent to which his or her symptoms correspond to what is known about posttraumatic states,[1] his or her past history of medical or mental

---

[1] PTSD-appropriate symptoms may be learned from reading books on trauma, however, and some lawyers have been accused of coaching their clients with regard to symptomatology.

health care if records are available (e.g., multiple brief admissions to a number of different treatment facilities, especially if records suggest malingering or factition), and, to some extent, the consistency of his or her reports of past history and previous symptoms.[2] Even when one or more of the above indices suggest malingering, however, in the absence of incontrovertible evidence it is appropriate only to hypothesize misrepresentation, not to conclude it definitively in a subsequent report.

In addition to gaining information from the assessment interview and review of prior records, the clinician may find that psychological tests are useful in the evaluation of potential malingering, as chapter 3 suggests. The two most common forms of test data in this regard are the results of instruments such as the Structured Interview of Reported Symptoms (SIRS) and the interpretation of validity scales within standard inventories (e.g., the MMPI-2, PAI, or MCMI-III). Because the effects of traumatic stress on the SIRS (and related instruments) are not well documented, and traumatized individuals tend to have higher scores on "fake bad" validity scales, conclusions based on these data—in either direction—should be made with care and qualified when appropriate.

Posttraumatic Response

After considering the various precursors to and moderators of posttraumatic stress, the final issue is the specific measurement of posttraumatic response. As indicated in chapters 5 and 7, there are a variety of useful instruments and interviews in this area. As a result, the final choice of measures is often determined by the specific assessment goals at hand and the relatively small differences between similar measures. In many cases, several instruments can be administered simultaneously to tap both the

---

[2] Although consistency of report is sometimes mentioned as a potential index of misrepresentation, some posttraumatic presentations (e.g., those involving significant dissociation or the normal waxing and waning of PTSD symptoms over time) can produce inconsistency that is not malingering.

specific posttraumatic responses of certain groups and yet evaluate general traumatic stress with more widely used measures. For example, when combat-related trauma is being examined, most researchers and clinicians typically include the Mississippi Scale for Combat-related PTSD in their test battery. Similarly, those evaluating the effects of torture and related trauma in Indochinese immigrants often administer the Harvard Trauma Questionnaire. Nevertheless, both groups of clinicians frequently include other, more generic measures of posttraumatic symptomatology as well.

Structured Interviews

If a structured interview is indicated, it is necessary to determine whether posttraumatic stress, alone, is the focus, or whether other potentially comorbid disorders also are being assessed. In the latter case, the SCID (with the optional PTSD module) probably is the most valid and useful, although it does not evaluate acute stress disorder or the dissociative disorders. If PTSD alone is being evaluated, the most helpful measure appears to be the Clinician-Administered PTSD Scale (CAPS-1). This interview has very good psychometric characteristics and yields additional useful data beyond the PTSD diagnosis per se. The extended time sometimes required to administer this measure (more than 1 hour in some cases), however, may make it less appealing when a quick diagnosis is needed.

Several structured interviews are available for the evaluation of dissociative disorders, each of which has its specific merits. Of these, the SCID-D is likely to be most useful, because it (a) is the only one to provide exact *DSM-IV* dissociative disorder diagnoses, and (b) it is one of the only interviews that assesses acute stress disorder. Published psychometric data on the SCID-D are relatively sparse thus far, although there is little reason to expect that this instrument does not perform as described.

Inventories and Scales

As described in chapter 7, two kinds of self-report measures tap posttraumatic states: those that suggest a dichotomous *DSM-III-R* or *DSM-IV* diagnosis (generally for PTSD) and those that measure the relative level of posttraumatic symptoms on one or more dimensions. Of the first group, most appear to operate in a similar fashion and probably work equally well in clinical practice. In fact, because they address the same diagnostic criteria (i.e., 17 items for the 17 PTSD criteria), the specific items of these various measures often are equivalent across instruments. One PTSD screen, however, is likely to be superior for clinical applications: the Posttraumatic Stress Diagnostic Scale (PDS; Foa, 1995). This instrument evaluates stressor characteristics, PTSD symptoms (including an overall severity rating), and level of impairment. It also provides comparison data from a sample of trauma victims.

The benefit of including one of these measures in an assessment battery is that they provide a simple screen for the presence of PTSD and thus may prompt the evaluator to consider PTSD in his or her diagnostic formulation. The clinician should not over-rely on these measures, however, because in most cases any given diagnostic criterion is tapped by a single item. As a result, a PTSD diagnosis may be inappropriately ruled in or out on the basis of simple client errors (e.g., overlooking or misunderstanding one or two items). For this reason, no diagnosis (or nondiagnosis) should be made on the basis of client response to these screening measures alone, and review of individual item responses may be more helpful than reliance on diagnostic prediction per se. Instead, diagnosis should arise from due consideration of test data and one or more diagnostic interviews.

Although most PTSD screens are somewhat limited in terms of their representation of posttraumatic symptoms, the clinician may find an intermediate point between brevity and content coverage in the Revised Civilian Mississippi Scale (RCMS). This scale consists of 30 items, several of which typically assess a single PTSD criterion; the availability of a parallel Spanish-language version is an additional advantage (Norris & Perilla, 1996). If this scale is used, the client should be told to respond to all items in terms of the same traumatic experience. Because this measure is new, however, only limited data are available on its psychometric properties.

Another measure that is likely to have clinical utility on further validation is the Stanford Acute Stress Reaction Questionnaire (SASRQ), which is used to evaluate the potential presence of acute stress disorder. Like the RCMS, the SASRQ uses multiple items to tap single diagnostic criteria and thus is less prey to client response reliability problems. Like the RCMS, the SASRQ has a Spanish version. As has been noted for other screening instruments, however, formal diagnosis of acute stress disorder should not be made on the basis of the SASRQ alone.

In contrast to diagnostic screening measures, there are a number of instruments whose primary function is to quantify the extent of a given posttraumatic state, rather than indicating the presence of a disorder per se. As noted in chapter 7, such measures have advantages and disadvantages. The primary advantage is that such tests allow the clinician to determine how traumatized an individual actually is, just as a depression measure typically indicates how depressed a given person may be. This information is often critical for the clinician because it indicates the severity of the problem and the extent to which immediate intervention is indicated. Moreover, for those who use repeat testing to measure the effects of treatment, such measures provide feedback regarding the client's improvement over time.

The most significant drawback of such trauma measures, however—at least at their current level of development—is that few of them have been normed in the general population. As a result, the clinician who determines that his or her client has a score of X on measure Y often has no empirical way of knowing the clinical significance of that score. A few measures have partially addressed this problem by deriving cutting scores for what is likely to be disorder-level symptomatology. Unfortunately, the appropriate cutting score often appears to vary by sample and study, and such procedures still leave the clinician with dichotomous data rather than clinically meaningful continuous scores. Alternatively, clinicians may chose to compare a given client's test score to relevant means reported in published studies. For example, some inference may be made if a client's score of X is equivalent to that of individuals with disorder Z in a published study. This approach is not always ideal, however, because the study mean may be specific to that sample (i.e., may not be generalizable to the client by virtue of disparent clinical, demographic, or socioeconomic status) or may be an unstable estimate because of insufficient sample size. Furthermore, the mean for a measure tells the clinician little unless its reliability and variance are also taken into account. As noted earlier, a major task of researchers in this area is to develop norms for the major continuous measures of posttraumatic symptomatology, so that a given score can be interpreted according to its extremity in the general population.

Even given this problem, some nonnormed scales may be sufficiently important that their use in a psychological test battery is justified. For example, the Dissociative Experiences Scale (DES) is a widely studied measure of a phenomenon for which there are few objective measures. Furthermore, the availability of cutoff scores for the DES, as well as data on DES variability in a large and diverse clinical sample of individuals (Carlson et al., 1993), allows some level of interpretation of specific scores. Elevated scores on the DES should be seen primarily as an indication for further investigation of dissociative disturbance (Armstrong, 1995), perhaps using the SCID-D or a regular clinical, DSM-IV-driven interview.

Another nonnormed instrument worthy of consideration is the Traumatic Stress Institute Belief Scale. Although this scale is not as well known or psychometrically supported as the DES, it has promise because it provides important information in an area highly relevant to posttraumatic disturbance: cognitive schema associated with needs and perceptions regarding safety, trust, esteem, intimacy, and control. Data in these areas can be quite helpful in the treatment of trauma survivors because they suggest areas where the client may have special vulnerabilities and strengths that reflect or moderate posttraumatic phenomena. However, because there are as yet little normative data on the Belief Scale, the clinician is limited to qualitative interpretation of item responses and scale scores.

As discussed in chapters 6 and 7, four standardized trauma-related scales are available to the clinician: three are PTSD scales of well-known psychological tests (the MMPI-2, PAI, and MCMI-III), and one is the Trauma Symptom Inventory (TSI). The primary advantage of the former scales is that they can be used any time these general tests are used. Furthermore, including at least two of these tests in the same battery provides the clinician with multiple sources of data on the same construct. The disadvantages of these scales are (a) the single "PTSD" score they render, as opposed to separate scores for each PTSD cluster; (b) their tendency to measure one component of PTSD over others (e.g., consisting of more intrusion items than avoidant or arousal ones); and (c) their frequent inclusion of non-PTSD symptoms such as depression. Nevertheless, the extensive standardization of the MMPI, PAI, and MCMI allow quantitative interpretation of specific scale scores—an important requirement for modern psychological tests.

The TSI measures a variety of posttraumatic states and includes three validity scales. In addition, because it is standardized on the general population, clinicians can interpret symptom severity on the basis of scale T scores. Its validity has only been established in terms of correlations with other measures and association with self-reported traumatic experiences, however; there are currently few data showing its sensitivity and specificity with regard to the prediction of actual stress disorders. Nevertheless, as a standardized, multiscale measure of posttraumatic states, the TSI may be a helpful addition to the trauma-relevant psychological test battery.

Summary

This chapter highlights a central principle of assessment in the area of posttraumatic stress: A complete psychological evaluation in this area involves the use of multiple psychological tests in the context of one or more detailed psychological interviews. Reliance on test data alone is insufficient to produce a *DSM-IV* diagnosis, let alone a reasonably complete clinical picture, and an interview alone (structured or otherwise) is unlikely to provide the wealth of data and normative comparisons potentially available from competent psychological testing.

The inclusion of multiple psychological tests within a given battery is paramount because of the breadth of potential posttraumatic responses and the limitations of any one psychological measure. The critical issue in test choice necessarily revolves around the specific assessment goals and the instruments best able to address those goals. In this regard, for example, a full trauma-relevant psychological test battery might include one of the traumatic events scales (e.g., the PSEI or TES), either the MMPI-2 or PAI, and each of the following: the MCMI-III, Rorschach, TSI, PDS, DES, and Traumatic Stress Institute Belief Scale. If the trauma was acute, the SASRQ may be added. In some cases, measures evaluating suicidality, substance abuse history, or eating disorders may be included. On the other hand, a more brief battery may consist solely of the TES, MMPI-2, and either the TSI, RCMS, or PDS.

Whatever the choice of instruments, the trauma-focused test battery should be considered as a tool to assist in the complex task of clinical judgment, not as a replacement for that judgment. Ultimately, the best clinical evaluations and diagnoses arise from as many sources of information as possible, ranging in some instances from review of records and interviews with collateral individuals, to the application of focused psychological tests and the results of one or more empathic and attuned clinical interviews.

Conclusion

As a perusal of any urban newspaper indicates, many people are exposed to interpersonal violence, accidents, disasters, and other traumatic events during their lifetimes. Yet, as noted in this volume, the concept of posttraumatic stress was more or less alien to both the person on the street and the mental health professional prior to *DSM-III*. How this could happen, and why it did, is a fascinating topic, one worthy of a book in itself. What this book documents, however, is the rapid growth of trauma-related research and clinical practice once PTSD became an acceptable concept. In a mere 15 years hundreds of articles have been written on the etiology, incidence, assessment, and treatment of posttraumatic states. At the same time, a new—albeit informal—mental health specialty has come into existence, with its primary focus being the diagnosis and clinical resolution of posttraumatic stress and disorder. Some of these specialists have come from Veterans Administration hospitals, some from rape crisis centers and battered women's shelters, some from disaster-oriented agencies such as the Red Cross, and some from the child abuse field.

What these researchers and clinicians have found is a collection of psychological disorders and conditions that are intrinsically related to traumatic events, yet have been largely overlooked in the past. These include acute stress disorder, posttraumatic stress disorder, brief psychotic disorder, a variety of dissociative disorders, and a number of other symptom clusters (e.g., involving somatization or disturbed relatedness) that arise at least partially from traumatic events. With each additional iteration of diagnostic systems used by mental health professionals (e.g., the progression from *DSM-I* to *DSM-IV*), these disorders and states have become more clearly defined, although there may have been some errors along the way. So, too, has an understanding grown of the complex interaction between person, history, stressor, and environment in the genesis of posttraumatic distress and disorder.

This book has considered one small piece of this growing knowledge-base, that is, the accurate assessment of posttraumatic states. Examination of the literature in this area highlights the tension between two phenomena: the primacy of those pre-*DSM-III* psychological tests and procedures typically used to assess basically nontrauma-based psychological disturbance, and the rapidly growing post-*DSM-II* need for tests of a whole new realm of trauma-related psychological disturbance. Traditional psychological instruments have tended to misinterpret what are now understood to be posttraumatic states, generally repackaging them as psychosis, personality disorder, and other less relevant psychological conditions. The net effect of this misinterpretation has been to provide clinicians with erroneous information, which, in turn, may lead to inadequate treatment outcomes.

As noted in this volume, however, mental health professionals are beginning to understand the phenomenology of posttraumatic disturbance and are increasingly able to provide an assessment approach that is supportive of the trauma survivor. In addition, we have begun to adapt traditional psychological tests to the assessment of posttraumatic states, both by developing new scoring systems and interpretation approaches and by creating more trauma-sensitive scales for these measures. We are also beginning what is likely to be an important part of psychological assessment in the future: the development of new psychological tests and structured interviews that directly tap posttraumatic stress and disorder.

Because all of this movement has been very recent, however, most traditional psychological tests still have less-than-optimal sensitivity and specificity with regard to posttraumatic stress, and most new trauma-specific tests lack the normative data necessary for full-fledged clinical use. This transitional phenomenon is likely to be short-lived, however, given the speed at which researchers and clinicians are working to produce increasingly more reliable and valid trauma-relevant measures. As a result, trauma survivors in both mental health and emergency-outreach populations are increasingly more likely to be understood clinically—an outcome that, in turn, can lead only to improved intervention and a better likelihood of recovery.

References

Addiction Research Foundation. (1985). *A Structured Addictions Assessment Interview for Selecting Treatment (ASIST)*. Toronto, Ontario, Canada: Author.

Affleck, G., Tennen, H., Croog, S., & Levine, S. (1987). Causal attribution, perceived benefits, and morbidity after a heart attack: An 8-year study. *Journal of Consulting and Clinical Psychology, 55*, 29–35.

Aldridge, M. R. (1994). A skeptical reflection on the diagnosis of multiple personality disorder. *Irish Journal of Psychological Medicine, 11*, 126–129.

Alexander, P. C. (1993). The differential effects of abuse characteristics and attachment in the prediction of long-term effects of sexual abuse. *Journal of Interpersonal Violence, 8*, 346–362.

Alexander, P. C., & Lupfer, S. L. (1987). Family characteristics and long-term consequences associated with sexual abuse. *Archives of Sexual Behavior, 16*, 235–245.

Allodi, F., & Cowgill, G. (1982). Ethical and psychiatric aspects of torture: A Canadian study. *Canadian Journal of Psychiatry, 27*, 88–102.

American Academy of Psychiatry and the Law. (1995). *Ethical guidelines for the practice of forensic psychiatry*. Washington, DC: Author.

American Psychiatric Association. (1952). *Diagnostic and statistical manual of mental disorders*. Washington, DC: Author.

American Psychiatric Association. (1968). *Diagnostic and statistical manual of mental disorders* (2nd ed.). Washington, DC: Author.

American Psychiatric Association. (1980). *Diagnostic and statistical manual of mental disorders* (3rd ed.). Washington, DC: Author.

American Psychiatric Association. (1987). *Diagnostic and statistical manual of mental disorders* (3rd ed., rev.). Washington, DC: Author.

American Psychiatric Association. (1994). *Diagnostic and statistical manual of mental disorders* (4th ed.). Washington, DC: Author.

Amnesty International. (1992). *Amnesty International report*. London: Author.

Anderson, G., Yasenik, L., & Ross, C. A. (1993). Dissociative experiences and disorders among women who identify themselves as sexual abuse survivors. *Child Abuse and Neglect, 17*, 677–686.

Anthony, J. C., Folstein, M., Romanoski, A. J., Vonkorff, M. R., Nestadt, C. R., Merchant, A., Brown, C. H., Shapiro, S., Kramer, M., & Gruenberg, E. M. (1985). Comparison of lay Diagnostic Interview Schedule and a standardized psychiatric diagnosis. *Archives of General Psychiatry, 42*, 667–676.

Arata, C. M., Saunders, B. E., & Kilpatrick, D. G. (1991). Concurrent validity of a crime-related Post Traumatic Stress Disorder scale for women within the Symptom Checklist–90—Revised. *Violence and Victims, 6*, 191–199.

Armstrong, J. (1991). The psychological organization of multiple personality disordered patients as revealed in psychological testing. *Psychiatric Clinics of North America, 14,* 533–546.

Armstrong, J. (1995). Psychological assessment. In J. L. Spira & I. D. Yalom (Eds.), *Treating dissociative identity disorder* (pp. 3–37). San Francisco: Jossey-Bass.

Armstrong, J., & Loewenstein, R. J. (1990). Characteristics of patients with multiple personality and dissociative disorders on psychological testing. *Journal of Nervous and Mental Disease, 178,* 448–454.

Astin, M. C., Lawrence, K. J., & Foy, D. W. (1993). Posttraumatic stress disorder among battered women: Risk and resiliency factors. *Violence and Victims, 8,* 17–29.

Astin, M. C., Ogland-Hand, S. M., Coleman, E. M., & Foy, D. W. (1995). Posttraumatic stress disorder and childhood abuse in battered women: Comparisons with maritally distressed women. *Journal of Consulting and Clinical Psychology, 63,* 308–312.

Atkeson, B., Calhoun, K., Resick, P., & Ellis, E. (1982). Victims of rape: Repeated assessment of depressive symptoms. *Journal of Consulting and Clinical Psychology, 50,* 96–102.

Bagley, C. (1991). The prevalence and mental health sequels of child sexual abuse in a community sample of women aged 18 to 27. *Canadian Journal of Community Mental Health, 10,* 103–116.

Baker, R. (1992). Psychosocial consequences for tortured refugees seeking asylum refugee status in Europe. In M. Basoglu (Ed.), *Torture and its consequences: Current treatment approaches* (pp. 83–106). Cambridge, England: Cambridge University Press.

Bartone, P., & Wright, K. (1990). Grief and group recovery following a military air disaster. *Journal of Traumatic Stress, 3,* 523–529.

Beck, A. T., Kovacs, M., & Weissman, A. (1979). Assessment of suicidal intention: The scale for suicide ideation. *Journal of Consulting and Clinical Psychology, 47,* 343–352.

Beck, A. T., Ward, C. H., Mandelson, M., Mock, J., & Erbaugh, J. (1961). An inventory for measuring depression. *Archives of General Psychiatry, 4,* 561–571.

Belkin, D. S., Greene, A. F., Rodrigue, J. R., & Boggs, S. R. (1994). Psychopathology and history of sexual abuse. *Journal of Interpersonal Violence, 9,* 535–547.

Berah, E. F., Jones, H. J., & Valent, P. (1984). The experience of a mental health team involved in the early phase of a disaster. *Australia and New Zealand Journal of Psychiatry, 18,* 354–358.

Berger, A. M., Knutson, J. F., Mehm, J. G., & Perkins, K. A. (1988). The self-report of punitive childhood experiences of young adults and adolescents. *Child Abuse and Neglect, 12,* 251–262.

Berliner, L., & Elliott, D. M. (1996). Sexual abuse of children. In J. Briere, L. Berliner, J. A. Bulkley, C. Jenny, & Reid, T. (Eds.), *The APSAC handbook on child maltreatment* (pp. 51–71). Newbury Park, CA: Sage.

Bernstein, D. P., Fink, L., Handelsman, L., Foote, J., Lovejoy, M., Wenzel, K.,

Sarapeto, E., & Ruggiero, J. (1994). Initial reliability and validity of a new retrospective measure of child abuse and neglect. *American Journal of Psychiatry, 151,* 1132–1136.

Bernstein, E. M., & Putnam, F. W (1986). Development, reliability, and validity of a dissociation scale. *Journal of Nervous and Mental Diseases, 174,* 727–734.

Blake, D. D., Weathers, F. W., Nagy, L. M., Kaloupek, D. G., Gusman, F. D., Charney, D. S., & Keane, T. M. (1995). The development of a clinician-administered PTSD scale. *Journal of Traumatic Stress, 8,* 75–90.

Blake, D. D., Weathers, F. W., Nagy, L. M., Kaloupek, D. G., Klauminzer, G., Charney, D. S., & Keane, T. M. (1990). A clinician rating scale for assessing current and lifetime PTSD: The CAPS-1. *The Behavior Therapist, 13,* 187–188.

Blanchard, E. B., Gerardi, R. J., Kolb, L. C., & Barlow, D. H. (1986). The utility of the Anxiety Disorders Schedule (ADIS) in the diagnosis of Post-traumatic Stress Disorder (PTSD) in Vietnam veterans. *Behavior Research and Therapy, 24,* 2701–2707.

Bliss, E. L. (1980). Multiple personalities: A report of 14 cases with implications for schizophrenia. *Archives of General Psychiatry, 37,* 1388–1397.

Bongar, B. (1991). *The suicidal patient: Clinical and legal standards of care.* Washington, DC: American Psychological Association.

Brabin, P. J., & Berah, E. F. (1995). Dredging up past traumas: Harmful or helpful? *Psychiatry, Psychology, and the Law, 2,* 165–171.

Branchey, L., Davis, W., & Lieber, C. S. (1984). Alcoholism in Vietnam and Korea veterans: A long term follow-up. *Alcoholism, 8,* 572–575.

Branscomb, L. (1991). Dissociation in combat-related post-traumatic stress disorder. *Dissociation: Progress in the Dissociative Disorders, 4,* 13–20.

Brassard, M. R., Hart, S. N., & Hardy, D. B. (1993). The Psychological Maltreatment Rating Scales. *Child Abuse and Neglect, 17,* 715–729.

Brauer, R., Harrow, M., & Tucker, G. (1970). Depersonalization phenomena in psychiatric patients. *British Journal of Psychiatry, 117,* 509–515.

Bremner, J. D., Steinberg, M., Southwick, S. M., Johnson, D. R., & Charney, D. S. (1993). Use of the Structured Clinical Interview for DSM–IV Dissociative Disorders for systematic assessment of dissociative symptoms in posttraumatic stress disorder. *American Journal of Psychiatry, 150,* 1011–1014.

Breslau, N., & Davis, G. C. (1987). Posttraumatic stress disorder: The stressor criterion. *Journal of Nervous and Mental Disease, 175,* 255–264.

Breslau, N., & Davis, G. C. (1992). Posttraumatic stress disorder in an urban population of young adults: Risk factors for chronicity. *American Journal of Psychiatry, 149,* 671–675.

Breslau, N. , Davis, G. C., & Andreski, P. (1995). Risk factors for PTSD-related traumatic events: A prospective analysis. *American Journal of Psychiatry, 152,* 529–535.

Breslau, N., Davis, G. C., Andreski, P., & Peterson, E. (1991). Traumatic events and posttraumatic stress disorder in an urban population of young adults. *Archives of General Psychiatry, 48,* 216–222.

Briere, J. (1989). *Therapy for adults molested as children: Beyond survival.* New York: Springer.

Briere, J. (1992a). *Child abuse trauma: Theory and treatment of the lasting effects.* Newbury Park, CA: Sage.

Briere, J. (1992b). Medical symptoms, health risk, and history of childhood sexual abuse (Editorial). *Mayo Clinic Proceedings, 67,* 603–604.

Briere, J. (1992c). Methodological issues in the study of sexual abuse effects. *Journal of Consulting and Clinical Psychology, 60,* 196–203.

Briere, J. (1995a). Child abuse, memory, and recall: A commentary. *Consciousness and Cognition, 4,* 83–87.

Briere, J. (1995b). Science versus politics in the delayed memory debate: A commentary. *The Counseling Psychologist, 23,* 290–293.

Briere, J. (1995c). *Trauma symptom inventory professional manual.* Odessa, FL: Psychological Assessment Resources.

Briere, J. (1996a). A self-trauma model for treating adult survivors of severe child abuse. In Briere, J., Berliner, L., Bulkley, J., Jenny, C, & Reid, T. (Eds.). *The APSAC handbook on child maltreatment* (pp. 140–157). Newbury Park, CA: Sage.

Briere, J. (1996b). *Therapy for adults molested as children, 2nd edition.* New York: Springer.

Briere, J. (1996c). *Trauma Symptom Checklist for Children (TSCC).* Odessa, FL: Psychological Assessment Resources.

Briere, J. (1996d). Psychological assessment of child abuse effects in adults. In J. Wilson & T. Keane (Eds.), *Assessing psychological trauma and PTSD* (pp. 43–68). New York: Guilford Press.

Briere, J., & Conte, J. (1993). Self-reported amnesia for abuse in adults molested as children. *Journal of Traumatic Stress, 6,* 21–31.

Briere, J., & Elliott, D. M. (1993). Sexual abuse, family environment, and psychological symptoms: On the validity of statistical control. *Journal of Consulting and Clinical Psychology, 61,* 284–288.

Briere, J., & Elliott, D. M. (1996a). *The Impacts of Event Scale in the general population: Psychometrics and prediction of trauma.* Unpublished manuscript, Department of Psychiatry, University of Southern California School of Medicine.

Briere, J., & Elliott, D. M. (1996b). *The Los Angeles Symptom Checklist: Psychometrics in a general population sample.* Unpublished manuscript, Department of Psychiatry, University of Southern California School of Medicine.

Briere, J., Elliott, D. M., Harris, K., & Cotman, A. (1995). Trauma Symptom Inventory: Psychometrics and association with childhood and adult trauma in clinical samples. *Journal of Interpersonal Violence, 10,* 387–401.

Briere, J., & Runtz, M. (1986). Suicidal thoughts and behaviours in former sexual abuse victims. *Canadian Journal of Behavioural Science, 18,* 413–423.

Briere, J., & Runtz, M. (1987). Post-sexual abuse trauma: Data and implications for clinical practice. *Journal of Interpersonal Violence, 2,* 367–379.

Briere, J., & Runtz, M. (1988). Symptomatology associated with childhood sexual victimization in a nonclinical adult sample. *Child Abuse and Neglect, 12,* 51–59.

Briere, J., & Runtz, M. (1989). The Trauma Symptom Checklist (TSC-33): Early data on a new scale. *Journal of Interpersonal Violence, 4*, 151–163.

Briere, J., & Runtz, M. (1990a). Augmenting Hopkins SCL scales to measure dissociative symptoms: Data from two nonclinical samples. *Journal of Personality Assessment, 55*, 376–379.

Briere, J., & Runtz, M. (1990b). Differential adult symptomatology associated with three types of child abuse histories. *Child Abuse & Neglect, 14*, 357–364.

Briere, J., & Runtz, M. (1993). Child sexual abuse: Long-term sequelae and implications for psychological assessment. *Journal of Interpersonal Violence, 8*, 312–330.

Briere, J., Woo, R., McRae, B., Foltz, J., & Sitzman, R. (in press). Lifetime victimization history, demographics, and clinical status in female psychiatric emergency room patients. *Journal of Nervous and Mental Disease.*

Briere, J., & Zaidi, L.Y. (1989). Sexual abuse histories and sequelae in female psychiatric emergency room patients. *American Journal of Psychiatry, 146*, 1602–1606.

Browne, A., & Finkelhor, D. (1986). Impact of child sexual abuse: A review of the research. *Psychological Bulletin, 99*, 66–77.

Bryant, R. A., & Harvey, A. G. (1996). Posttraumatic stress reactions in volunteer firefighters. *Journal of Traumatic Stress, 9*, 51–62.

Bryer, J. B., Nelson, B. A., Miller, J. B., & Krol, P. A. (1987). Childhood sexual and physical abuse as factors in adult psychiatric illness. *American Journal of Psychiatry, 144*, 1426–1430.

Burgess, A. W., & Holmstrom, L. L. (1979). *Rape: Crisis and recovery.* Bowie, MD: Robert Brady Co.

Burnam, M. A., Stein, J. A., Golding, J. M., Siegel, J. M., Sorenson, S. B., Forsythe, A. B., & Telles, C. A. (1988). Sexual assault and mental disorders in a community population. *Journal of Consulting and Clinical Psychology, 56*, 843–850.

Busby, D. M., Glenn, E., Steggell, G. L., & Adamson, D. W. (1993). Treatment issues for survivors of physical and sexual abuse. *Journal of Marital and Family Therapy, 19*, 377–391.

Butcher, J. N., Dahlstrom, W. G., Graham, J. R., Tellegen, A., & Kaemmer, B. (1989). *Minnesota Multiphasic Personality Inventory (MMPI-2). Manual for administration and scoring.* Minneapolis: University of Minnesota Press.

Butler, R. W., Foy, D. W., Snodgrass, L., Lea-Hurwicz, M., & Goldfarb, J. (1988). Combat-related posttraumatic stress disorder in a nonpsychiatric population. *Journal of Anxiety Disorders, 2*, 111–120.

Cacciola, J., Griffith, J., & McLellan, A. T. (1987). *Addiction Severity Index instruction manual* (4th ed.). Philadelphia: University of Pennsylvania, School of Medicine, Department of Psychiatry/Veterans Administration Medical Center. Mimeographed.

Caldwell, A. B., & O'Hare, C. (1975). *A handbook of MMPI personality types.* Santa Monica, CA: Clinical Psychological Services.

Canino, G., Bird, H., Shrout, P. E., Rubio-Stipec, M. , Bravo, M., Matinez, R.,

Sesman, M., & Guevara, L. M. (1987). The prevalence of specific psychiatric disorders in Puerto Rico. *Archives of General Psychiatry, 44*, 127–133.

Canon, D. S., Bell, W. E., Andrews, R. H., & Finkelstein, A. S. (1987). Correspondence between MMPI PTSD measures and clinical diagnosis. *Journal of Personality Assessment, 51*, 517–521.

Card, J. J. (1987). Epidemiology of PTSD in a national cohort of Vietnam veterans. *Journal of Clinical Psychology, 43*, 6–17.

Cardeña, E. (1994). The domains of dissociation. In S. J. Lynn & J. W. Rhue (Eds.), *Dissociation: Clinical, theoretical, and research perspectives* (pp. 15–31). New York: Guilford Press.

Cardeña, E., Classen, C. & Spiegel, D. (1991). *Stanford Acute Stress Reaction Questionnaire (SASRQ)*. Unpublished manuscript, Department of Psychiatry and Behavioral Sciences, Stanford University.

Cardeña, E., Holen, A., McFarlane, A., Solomon, Z., Wilkenson, C., & Spiegel, D. (in press). A multi-site study of acute stress reactions to a disaster. In American Psychiatric Association (Ed.), *DSM-IV sourcebook, Volume 4*. Washington, DC: Author.

Cardeña, E., Koopman, C., Classen, C., & Spiegel, D. (1996). Review of the Stanford Acute Stress Reaction Questionnaire. In B. H. Stamm (Ed.), *Measurement of stress, trauma and adaptation* (pp. 293–295). Lutherville, MD: Sidran Press.

Cardeña, E., Lewis-Fernandez, R., Bear, D., Pakianathan, I., & Spiegel, D. (1996). Dissociative disorders. In American Psychiatric Association (Ed.), *DSM-IV sourcebook, Volume 2*. Washington, DC: Author.

Cardeña, E., & Spiegel, D. (1993). Dissociative reactions to the San Francisco Bay Area earthquake of 1989. *American Journal of Psychiatry, 150*, 474–478.

Carlin, A. S., & Ward, N. G. (1992). Subtypes of psychiatric inpatient women who have been sexually abused. *Journal of Nervous and Mental Disease, 180*, 392–397.

Carlson, E. B. (in press). *The clinician's guide to understanding and assessing trauma and trauma responses*. New York: Guilford Press.

Carlson, E. B., & Armstrong, J. (1995). The diagnosis and assessment of dissociative disorders. In S. J. Lynn & J. L. Rhue (Eds.), *Dissociation: Clinical and theoretical perspectives* (pp. 159–174). New York: Guilford Press.

Carlson, E. B., Putnam, F. W., Ross, C. A., Anderson, G., Clark, P., Torem, M., Coons, P., Bowman, E., Chu, J. A., Dill, D., Loewenstein, R. J., & Braun, B. G. (1991). Factor analysis of the Dissociative Experiences Scale: A multicenter study. In B. G. Braun & E. B. Carlson (Eds.), *Proceedings of the Eighth International Conference on Multiple Personality and Dissociative States* (p. 30). Chicago: Rush Presbyterian.

Carlson, E. B., Putnam, F. W., Ross, C. A., Torem, M., Coons, P., Dill, D., Loewenstein, R. J., & Braun, B. G. (1993). Validity of the Dissociative Experiences Scale in screening for multiple personality disorder: A multicenter study. *American Journal of Psychiatry, 150*, 1030–1036.

Carlson, E. B., & Rosser-Hogan, R. (1991). Trauma experiences, posttraumatic stress, dissociation, and depression in Cambodian refugees. *American Journal of Psychiatry, 148*, 1548–1551.

Cascardi, M., O'Leary, D., Lawrence, E. E., & Schlee, K. A. (1995). Characteristics of women physically abused by their spouses and who seek treatment regarding marital conflict. *Journal of Consulting and Clinical Psychology, 63,* 616–623.

Cattell, J. P., & Cattell, J. R. (1974). Depersonalization: Psychological and social perspectives. In S. Arieti (Ed.), *American handbook of psychiatry* (pp. 767–799). New York: Basic Books.

Centers for Disease Control. (1987). Postservice mortality among Vietnam veterans. *Journal of the American Medical Association, 257,* 790–795.

Cerney, M. (1990). The Rorschach and traumatic loss: Can the presence of traumatic loss be detected from the Rorschach? *Journal of Personality Assessment, 55,* 781–789.

Chakraborty, A. (1991). Culture, colonialism, and psychiatry. *Lancet, 337,* 1204–1207.

Chan, C. S. (1987). Asian-American women: Psychological responses to sexual exploitation and cultural stereotypes. *Women & Therapy, 6,* 33–38.

Cheperon, J. A., & Prinzhorn, B. (1994). Personality Assessment Inventory (PAI): Profiles of adult female abuse survivors. *Assessment, 1,* 393–399.

Choca, J. P., Shanley, L. A., & Van Denburg, E. (1992). *Interpretative guide to the Millon Clinical Multiaxial Inventory.* Washington, DC: American Psychological Association.

Chu, J. A., & Dill, D. L. (1990). Dissociative symptoms in relation to childhood physical and sexual abuse. *American Journal of Psychiatry, 147,* 887–892.

Cloitre, M., Tardiff, K., Marzuk, P. M., Leon, A. C., & Portera, L. (1996). Childhood abuse and subsequent sexual assault among female inpatients. *Journal of Traumatic Stress, 9,* 473–482.

Cohen, L. J., & Roth, S. (1987). The psychological aftermath of rape: Long-term effects and individual differences in recovery. *Journal of Social and Clinical Psychology, 5,* 525–534.

Cole, P. M., & Putnam, F. W. (1992). Effect of incest on self and social functioning: A developmental psychopathology perspective. *Journal of Consulting and Clinical Psychology, 60,* 174–184.

Coons, P. M., & Milstein, V. (1986). Psychosexual disturbances in multiple personality. *Journal of Nervous and Mental Disease, 47,* 106–110.

Coons, P. M., & Milstein, V. (1994). Factitious or malingered multiple personality disorder: Eleven cases. *Dissociation: Progress in the Dissociative Disorders, 7,* 81–85.

Courtois, C. (1995). Assessment and diagnosis. In C. Classen & I. Yalom (Eds.), *Treating women molested in childhood* (pp. 1–34). San Francisco: Jossey-Bass.

Craine, L. S., Henson, C. H., Colliver, J. A., & MacLean, D. G. (1988). Prevalence of a history of sexual abuse among female psychiatric patients in a state hospital system. *Hospital and Community Psychiatry, 39,* 300–304.

Dancu, C. V., Riggs, D. S., Hearst-Ikeda, D., Shoyer, B. G., & Foa, E. B. (1996). Dissociative experiences and posttraumatic stress disorder among female victims of criminal assault and rape. *Journal of Traumatic Stress, 9,* 253–267.

Davidson, J. R. T. (1994). Issues in the diagnosis of posttraumatic stress disorder.

In R. S. Pynoos (Ed.), *Posttraumatic stress disorder: A clinical review* (pp. 1–15). Lutherville, MD: Sidran.

Davidson, J. R. T., & Fairbank, J. A. (1993). The epidemiology of posttraumatic stress disorder. In J. R. T. Davidson & E. B. Foa (Eds.), *Posttraumatic stress disorder: DSM-IV and beyond* (pp. 147–169). Washington, DC: American Psychiatric Press.

Davidson, J. R. T., & Foa, E. B. (1991). Diagnostic issues in posttraumatic stress disorder: Considerations for the DSM–IV. *Journal of Abnormal Psychology, 100,* 346–355.

Davidson, J. R. T., & Foa, E. B. (Eds.). (1993). *Posttraumatic stress disorder: DSM-IV and beyond.* Washington, DC: American Psychiatric Press.

Davidson, J. R. T., Hughes, D., Blazer, D., & George, L. K. (1991). Posttraumatic stress disorder in the community: An epidemiologic study. *Psychological Medicine, 21,* 1–9.

Davidson, J. R. T., Kudler, H. S., Saunders, W. B., & Smith, R. D. (1990). Symptom and comorbidity patterns in World War II and Vietnam veterans with posttraumatic stress disorder. *Comprehensive Psychiatry, 31,* 162–170.

Davidson, J., Kudler, H., & Smith, R. (1990). *The Structured Interview for PTSD (SI-PTSD).* Unpublished manuscript, Department of Psychiatry, Duke University, Durham, NC.

Davidson, J., Smith, R., & Kudler, H. (1989). The validity and reliability of the *DSM–III* criteria for post-traumatic stress disorder. *Journal of Nervous and Mental Disease, 177,* 336–341.

Demaré, D. (1993). *The Childhood Maltreatment Questionnaire.* Unpublished manuscript, University of Manitoba, Winnipeg, Manitoba, Canada.

Demaré, D., & Briere, J. (1994, August). *Childhood maltreatment and current symptomatology in 1,179 university students.* Paper presented at the 102nd Annual Convention of the American Psychological Association, Los Angeles, CA.

Demaré, D., & Briere, J. (1995, August). *Trauma Symptom Checklist—40: Validation with sexually abused and nonabused university students.* Paper presented at the 103rd Annual Convention of the American Psychological Association, New York.

Demaré, D., & Briere, J. (1996). *Validation of the Trauma Symptom Inventory with abused and nonabused university students.* Unpublished manuscript, University of Manitoba, Winnipeg, Manitoba, Canada.

Dembo, R., Williams, L., LaVoie, L., Barry, E., Getreu, A., Wish, E., Schmeider, J., & Washburn, M. (1989). Physical abuse, sexual victimization, and illicit drug use: Replication of a structural analysis among a new sample of high-risk youths. *Violence and Victims, 4,* 121–138.

Derogatis, L.R. (1977). *SCL-90: Administration, scoring, and procedure manual-I for the R (revised) version.* Baltimore: John Hopkins University School of Medicine.

Derogatis, L. R. (1983). *SCL-90-R administration, scoring, and procedures manual II for the revised version* (2nd ed.). Towson, MD: Clinical Psychometrics Research.

Derogatis, L. R., Lipman, R. S., Rickels, K., Ulenhuth, E. H., & Covi, L. (1974).

The Hopkins Symptom Checklist (HSCL): A self-report symptom inventory: *Behavioral Science, 19,* 1–15.

Derogatis, L. R., & Spencer, P. M. (1982). *The Brief Symptom Inventory administration, scoring, and procedures.* Baltimore: Clinical Psychometric Research Institute.

DiNardo, P. A., & Barlow, D. H. (1988). *Anxiety Disorders Interview Scale—Revised.* Albany, NY: Center for Phobia and Anxiety Disorders.

DiNardo, P. A., O'Brien, G. T., Barlow, D. H., Waddell, M. T., & Banchard, E. B. (1983). Reliability of DSM-III anxiety disorder categories using a new structured interview. *Archives of General Psychiatry, 40,* 1070–1074.

DiTomasso, M. J., & Routh, D. K. (1993). Recall of abuse in childhood and three measures of dissociation. *Child Abuse and Neglect, 17,* 477–485.

Drossman, D. A., Lesserman, J., Nachman, G., Li, Z., Gluck, H., Toomey, T. C., Mitchell, C. M. (1990). Sexual and physical abuse in women with functional or organic gastrointestinal disorders. *Annuals of Internal Medicine, 113,* 828–833.

Dubester, K. A., & Braun, B. G. (1995). Psychometric properties of the dissociative experiences scale. *Journal of Nervous and Mental Disease, 183,* 231–235.

Durkin, M. E. (1993). Major depression and post-traumatic stress disorder following the Coalinga (California) and Chile earthquakes: A cross-cultural comparison. *Journal of Social Behavior and Personality, 8,* 405–420.

Dutton, D. G. (1992). Theoretical and empirical perspectives on the etiology and prevention of wife assault. In R. D. Peters, R. J. McMahon, & V. L. Quinsey (Eds.), *Aggression and violence throughout the life span* (pp. 192–221). Newbury Park, CA: Sage.

Dutton, M. A., Burghardt, K., Perrin, S., Chrestman, K., & Halle, P. (1994). Battered women's cognitive schemata. *Journal of Traumatic Stress, 7,* 237–255.

Dutton, D. G., & Painter, S. (1981). Traumatic bonding: The development of emotional attachments in battered women and other relationships of intermittent abuse. *Victimology, 6,* 139–155.

Dutton, D. G., & Painter, S. (1993). The battered woman syndrome: Effects of severity and intermittency of abuse. *American Journal of Orthopsychiatry, 63,* 614–622.

Dutton, M. A., Hohnecker, L. C., Halle, P. M., & Burghardt, K. J. (1994). Traumatic responses among battered women who kill. *Journal of Traumatic Stress, 7,* 549–564.

Edwards, G., & Angus, J. (1972). Depersonalization. *British Journal of Psychiatry, 120,* 242–244.

Eisendrath, S. J., Way, L. W., Ostroff, J. W., & Johanson, C. A. (1986). Identification of psychogenic abdominal pain. *Psychosomatics, 27,* 705–712.

El Sarraj, E., Punamaki, R., Salmi, S., & Summerfield, D. (1996). Experiences of torture and ill-treatment and posttraumatic stress disorder symptoms among Palestinian prisoners. *Journal of Traumatic Stress, 9,* 595–606.

Elliott, D. M. (1992). *Traumatic Events Survey.* Unpublished psychological test, Harbor-UCLA Medical Center, Los Angeles.

Elliott, D. M. (1993, November). *Assessing the psychological impact of recent violence in an inpatient setting.* Paper presented at the meeting of the International Society for Traumatic Stress Studies, San Antonio, TX.

Elliott, D. M. (1994a). Assessing adult victims of interpersonal violence. In J. Briere (Ed.), *Assessing and treating victims of violence* (New Directions for Mental Health Services Series No. 64, pp. 5–16). San Francisco: Jossey-Bass.

Elliott, D. M. (1994b). Impaired object relations in professional women molested as children. *Psychotherapy, 31,* 79–86.

Elliott, D. M. (1995, August). *Trauma, memory loss, and subsequent recall: Prevalence and triggers to memory recall.* Paper presented at the 105th Annual Convention of the American Psychological Association, New York.

Elliott, D. M., & Briere, J. (1992). Sexual abuse trauma among professional women: Validating the Trauma Symptom Checklist—40 (TSC-40). *Child Abuse and Neglect, 16,* 391–398.

Elliott, D. M., & Briere, J. (1994). Forensic sexual abuse evaluations of older children: Disclosures and symptomatology. *Behavioral Sciences and the Law, 12,* 261–277.

Elliott, D. M., & Briere, J. (1995). Posttraumatic stress associated with delayed recall of sexual abuse: A general population study. *Journal of Traumatic Stress, 8,* 629–647.

Elliott, D. M., & Mok, D. (1995, April). *Adult sexual assault: Prevalence, symptomatology, and sex differences.* Paper presented at the annual meeting of the Western Psychological Association, San Francisco, CA.

Engdahl, B. E., & Eberly, R. E. (1990). The effects of torture and other maltreatment: Implications for psychology. In P. Suedfeld (Ed.), *Psychology and torture* (pp. 31–47). New York: Hemisphere.

Engdahl, B. E., Speed, N., Eberly, R. E., & Schwartz, J. (1991). Comorbidity of psychiatric disorders and personality profiles of American World War II prisoners of war. *Journal of Nervous and Mental Disease, 179,* 181–187.

Engles, M. L., Moisan, D., & Harris, R. (1994). MMPI indices of childhood trauma among 110 female outpatients. *Journal of Personality Assessment, 63,* 135–147.

Enns, C. Z., McNeilly, C. L., Corkery, J. M., & Gilbert, M. S. (1995). The debate about delayed memories of child sexual abuse: A feminist perspective. *The Counseling Psychologist, 23,* 181–279.

Epstein, R. S. (1993). Avoidant symptoms cloaking the diagnosis of PTSD in patients with severe accidental injury. *Journal of Traumatic Stress, 6,* 451–458.

Escobar, J. I., Canino, F., Rubio-Stipec, M., & Bravo, M. (1992). Somatic symptoms after a natural disaster: A prospective study. *American Journal of Psychiatry, 149,* 965–967.

Exner, J. E. (1979). *The Rorschach: A comprehensive system.* New York: Wiley.

Exner, J. E. (1986). *The Rorschach: A comprehensive system* (2nd ed.). New York: Wiley.

Fairbank, J. A., Caddell, J. M., & Keane, T. M. (1985, August). *Black–White differences on the MMPI and PTSD subscale.* Paper presented at the 93rd Annual Convention of the American Psychological Association, Los Angeles, CA.

Fairbank, J. A., Hansen, D. J., & Fitterling, J. M. (1991). Patterns of appraisal and coping across different stressor conditions among former prisoners of war with and without posttraumatic stress disorder. *Journal of Consulting and Clinical Psychology, 59*, 274–281.

Fairbank, J. A., Keane, T. M., & Malloy, P. F. (1983). Some preliminary data on the psychological characteristics of Vietnam veterans with post-traumatic stress disorder. *Journal of Consulting and Clinical Psychology, 51*, 912–919.

Fairbank, S. A., McCaffrey, R. J., & Keane, T. M. (1985). Psychometric detection of fabricated symptoms of post-traumatic stress disorder in Vietnam veterans. *Journal of Clinical Psychology, 43*, 44–55.

Falsetti, S. A., & Resnick, H. S. (1995). Helping the victims of violent crime. In J. R. Freedy & S. E. Hobfoll (Eds.), *Traumatic stress: From theory to practice* (pp. 263–285). New York: Plenum Press.

Falsetti, S. A., Resnick, H. S., Kilpatrick, D. G., & Freedy, J. R. (1994). A review of the "Potential Stressful Events Interview": A comprehensive assessment instrument of high and low magnitude stressors. *The Behavior Therapist, 17*, 66–67.

Falsetti, S. A., Resnick, H. S., Resick, P. A., & Kilpatrick, D. G. (1993). The Modified PTSD Symptom Scale: A brief self-report measure of post-traumatic stress disorder. *Behavior Therapist, 17*, 66–67.

Feldman-Summers, S., & Pope, K. S. (1994). The experience of "forgetting" childhood abuse: A national survey of psychologists. *Journal of Consulting and Clinical Psychology, 62*, 636–639.

Finkelhor, D. (1990). Early and long-term effects of child sexual abuse: An update. *Professional Psychology: Research and Practice, 21*, 325–330.

Finkelhor, D., Hotaling, G. T., Lewis, I. A., & Smith, C. (1989). Sexual abuse and its relationship to later sexual satisfaction, marital status, religion, and attitudes. *Journal of Interpersonal Violence, 4*, 379–399.

Fisher, P. M., Winne, P. H., & Ley, R. G. (1993). Group therapy for adult women survivors of child sexual abuse: Differentiation of completers versus dropouts. *Psychotherapy, 30*, 616–624.

Foa, E. B. (1995). *Posttraumatic Stress Diagnostic Scale (PDS) manual*. Minneapolis, MN: National Computer Systems.

Foa, E. B., Riggs, D. S., Dancu, & C. V., Rothbaum, B. O. (1993). Reliability and validity of a brief instrument assessing post-traumatic stress disorder. *Journal of Traumatic Stress, 6*, 459–474.

Foa, E. B., Zinbarg, R. E., & Rothbaum, B. O. (1992). Uncontrollability and unpredictability in post-traumatic stress disorder: An animal model. *Psychological Bulletin, 112*, 218–238.

Follette, V. M., Polusny, M. A., Bechtle, A. E., & Naugle, A. E. (1996). Cumulative trauma: The impact of child sexual abuse, adult sexual assault, and spouse abuse. *Journal of Traumatic Stress, 9*, 25–35.

Follingstad, D. R., Brennan, A. F., Hause, E. S., Polek, D. S., & Rutledge, L. L. (1991). Factors moderating physical and psychological symptoms of battered women. *Journal of Family Violence, 6*, 81–95.

Forman, B. D. (1982). Reported male rape. *Victimology, 7*, 235–236.

Forster, P. (1992). Nature and treatment of acute stress reactions. In L. S. Austin (Ed.), *Responding to disaster: A guide for mental health professionals* (pp. 25–51). Washington, DC: American Psychiatric Press.

Foy, D. W., Resnick, H. S., Sipprelle, R. C., & Carroll, E. M. (1987). Premilitary, military, and postmilitary factors in the development of combat-related posttraumatic stress disorder. *The Behavior Therapist, 10,* 3–9.

Foy, D. W., Sipprelle, R. C., Rueger, D. B., & Carroll, E. M. (1984). Etiology of posttraumatic stress syndrome in Vietnam veterans: Analysis of premilitary, military, and combat exposure influences. *Journal of Consulting and Clinical Psychology, 52,* 79–87.

Freedy, J. R., Shaw, D. L., Jarrell, M. P., & Masters, C. R. (1992). Toward an understanding of the psychological impact of natural disasters: An application of the Conservation Resources Stress model. *Journal of Traumatic Stress, 5,* 441–454.

Freinkel, A., Koopman, C., & Spiegel, D. (1994). Dissociative symptoms in media execution witnesses. *American Journal of Psychiatry, 151,* 1335–1339.

Friedman, M. J., & Jaranson, J. M. (1994). The applicability of the PTSD concept to refugees. In A. J. Marsella, T. H. Borneman, S. Ekblad, & J. Orley (Eds.), *Amidst peril and pain: The mental health and well-being of the world's refugees* (pp. 207–228). Washington, DC: American Psychological Association.

Friedrich, W. N. (1994). Assessing children for the effects of sexual victimization. In J. Briere (Ed.), *Assessing and treating victims of violence* (New Directions for Mental Health Services Series No. 64, pp. 17–27). San Francisco: Jossey-Bass.

Friedrich, W. N. (in press). *Psychological assessment of sexually abused children and adolescents.* Newbury Park, CA: Sage.

Frischholz, E. J., Braun, B. G., Sachs, R. G., Hopkins, L., Shaeffer, D. M., Lewis, J., Leavitt, F., Pasquotto, J. N., & Schwartz, D. R. (1990). The Dissociative Experiences Scale: Further replication and validation. *Dissociation: Progress in the Dissociative Disorders, 3,* 151–153.

Frye, S., & Stockton, R. (1982). Discriminant analysis of posttraumatic stress disorder among a group of Vietnam combat veterans. *American Journal of Psychiatry, 139,* 52–56.

Ganley, A. L. (1981). *Court mandated counseling for men who batter: Participants' and trainers' manuals.* Washington, DC: Center for Women's Policy Studies.

Garner, D. M. (1991). *Eating Disorder Inventory—2 Professional Manual.* Odessa, FL: Psychological Assessment Resources.

Garner, D. M., Olmstead, M. P., & Polivney, J. (1983). Development and validation of a multidimensional eating disorder inventory for anorexia nervosa and bulimia. *International Journal of Eating Disorders, 2,* 15–34.

Gayford, J. J. (1975). Wife-battering: A preliminary study of 100 cases. *British Medical Journal, 1,* 194–197.

Gayton, W. F., Burchstead, G. N., & Matthews, G. R. (1986). An investigation of the utility of an MMPI post-traumatic stress scale. *Journal of Clinical Psychology, 42,* 916–917.

Gidycz, C. A., & Koss, M. P. (1990). A comparison of group and individual sexual assault victims. *Psychology of Women Quarterly, 14,* 325–342.

Gilbert, B. (1994). Treatment of adult victims of rape. In J. Briere (Ed.), *Assessing and treating victims of violence* (New Directions for Mental Health Series No. 64, pp. 67–78). San Francisco: Jossey-Bass.

Gleason, W. J. (1993). Mental disorders in battered women: An empirical study. *Violence and Victims, 8*, 53–68.

Goff, D. C., Brotman, A. W., Kindlon, D., & Waites, M. (1991). Self-reports of childhood abuse in chronically psychotic patients. *Psychiatry Research, 37*, 73–80.

Gold, S. R., Milan, L. D., Mayall, A., & Johnson, A. E. (1994). A cross-validation study of the Trauma Symptom Checklist: The role of mediating variables. *Journal of Interpersonal Violence, 9*, 12–26.

Goldberg, J., True, W. R., Eisen, S. A., & Henderson, W. G. (1990). A twin study of the effects of the Vietnam war on posttraumatic stress disorder. *Journal of the American Medical Association, 263*, 1227–1232.

Golding, J. M. (1996). Sexual assault history and women's reproductive health. *Psychology of Women Quarterly, 20*, 101–121.

Goldwater, L., & Duffy, J. F. (1990). Use of the MMPI to uncover histories of childhood abuse in adult female psychiatric patients. *Journal of Clinical Psychology, 46*, 392–398.

Graham, J. R. (1987). *The MMPI: A practical guide* (2nd ed.). New York: Oxford University Press.

Graham, J. R. (1990). *MMPI-2: Assessing personality and psychopathology.* New York: Oxford University Press.

Green, B. (1994). Traumatic stress and disaster: Mental health effects and factors influencing adaptation. In F. Liehmac & C. C. Nadelson (Eds.), *International review of psychiatry, Vol. 2* (pp. 117–210). Washington, DC: American Psychiatric Press.

Green, B., Grace, M. C., & Gleser, C. G. (1985). Identifying survivors at risk: Long-term impairment following the Beverly Hills Supper Club fire. *Journal of Consulting and Clinical Psychology, 53*, 672–678.

Green, B. L., Grace, M. C., Lindy, J. D., & Gleser, G. C. (1990). War stressor and symptom persistence in posttraumatic stress disorder. *Journal of Anxiety Disorder, 4*, 31–39.

Green, B. L., Grace, M. C., Lindy, J. D., Gleser, G. C., & Leonard, A. (1990). Risk factors for PTSD and other diagnoses in a general sample of Vietnam veterans. *American Journal of Psychiatry, 147*, 729–733.

Green, B. L., Grace, M. C., Lindy, J. D., Tichener, J. L., & Lindy, J. G. (1983). Levels of functional impairment following a civilian disaster: The Beverly Hills Supper Club fire. *Journal of Consulting and Clinical Psychology, 51*, 573–580.

Green, B. L., Lindy, J. D., Grace, M. C., & Gleser, G. C. (1989). Multiple diagnosis in post-traumatic stress disorder: The role of war stressors. *Journal of Nervous and Mental Disease, 177*, 329–335.

Green, B. L., Lindy, J. D., Grace, M. C., Gleser, G. C., Leonard, A. C., Korol, M., & Winget, C. (1990). Buffalo Creek survivors in the second decade: Stability of stress symptoms. *American Journal of Orthopsychiatry, 60*, 45–54.

Gregg, G. R., & Parks, E. D. (1995). Selected Minnesota Multiphasic Personality

Inventory-2 Scales for identifying women with a history of sexual abuse. *Journal of Nervous and Mental Disease, 183,* 53–56.

Guarnaccia, P., Canino, G., Rubio-Stipec, M., & Bravo, M. (1993). The prevalence of *ataques de nervios* in the Puerto Rico disaster study. *Journal of Nervous and Mental Disease, 181,* 157–165.

Hagström, R. (1995). The acute psychological impact on survivors following a train accident. *Journal of Traumatic Stress, 8,* 391–402.

Hammarberg, M. (1992). Penn Inventory for Posttraumatic Stress Disorder: Psychometric properties. *Psychological Assessment, 4,* 67–76.

Hanson, R. F., Kilpatrick, D. G., Falsetti, S. A., & Resnick, H. S. (1995). Violent crime and mental health. In J. R. Freedy & S. E. Hobfoll (Eds.), *Traumatic stress: From theory to practice* (pp. 129–161). New York: Plenum Press .

Hardesty, L., & Greif, G. L. (1994). Common themes in a group for female iv drug users who are HIV positive. *Journal of Psychoactive Drugs, 26,* 289–293.

Harris, R., & Lingoes, J. (1968). *Subscales for the Minnesota Multiphasic Personality Inventory.* Unpublished materials, The Langley Porter Clinic, University of California, San Francisco.

Hartman, W., Clark, M., Morgan, M., Dunn, V., Perry, G., & Winsch, D. (1990). Rorschach structure of a hospitalized sample of Vietnam veterans with PTSD. *Journal of Personality Assessment, 54,* 149–159.

Hartsough, D. M. (1986). *Variables affecting duty-related stress after an air crash disaster.* Unpublished manuscript, Purdue University at West Lafayette, IN.

Hathaway, S. R., & McKinley, J. C. (1943). *The Minnesota Multiphasic Personality Inventory* (rev. ed.). Minneapolis: University of Minnesota Press.

Hauff, E., & Vaglum, P. (1994). Chronic posttraumatic stress disorder in Vietnamese refugees: A prospective community study of prevalence, course, psychopathology, and stressors. *Journal of Nervous and Mental Disease, 182,* 85–90.

Hazzard, A., Weston, J., & Gutterres, C. (1992). After a child's death: Factors related to parental bereavement. *Journal of Developmental and Behavioral Pediatrics, 13,* 24–30.

Helzer, J. K., Robins, L. N., & McEvoy, L. (1987). Post-traumatic stress disorder in the general population: Findings of the Epidemiologic Catchment Area survey. *New England Journal of Medicine, 317,* 1630–1634.

Henderson, J. L., & Moore, M. (1944). The psychoneuroses of war. *The New England Journal of Medicine, 230,* 273–279.

Hendrix, C. C., Anelli, L. M., Gibbs, J. P., & Fournier, D. G. (1994). Validation of the Purdue Post-Traumatic Stress Scale on a sample of Vietnam veterans. *Journal of Traumatic Stress, 7,* 311–318.

Hendrix, C. C, Jurich, A. P., & Schumm, W. R. (1994). Validation of the Impact of Event Scale of American Vietnam veterans. *Psychological Reports, 75,* 321–322.

Herman, D., Weathers, F., Litz, B., Joaquim, S., & Keane, T. (1993, October). *The PK Scale of the MMPI-2. Reliability and validity of the embedded and standalone versions.* Paper presented at the annual meeting of the International Society for Traumatic Stress Studies, San Antonio, TX.

Herman, J. L. (1992a). Complex PTSD: A syndrome in survivors of prolonged and repeated trauma. *Journal of Traumatic Stress, 5*, 377–392.

Herman, J. L. (1992b). *Trauma and recovery: The aftermath of violence—from domestic abuse to political terror.* New York: Basic Books.

Herman, J. L., Perry, C., & van der Kolk, B. A. (1989). Childhood trauma in borderline personality disorder. *American Journal of Psychiatry, 146*, 490–494.

Herman, J. L., & Schatzow, E. (1987). Recovery and verification of memories of childhood sexual trauma. *Psychoanalytic Psychology, 4*, 1–14.

Hillman, R. G. (1981). The psychopathology of being held hostage. *American Journal of Psychiatry, 138*, 1193–1197.

Hobfoll, S. E. (1988). *The ecology of stress.* Washington, DC: Hemisphere.

Hobfoll, S. E., Dunahoo, C. A., & Monnier, J. (1995). Conservation of resources and traumatic stress. In J. R. Freedy & S. E. Hobfoll (Eds.), *Traumatic stress: From theory to practice* (pp. 29–47). New York: Plenum Press.

Hodgkinson, P. E., & Shepherd, M. A. (1994). The impact of disaster support work. *Journal of Traumatic Stress, 7*, 587–600.

Hofmann-Patsalides, B. M. (1994). *Paternal incest, somatization, and disturbances in affect symbolization (alexithymia): A Rorschach study.* Unpublished doctoral dissertation, California Institute of Integral Studies, San Francisco.

Holen, A. (1993). The north sea oil rig disaster. In J. P. Wilson & B. Raphael (Eds.), *International handbook of traumatic stress syndromes* (pp. 471–478). New York: Plenum Press.

Holloway, H. C., & Fullerton, C. S. (1994). The psychology of terror and its aftermath. In R. J. Ursano, C. S. Fullerton, & B. G. McCaughey (Eds.), *Individual and community response to trauma and disaster: The structure of human chaos* (pp. 31–45). Cambridge, England: Cambridge University Press.

Horowitz, M. J. (1976). *Stress response syndromes.* New York: Jason Aronson.

Horowitz, M. J., Weiss, D. S., & Marmar, C. R. (1987). Diagnosis of posttraumatic stress disorder. *Journal of Nervous and Mental Disease, 175*, 267–268.

Horowitz, M. J., Wilner, N., & Alvarez, W. (1979). Impacts of Event Scale: A measure of subjective stress. *Psychosomatic Medicine, 41*, 209–218.

Hougen, H. P., Kelstrup, J., Petersen, H. D., & Rasmussen, O. V. (1988). Sequelae to torture: A controlled study of torture victims living in exile. *Forensic Science International, 36*, 153–160.

Hough, R. L., Canino, G. J., Abueg, F. R., & Gusman, F. D. (1996). PTSD and related stress disorders among Hispanics. In A. J. Marsella, M. J. Friedman, E. T. Gerrity, & R. M. Scurfield (Eds.), *Ethnocultural aspects of posttraumatic stress disorder: Issues, research, and clinical applications* (pp. 301–338). Place of publication: Publisher.

Houskamp, B. M. (1994). Assessing and treating battered women: A clinical review of issues and approaches. In J. Briere (Ed.), *Assessing and treating victims of violence* (New Directions for Mental Health Series No. 64, pp. 79–89). San Francisco: Jossey-Bass.

Houskamp, B. M., & Foy, D. W. (1991). The assessment of posttraumatic stress disorder in battered women. *Journal of Interpersonal Violence, 6*, 368–376.

Hunter, J. A. (1991). A comparison of the psychosocial maladjustment of adult males and females sexually molested as children. *Journal of Interpersonal Violence, 6,* 205–217.

Hyer, L. A., Davis, H., Albrecht, J. W., Boudewns, P. A., & Woods, M. G. (1994). Cluster analysis of MCMI-II on chronic PTSD victims. *Journal of Clinical Psychology, 50,* 502–515.

Hyer, L. A., Davis, H., Woods, G., Albrecht, J., & Boudewyns, P. A. (1992). Relationship between the Millon Clinical Multiaxial Inventory and the Millon-II: Value of scales for aggressive and self-defeating personalities in posttraumatic stress disorder. *Psychological Reports, 71,* 687–689.

Hyer, L. A., Fallon, J. H., Harrison, W. R., & Boudewyns, P. A. (1987). MMPI overreporting by Vietnam combat veterans. *Journal of Clinical Psychology, 43,* 79–83.

Hyer, L.A., Summers, M. N., Boyd, S., Litaker, M., & Boudewyns, P. (1996). Assessment of older combat veterans with the Clinician-Administered PTSD Scale. *Journal of Traumatic Stress, 9,* 587–593.

Hyer, L. A., Woods, M. G., Boudewyns, P. A., Bruno, R. D., & O'Leary, W. C. (1988). Concurrent validation of the Millon Clinical Multiaxial Inventory among Vietnam veterans with posttraumatic stress disorder. *Psychological Reports, 63,* 271–278.

Hyer, L. A., Woods, M. G., Boudewyns, P. A., Harrison, W. R., & Tamkin, A. S. (1990). MCMI and 16-PF with Vietnam veterans: Profiles and concurrent validation of MCMI. *Journal of Personality Disorders, 4,* 391–401.

Hyer, L. A., Woods, M. G., Harrison, W., Boudewyns, P. , & O'Leary, W. C. (1989). MMPI F-K index among hospitalized Vietnam veterans. *Journal of Clinical Psychology, 45,* 250–254.

Jacobson, G. R. (1989). A comprehensive approach to pretreatment evaluation: I. Detection, assessment, and diagnosis of alcoholism. In R. K. Hester & W. R. Miller (Eds.), *Handbook of alcoholism treatment approaches: Effective alternatives* (pp. 17–43). New York: Pergamon Press.

Jaffe, R. (1968). Dissociative phenomena in former concentration camp inmates. *International Journal of Psychoanalysis, 49,* 310–312.

Jordan, R. G., Nunley, T. V., & Cook, R. R. (1992). Symptom exaggeration in a PTSD inpatient population: Response set or claim for compensation. *Journal of Traumatic Stress, 5,* 633–642.

Joseph, S., Yule, W., Williams, R., & Andrews, B. (1993). Crisis support in the aftermath of disaster: A longitudinal perspective. *British Journal of Clinical Psychology, 32,* 177–185.

Kardiner, A., & Spiegel, H. (1947). *War stress and neurotic illness.* New York: Harper.

Kaser-Boyd, N. (1993). Post-traumatic stress disorder in children and adults: The legal relevance. *Western State University Law Review, 20,* 319–334.

Kaufman, A., Divasto, P., Jackson, R., Voorhees, D., & Christy, J. (1980). Male rape victims: Noninstitutionalized assault. *American Journal of Psychiatry, 137,* 221–223.

Keane, T. M., Caddell, J. M., & Taylor, K. L. (1988). Mississippi scale for combat-related posttraumatic stress disorder: Three studies in reliability and validity. *Journal of Consulting and Clinical Psychology, 56,* 85–90.

Keane, T. M., Fairbank, J. A., Caddell, J. M., Zimering, R. T., Taylor, K. L., & Mora, C. A. (1989). Clinical evaluation of a measure to assess combat exposure. *Psychological Assessment, 1*, 53–55.

Keane, T. M., Kolb, L. C., & Thomas, R. T. (1990). *A psychophysiological study of chronic PTSD* (Department of Veterans Affairs Cooperative Study No. 334).

Keane, T. M., Malloy, P. F., & Fairbank, J. A. (1984). Empirical development of an MMPI subscale for the assessment of combat-related posttraumatic stress disorder. *Journal of Consulting and Clinical Psychology, 52*, 888–891.

Kemp, A., Green, B. L., Hovanitz, C., & Rawlings, E. I. (1995). Incidence and correlates of posttraumatic stress disorder in battered women: Shelter and community samples. *Journal of Interpersonal Violence, 10*, 43–55.

Kennedy, L. W., & Dutton, D. G. (1989). The incidence of wife assault in Alberta. *Canadian Journal of Behavioural Science, 21*, 40–54.

Kernberg, O. F. (1976). *Borderline conditions and pathological narcissism.* New York: Aronson.

Kessler, R. C., Sonnega, A., Bromet, E., Hughes, M., & Nelson, C. B. (1995). Posttraumatic stress disorder in the national comorbidity survey. *Archives of General Psychiatry, 52*, 1048–1060.

Khan, F. I., Welch, T. L., & Zillmer, E. A. (1993). MMPI-2 profiles of battered women in transition. *Journal of Personality Assessment, 60*, 100–111.

Kilpatrick, D. G., Best, C. L., Veronen, L. J., Amick, A. E., Villeponteaux, L. A., & Ruff, G. (1985). Mental health correlates of criminal victimization: A random community survey. *Journal of Consulting and Clinical Psychology, 53*, 866–873.

Kilpatrick, D. G., Edmunds, C. N., & Seymour, A. K. (1992). *Rape in America: A report to the nation.* Arlington, VA: National Victim Center.

Kilpatrick, D. G., & Resnick, H. S. (1993). Posttraumatic stress disorder associated with exposure to criminal victimization in clinical and community populations. In J. R. T. Davidson & E. B. Foa (Eds.), *Posttraumatic stress disorder: DSM-IV and beyond* (pp. 113–143). Washington, DC: American Psychiatric Press.

Kilpatrick, D., Resnick, H. S., & Freedy, J. R. (1991a). *High and low magnitude events structured interview.* Charleston: Crime Victims Research and Treatment Center, Medical University of South Carolina.

Kilpatrick, D., Resnick, H., & Freedy, J. (1991b). *The Potential Stressful Events Interview.* Unpublished instrument, University of South Carolina, Charleston.

Kilpatrick, D. G., Saunders, B. E., Amick-McMullan, A., Best, C. L., Veronen, L. J., & Resick, H. S. (1989). Victim and crime factors associated with the development of crime-related post-traumatic stress disorder. *Behavior Therapy, 20*, 199–214.

Kilpatrick, D. G, Saunders, B. E., Veronen, L. J., Best, C. L., & Von, J. M. (1987). Criminal victimization: Lifetime prevalence, reporting to police, and psychological impact. *Crime and Delinquency, 33*, 479–489.

Kimerling, R., & Calhoun, K. S. (1994). Somatic symptoms, social support, and treatment seeking among sexual assault victims. *Journal of Consulting and Clinical Psychology, 62,* 333–340.

King, D. W., King, L. A., Foy, D. W., & Gudanowski, D. M. (1996). Prewar factors in combat-related posttraumatic stress disorder: Structural equation modeling with a national sample of female and male vietnam veterans. *Journal of Consulting and Clinical Psychology, 64,* 520–531.

King, L. A., King, D. W., Leskin, G., & Foy, D. W. (1995). The Los Angeles Symptom Checklist: A self-report measure of posttraumatic stress disorder. *Assessment, 2,* 1–17.

Kinzie, J. D., & Boehnlein, J. K. (1989). Post-traumatic psychosis among Cambodian refugees. *Journal of Traumatic Stress, 2,* 185–198.

Kirmayer, L. J. (1996). Confusion of the senses: Implications of ethnocultural variation in somatoform and dissociative disorders for PTSD. In A. J. Marsella, M. J. Friedman, E. T. Gerrity, & R. M. Scurfield (Eds.), *Ethnocultural aspects of posttraumatic stress disorder: Issues, research, and clinical applications* (pp. 131–163). Washington, DC: American Psychological Association.

Kissen, M. (Ed.). (1986). *Assessing object relations phenomena.* New York: International Universities Press.

Kluft, R. P. (1988). The phenomenology and treatment of extremely complex multiple personality disorder. *Dissociation: Progress in the Dissociative Disorders, 1,* 47–58.

Kluft, R. P. (1993). Multiple personality disorder. In D. Spiegel (Ed.), *Dissociative disorders: A clinical review* (pp. 17–44). Lutherville, MD: Sidran Press.

Kolko, D. J. (1996). Child physical abuse. In J. Briere, L. Berliner, J. A. Bulkley, C. Jenny, & T. Reid (Eds.), *The APSAC handbook on child maltreatment* (pp. 21–50). Newbury Park, CA: Sage.

Koopman, C., Classen, C., Cardeña, E., & Spiegel, D. (1995). When disaster strikes, acute stress disorder may follow. *Journal of Traumatic Stress, 8,* 29–46.

Koopman, C., Classen, C., & Spiegel, D. (1994). Predictors of posttraumatic stress symptoms among survivors of the Oakland/Berkeley, California, firestorm. *American Journal of Psychiatry, 151,* 888–894.

Koopman, C., Classen, C., & Spiegel, D. (1996). Dissociative responses in the immediate aftermath of the Oakland/Berkeley firestorm. *Journal of Traumatic Stress, 9,* 521–540.

Koretzky, M. B., & Peck, A. H. (1990). Validation and cross-validation of the PTSD subscale of the MMPI with civilian trauma victims. *Journal of Clinical Psychology, 45,* 72–76.

Koss, M. P. (1983). The scope of rape: Implications for the clinical treatment of victims. *The Clinical Psychologist, 36,* 88–91.

Koss, M. P. (1993). Detecting the scope of rape: A review of prevalence research methods. *Journal of Interpersonal Violence, 8,* 198–222.

Koss, M. P., & Gidycz, C. A. (1985). Sexual experiences survey: Reliability and validity. *Journal of Consulting and Clinical Psychology, 53,* 422–423.

Koss, M. P., & Harvey, M. R. (1991). *The rape victim: Clinical and community interventions.* Newbury Park, CA: Sage.

Kramer, T. L., & Green, B. L. (1991). Posttraumatic stress disorder as an early response to sexual assault. *Journal of Interpersonal Violence, 6*, 160–173.

Krinsley, K. E., & Weathers, F. W. (1995). The assessment of trauma in adults. *PTSD Research Quarterly, 6*, 1–6.

Kroll, J. (1993). *PTSD/borderlines in therapy: Finding the balance.* New York: Norton.

Kroll, J., Habenicht, M., Mackenzie, T., Yang, M., Chan, S., Vang, T., Nguyen, T., Ly, M., Phommasouvanh, B., Nguyen, H., Vang, Y., Souvannasoth, L., & Cabugao, R. (1989). Depression and posttraumatic stress disorder in Southeast Asian refugees. *American Journal of Psychiatry, 146*, 1592–1597.

Kubany, E. S. (1994). A cognitive model of guilt typology in combat-related PTSD. *Journal of Traumatic Stress, 7*, 3–19.

Kudler, H., & Davidson, R. T. (1995). General principles of biological intervention following trauma. In J. R. Freedy & S. E. Hobfoll (Eds.), *Traumatic stress: From theory to practice* (pp. 73–98). New York: Plenum Press.

Kulka, R. A., Schlenger, W. E., Fairbank, J. A., Hough, R. L., Jordan, B. K., Marmar, C. R., & Weiss, D. S. (1988). *The National Vietnam Veterans Readjustment Study (NVVRS): Description, current status, and initial PTSD prevalence estimates.* Washington, DC: Veteran's Administration.

Kulka, R. A., Schlenger, W. E., Fairbank, J. A., Hough, R. L., Jordan, B. K., Marmar, C. R., & Weiss, D. S. (1990). *Trauma and the Vietnam War generation.* New York: Brunner/Mazel.

Kwawer, J., Lerner, H., Lerner, P., & Sugarman, A. (Eds.). (1980). *Borderline phenomena and the Rorschach test.* New York: International University Press.

Labott, S., Leavitt, F. Braun, B., & Sachs, R. (1992). Rorschach indicators of multiple personality disorder. *Perceptual and Motor Skills, 75*, 147–158.

Lanktree, C. B., Briere, J., & Zaidi, L. Y. (1991). Incidence and impacts of sexual abuse in a child outpatient sample: The role of direct inquiry. *Child Abuse and Neglect, 15*, 447–453.

Lating, J. M., Zeichner, A., & Keane, T. M. (1995). Psychological assessment of PTSD. In G. S. Everly & J. M. Lating (Eds.), *Psychotraumatology* (pp. 129–145). New York: Plenum Press.

Lauterbach, D., & Vrana, S. (1996). Three studies on the reliability and validity of a self-report measure of posttraumatic stress. *Assessment, 3*, 17–25.

Lawrence, K. J., Cozolino, L. J., & Foy, D. W. (1995). Psychological sequelae in adult females reporting childhood ritualistic abuse. *Child Abuse and Neglect, 19*, 975–984.

Leavitt, F., & Labott, S. M. (1996). Authenticity of recovered sexual abuse memories: A Rorschach study. *Journal of Traumatic Stress, 9*, 483–496.

Leff, J. (1988). *Psychiatry around the globe: A transcultural view.* London: Gaskell.

Levin, P. (1993). Assessing PTSD with the Rorschach projective technique. In J. Wilson & B. Raphael (Eds.), *The international handbook of traumatic stress syndromes* (pp. 189–200). New York: Plenum Press.

Levin, P., & Reis, B. (1996). The use of the Rorschach in assessing trauma. In J. Wilson & T. Keane (Eds.), *Assessing psychological trauma and PTSD* (pp. 529–543). New York: Guilford Press.

Lindsay, D. S. (1994). Contextualizing and clarifying criticisms of memory work [Special issue]. *Consciousness and Cognition: An International Journal, 3*, 426–437.

Lindsay, D. S. (1995). Beyond backlash: Comments on Enns, McNeilly, Corkery, and Gilbert. *The Counseling Psychologist, 23*, 280–289.

Linehan, M. M. (1993). *Cognitive–behavioral treatment of borderline personality disorder.* New York: Guilford Press.

Lisak, D. (1994). The psychological impact of sexual abuse: Content analysis of interviews with male survivors. *Journal of Traumatic Stress, 7*, 525–548.

Litz, B. T., Penk, W. F., Gerardi, R. J., & Keane, T. M. (1992). Assessment of post-traumatic stress disorder. In P. A. Saigh (Ed.), *Posttraumatic stress disorder: A behavioral approach to assessment and treatment* (pp. 50–84). Boston: Allyn & Bacon.

Litz, B. T., Penk, W. E., Walsh, S., Hyer, L., Blake, D. D., Marx, B., Keane, T. M., & Bitman, D. (1991). Similarities and differences between MMPI and MMPI-2 applications to the assessment of post-traumatic stress disorder. *Journal of Personality Assessment, 57*, 238–254.

Loewenstein, R. J. (1990). Somatoform disorders in victims of incest and child abuse. In R. P. Kluft (Ed.), *Incest-related syndromes of adult psychopathology* (pp. 75–111). Washington, DC: American Psychiatric Press.

Loewenstein, R. J. (1991). An office mental status examination for chronic complex dissociative symptoms and multiple personality disorder. *Psychiatric Clinics of North America, 14*, 567–604.

Loewenstein, R. J. (1993). Psychogenic amnesia and psychogenic fugue: A comprehensive review. In D. Spiegel (Ed.), *Dissociative disorders: A clinical review* (pp. 45–78). Lutherville, MD: Sidran Press.

Loftus, E. F. (1993). The reality of repressed memories. *American Psychologist, 48*, 518–537.

Loftus, E. F., & Ketcham, K. (1994). *The myth of repressed memory: False memories and allegations of sexual abuse.* New York: St. Martin's Press.

Loftus, E. F., Polonsky, S., & Fullilove, M. T. (1994). Memories of childhood sexual abuse: Remembering and repressing. *Psychology of Women Quarterly, 18*, 67–84.

Loring, D. W., Lee, G. P., Martin, R. C., & Meador, K. J. (1989). Verbal and visual memory index discrepancies from the Wechsler Memory Scale—Revised: Cautions in interpretation. *Psychological Assessment, 1*, 198–202.

Lovitt, R., & Lefkoff, G. (1985). Understanding multiple personality disorder with the comprehensive Rorschach system. *Journal of Personality Assessment, 58*, 289–294.

Lundberg-Love, P. K., Marmion, S., Ford, K., Geffner, R., & Peacock, L. (1992). The long-term consequences of childhood incestuous victimization upon adult women's psychological symptomatology. *Journal of Child Sexual Abuse, 1*, 81–102.

Lundin, T. (1995). Transportation disasters: A review. *Journal of Traumatic Stress, 8*, 381–389.

Lundin, T., & Bodegard, M. (1993). The psychological impact of an earthquake on rescue workers: A follow-up study of the Swedish group of rescue workers in Armenia, 1988. *Journal of Traumatic Stress, 6*, 129–139.

Lyons, J. A., Caddell, J. M., Pittman, R. L., Rawls, R., & Perrin, S. (1994). The potential for faking on the Mississippi Scale for Combat-related PTSD. *Journal of Traumatic Stress, 7*, 441–445.

Lyons, J. A., & Keane, T. M. (1992). Keane PTSD scale: MMPI and MMPI-2 update. *Journal of Traumatic Stress, 5*, 111–117.

MacAndrew, C. (1965). The differentiation of male alcoholic outpatients from nonalcoholic psychiatric outpatients by means of the MMPI. *Quarterly Journal of Studies on Alcohol, 26*, 238–246.

Madakasira, S., & O'Brien, K. F. (1987). Acute posttraumatic stress disorder in victims of a natural disaster. *Journal of Nervous and Mental Disease, 175*, 286–290.

Magana, D. (1990). *The impact of client–therapist sexual intimacy and child sexual abuse on psychosexual and psychological functioning.* Unpublished doctoral dissertation, University of California at Los Angeles, Los Angeles.

Mann, B. J. (1995). The North Carolina Dissociation Index: A measure of dissociation using items from the MMPI-2. *Journal of Personality Assessment, 64*, 349–359.

Mansour, F. (1987). Egyptian psychiatric casualties in the Arab-Israeli wars. *Contemporary studies in combat psychiatry, 62*, 157–163.

March, J. S. (1993). What constitutes a stressor? The "criterion A" issue. In J. R. T. Davidson & E. B. Foa (Eds.), *Posttraumatic stress disorder: DSM-IV and beyond* (pp. 37–54). Washington, DC: American Psychiatric Press.

Marmar, C. R., Weiss, D. S., and Metzler, T. (1996). The Peritraumatic Dissociative Experiences Questionnaire. In J. Wilson & T. Keane (Eds.), *Assessing psychological trauma and PTSD* (pp. 412–428). New York: Guilford Press.

Marmar, C. R., Weiss, D. S., Metzler, T. J., & Delucchi, K. (1996). Characteristics of emergency services personnel related to peritraumatic dissociation during critical incident exposure. *American Journal of Psychiatry, 153*, 94–102.

Marmar, C. R., Weiss, D. S., Metzler, T. J., Ronfeldt, H. M., & Foreman, C. (1996). Stress responses of emergency services personnel to the Loma Prieta earthquake Interstate 880 freeway collapse and control traumatic incidents. *Journal of Traumatic Stress, 9*, 63–85.

Marsella, A. J., Friedman, M. J., Gerrity, E. T., & Scurfield, R. M. (1996). Ethnocultural aspects of PTSD: Some closing thoughts. In A. J. Marsella, M. J. Friedman, E. T. Gerrity, & R. M. Scurfield (Eds.), *Ethnocultural aspects of posttraumatic stress disorder: Issues, research, and clinical applications* (pp. 529–538). Washington, DC: American Psychological Association.

Marsella, A. J., Friedman, M. J., & Spain, E. H. (1996). Ethnocultural aspects of PTSD: An overview of issues and research directions. In A. J. Marsella, M. J. Friedman, E. T. Gerrity, & R. M. Scurfield (Eds.), *Ethnocultural aspects of posttraumatic stress disorder: Issues, research, and clinical applications* (pp. 105–129). Washington, DC: American Psychological Association.

Mas, K. (1992). *Disrupted schemata in psychiatric patients with a history of childhood sexual abuse.* Unpublished doctoral dissertation, California School of Professional Psychology, Fresno.

Masterson, J. F. (1976). *Psychotherapy of the borderline adult: A developmental approach.* New York: Brunner/Mazel.

McCahill, T. W., Meyer, L. C., & Fishman, A. M. (1979). *The aftermath of rape.* Lexington, MA: DC Heath.

McCann, I. L., & Pearlman, L. A. (1990). *Psychological trauma and the adult survivor: Theory, therapy, and transformation.* New York: Brunner/Mazel.

McDermott, W. F. (1987). The diagnosis of post-traumatic stress disorder using the Millon Clinical Multiaxial Inventory. In C. Green (Ed.), *Conference of the Millon Clinical Inventories (MCMI, MBHI, MAPI,* pp. 257–262). Minneapolis, MN: National Computer Systems.

McFall, M. E., Smith, D. E., McKay, P. W., & Tarver, D. J. (1990). Reliability and validity of Mississippi Scale for Combat-Related Posttraumatic Stress Disorder. *Psychological Assessment, 2,* 114–121.

McFall, M. E., Smith, D. E., Roszell, D. K., Tarver, D. J., & Malas, K. L. (1990). Convergent validity of measures of PTSD in Vietnam combat veterans. *American Journal of Psychiatry, 147,* 645–648.

McFarlane, A. C. (1988). Relationship between psychiatric impairment and a natural disaster: The role of distress. *Psychological Medicine, 18,* 129–139.

McFarlane, A. C. (1989). The aetiology of post-traumatic morbidity: Predisposing, precipitating and perpetuating factors. *British Journal of Psychiatry, 154,* 221–228.

McMillen, C., Zuravin, S., & Rideout, G. (1995). Perceived benefit from child sexual abuse. *Journal of Consulting and Clinical Psychology, 63,* 1037–1043.

Meichenbaum, D. (1994). *A clinical handbook/practical therapist manual for assessing and treating adults with post-traumatic stress disorder (PTSD).* Waterloo, Ontario, Canada: Institute Press.

Melamed, B. G., Melamed, J. L., & Bouhoutsos, J. C. (1990). Psychological consequences of torture: A need to formulate new strategies for research. In P. Suedeld (Ed.), *Psychology and torture* (pp. 13–30). New York: Hemisphere.

Meyers, J. (1988). The Rorschach as a tool for understanding the dynamics of women with histories of incest. In H. D. Lerner & P. M. Lerner (Eds.), *Primitive mental states and the Rorschach* (pp. 203–228). Madison, CT: International Universities Press.

Meyers, J. E. B. (1995). Expert testimony. In J. Briere, L. Berliner, J. A. Bulkley, C. Jenny, & T. Reid (Eds.), *The APSAC handbook on child maltreatment* (pp. 319–340). Newbury Park, CA: Sage.

Michigan Stat. Ann. 28.788 (1)(h) (Callaghan Cum. Supp. 1980).

Mikulincer, M., & Solomon, Z. (1988). Attributional style and combat-related posttraumatic stress disorder. *Journal of Abnormal Psychology, 97,* 308–313.

Millon, T. (1983). *Millon Clinical Multiaxial Inventory manual.* Minneapolis, MN: Interpretive Scoring System.

Millon, T. (1987). *Manual for the MCMI-II* (2nd ed.). Minneapolis, MN: National Computer Systems.

Millon, T. (1994). *Manual for the MCMI-III*. Minneapolis, MN: National Computer Systems.

Mollica, R., Caspi-Yavin, Y., Bollini, P., Truong, T., Tor, S., & Lavelle, J. (1992). Harvard Trauma Questionnaire: Validating a cross-cultural instrument for measuring torture, trauma, and posttraumatic stress disorder in Indochinese refugees. *Journal of Nervous and Mental Disease, 180*, 111–116.

Mollica, R., Caspi-Yavin, Y., Lavelle, J., Tor, S., Yang, T., Chan, S., Pham, T., Ryan, A., & de Marneffe, D. (1995). *Manual for the Harvard Trauma Questionnaire*. Brighton, MA: Indochinese Psychiatry Clinic.

Mollica, R., Wyshak, G., & Lavelle, J. (1987). The psychosocial impact of war trauma and torture on Southeast Asian refugees. *American Journal of Psychiatry, 144*, 1567–1572.

Moran, C. (1986). Depersonalization and agoraphobia associated with marijuana use. *British Journal of Medical Psychology, 59*, 187–196.

Morey, L. C. (1991). *Personality Assessment Inventory: Professional manual*. Odessa, FL: Psychological Assessment Resources.

Morrison, J. (1989). Childhood sexual histories of women with somatization disorder. *American Journal of Psychiatry, 146*, 239–241.

Munley, P. H., Bains, D. S., Bloem, W. D., & Busby, R. M. (1995). Post-traumatic stress disorder and the MMPI-2. *Journal of Traumatic Stress, 8*, 171–178.

Murphy, S. M., Kilpatrick, D. G., Amick-McMullan, A., Veronen, L. J., Paduhovich, J., Best, C. L., Villeponteaux, L. A. & Saunders, B. E. (1988). Current psychological functioning of child sexual assault survivors: A community study. *Journal of Interpersonal Violence, 3*, 55–79.

Murray, E. J., & Segal, D. L. (1994). Emotional processing in vocal and written expression of feelings about traumatic experiences. *Journal of Traumatic Stress, 7*, 391–405.

Nader, K. (1996). Assessing traumatic experiences in children. In J. Wilson & T. Keane (Eds.), *Assessing psychological trauma and PTSD* (pp. 291–348). New York: Guilford Press.

Nash, M. R., Hulsey, T. L., Sexton, M. C., Harralson, T. L., & Lambert, W. (1993). Long-term sequelae of childhood sexual abuse: Perceived family environment, psychopathology, and dissociation. *Journal of Consulting and Clinical Psychology, 61*, 276–283.

Neiderland, W. G. (1968). Clinical observations on the "survivor syndrome." *International Journal of Psychoanalysis, 49*, 313–315.

Neill, J. R. (1993). How psychiatric symptoms varied in World War I and II. *Military Medicine, 158*, 149–151.

Nemiah, J. C. (1993). Dissociation, conversion, and somatization. In D. Spiegel (Ed.), *Dissociative disorders: A clinical review* (pp. 104–116). Lutherville, MD: Sidran Press.

Neumann, D. A., Houskamp, B. M., Pollock, V. E., & Briere, J. (1996). The long-term sequelae of childhood sexual abuse in women: A meta-analytic review. *Child Maltreatment, 1*, 6–16.

Newman, E., Kaloupek, D. G., & Keane, T. M. (1996). Assessment of post-traumatic stress disorder in clinical and research settings. In B. A. van der

Kolk, A. C. McFarlane, & L. Weisaeth (Eds.), *Traumatic stress: The effects of overwhelming experience on mind, body, and society* (pp. 242–275). New York: Guilford Press.

Nichter, M. (1981). Idioms of distress: Alternatives in the expression of psychological distress: A case study from India. *Culture, Medicine, and Psychiatry, 5,* 379–408.

Norris, F. H. (1990). Screening for traumatic stress: A scale for use in the general population. *Journal of Applied Social Psychology, 20,* 1704–1718.

Norris, F. H. (1992). Epidemiology of trauma: Frequency and impact of different potentially traumatic events on different demographic groups. *Journal of Consulting and Clinical Psychology, 60,* 409–418.

Norris, F. H., & Perilla, J. (1996). Reliability, validity, and cross-language stability of the Revised Civilian Mississippi Scale for PTSD. *Journal of Traumatic Stress, 9,* 285–298.

Norris, F. H., Phifer, J. F., & Kaniasty, K. (1994). Individual and community reactions to the Kentucky floods: Findings from a longitudinal study of older adults. In R. J. Ursano, C. S. Fullerton, & B. G. McCaughey (Eds.), *Individual and community response to trauma and disaster: The structure of human chaos* (pp. 378–400). Cambridge, England: Cambridge University Press.

Norris, F. H. & Riad, J. K. (1996). Standardized self-report measures of civilian trauma and PTSD. In J. Wilson & T. Keane (Eds.), *Assessing psychological trauma and PTSD: A practitioner's handbook.* New York: Guilford Press.

Norris, F., & Thompson, M. P. (1995). Applying community psychology to the prevention of trauma and traumatic life events. In J. R. Freedy & S. E. Hobfoll (Eds.), *Traumatic stress: From theory to practice* (pp. 49–71). New York: Plenum Press.

Noyes, R., Hoenk, P., Kuperman, S., & Slyman, D. J. (1977). Depersonalization in accident victims and psychiatric patients. *Journal of Nervous and Mental Diseases, 164,* 401–407.

Noyes, R., & Kletti, R. (1977). Depersonalization in response to life-threatening danger. *Comparative Psychiatry, 18,* 375–384.

Ofshe, R., & Watters, E. (1993). Making monsters. *Society, 30,* 4–16.

Ogata, S. N., Silk, K. R., Goodrich, S., Lohr, N. E., Westen, D., & Hill, E. M. (1990). Childhood sexual and physical abuse in adult patients with borderline personality disorder. *American Journal of Psychiatry, 147,* 1008–1013.

Ornitz, E. M., & Pynoos, R. S. (1989). Startle modulation in children with posttraumatic stress disorder. *American Journal of Psychiatry, 146,* 866–870.

Orr, S. P., Claiborn, J. M., Altman, B., Forgue, D. F., de Jong, J. B., Pitman, R. K., & Herz, L. R. (1990). Psychometric profile of post-traumatic stress disorder, anxious, and healthy Vietnam veterans: Correlations with psychophysiological responses. *Journal of Consulting and Clinical Psychology, 58,* 329–335.

Owens, T. H. (1984). Personality traits of female psychotherapy patients with a history of incest: A research note. *Journal of Personality Assessment, 48,* 606–608.

Parfit, D. N., & Gall, C. M. C. (1944). Psychogenic amnesia: The refusal to remember. *The Journal of Mental Science, 379*, 519–531.

Paris, J., Zweig, F. H., & Guzder, J. (1994). Risk factors for borderline personality in male outpatients. *Journal of Nervous and Mental Disease, 182*, 375–380.

Pearlman, L.A. (1996). Review of TSI Belief Scale, Revision L. In B. H. Stamm (Ed.), *Measurement of stress, trauma, and adaptation* (pp. 415–419). Lutherville, MD: Sidran Press.

Pearlman, L. A., & Mac Ian, P. S. (1995). Vicarious traumatization: An empirical study of the effects of trauma work on trauma therapists. *Professional Psychology: Research and Practice, 26*, 558–565.

Pearlman, L. A., Mac Ian, P. S., Johnson, G., & Mas, K. (1992, October). *Understanding cognitive schemas across groups: Empirical findings and their implications.* Paper presented at the annual meeting of the International Society for Traumatic Stress Studies, Los Angeles, CA.

Pearlman, L. A., & Saakvitne, K. W. (1995). *Trauma and the therapist: Countertransference and vicarious traumatization in psychotherapy with incest survivors.* New York: Norton.

Pelcovitz, D., van der Kolk, B. A., Roth, S., Mandel, F., Kaplan, S., & Resick, P. (in press). Development and validation of the Structured Interview for Disorders of Extreme Stress. *Journal of Traumatic Stress.*

Penk, W. E., Peck, R. F., Robinowitz, R., Bell, W., & Little, D. (1988). Coping and defending styles among Vietnam combat veterans seeking treatment for post-traumatic stress disorder and substance abuse disorder. In M. Galanter (Ed.), *Recent developments in alcoholism* (Vol. 6, pp. 69–88). New York: Plenum Press.

Pennebaker, J. W., Kiecolt-Glaser, J. K., & Glaser, R. (1988). Disclosure of trauma and immune function: Health implications for psychotherapy. *Journal of Consulting and Clinical Psychology, 56*, 239–245.

Petrie, K. J., Booth, R. J., Pennebaker, J. W., Davison, K. P., & Thomas, M. G. (1995). Disclosure of trauma and immune response to a Hepatitis B vaccination program. *Journal of Consulting and Clinical Psychology, 63*, 787–792.

Phillips, D. W. (1994). Initial development and validation of the Phillips Dissociation Scale (PDS) of the MMPI. *Progress in the Dissociative Disorders, 7*, 92–100.

Pickens, J., Field, T., Prodromidis, M., Pelaez-Nogueras, M., & Hossain, Z.. (1995). Posttraumatic stress, depression and social support among college students after Hurricane Andrew. *Journal of College Student Development, 36*, 152–161.

Pinto, P. A., & Gregory, R. J. (1995). Posttraumatic stress disorder with psychotic features. *American Journal of Psychiatry, 152*, 471.

Piotrowski, C., & Lubin, B. (1990). Assessment practices of health psychologists: Survey of APA Division 38 clinicians. *Professional Psychology: Research and Practice, 21*, 99–106.

Polusny, M. A., & Follette, V. M. (1995). Long-term correlates of child sexual abuse: Theory and review of the empirical literature. *Applied and Preventive Psychology, 4*, 143–166.

Pope, K. S. (1994). *Sexual involvement with therapists: Patient assessment, subsequent therapy, forensics.* Washington, DC: American Psychological Association.

Putnam, F. W. (1985). Dissociation as a response to extreme trauma. In R. P. Kluft (Ed.), *Childhood antecedents of multiple personality* (pp. 66–97). Washington, DC: American Psychiatric Press.

Putnam, F. W. (1989). *Diagnosis and treatment of multiple personality disorder.* New York: Guilford Press.

Putnam, F. W. (1993). Dissociative phenomena. In D. Spiegel (Ed.), *Dissociative disorders: A clinical review* (pp. 1–16). Lutherville, MD: Sidran Press.

Putnam, F. W., Guroff, J. J., Silberman, E. K., Barban, L., & Post, R. M. (1986). The clinical phenomenology of multiple personality disorder: Review of 100 recent cases. *Journal of Clinical Psychiatry, 47,* 285–293.

Raphael, B. (1977). The Granville train disaster: Psychological needs and their management. *The Medical Journal of Australia, 1,* 303–305.

Raphael, B. (1981). Personal disaster. *Australian and New Zealand Journal of Psychiatry, 15,* 183–198.

Rappaport, D., Gil, M., & Schafer, R. (1945–1946). *Diagnostic psychological testing: The theory, statistical evaluation, and diagnostic application of a battery of tests* (Vols. 1–2). Chicago: Year Books Publishers.

Rausch, K., & Knutson, J. F. (1991). The self-report of personal punitive childhood experiences and those of siblings. *Child Abuse and Neglect, 15,* 29–36.

Reifman, A., & Windle, M. (1996). Vietnam combat exposure and recent drug use: A national study. *Journal of Traumatic Stress, 9,* 557–568.

Resick, P. A. (1993). The psychological impact of rape. *Journal of Interpersonal Violence, 8,* 223–255.

Resick, P. A., & Schnicke, M. K. (1993). *Cognitive processing therapy for rape victims: A treatment manual.* Newbury Park, CA: Sage.

Resnick, H. S. (1996). Psychometric review of Trauma Assessment for Adults. In B. H. Stamm (Ed.), *Measurement of stress, trauma, and adaptation.* Lutherville, MD: Sidran Press.

Resnick, H. S., Best, C. L., Freedy, J. R., & Kilpatrick, D. G. (1993). *Traumatic Events Assessment for Adults.* Unpublished manual, Medical University of South Carolina, Crime Victims Research and Treatment Center, Charleston.

Resnick, H., Kilpatrick, D., Dansky, B., Saunders, B., & Best, C. (1993). Prevalence of civilian trauma and posttraumatic stress disorder in a representative national sample of women. *Journal of Consulting and Clinical Psychology, 61,* 984–991.

Resnick, H. S., Kilpatrick, D. G., & Lipovsky, J. A. (1991). Assessment of rape-related post-traumatic stress disorder: Stressor and symptom dimensions. *Psychological Assessment, 3,* 561–572.

Reynolds, W. M. (1991). Psychometric characteristics of the Adult Suicidal Ideation Questionnaire in college students. *Journal of Personality Assessment, 56,* 289–307.

Rhodes, N. R. (1992). Comparison of MMPI psychopathic deviate scores of battered and nonbattered women. *Journal of Family Violence, 7,* 297–307.

Riether, A. M., & Stoudemire, A. (1988). Psychogenic fugue states: A review. *Southern Medical Journal, 81,* 568–571.

Riggs, D. S., Kilpatrick, D. G., & Resnick, H. S. (1992). Long-term psychological distress associated with marital rape and aggravated assault: A comparison to other crime victims. *Journal of Family Violence, 7,* 283–296.

Rinsley, D. B. (1980). *Treatment of the severely disturbed adolescent.* New York: Aronson.

Robins, L. N., & Heltzer, J. E. (1985). *Diagnostic Interview Schedule (DIS).* Department of Psychiatry, Washington University, St. Louis, MO.

Roesler, T. A., & McKenzie, N. (1994). Effects of childhood trauma on psychological functioning in adults sexually abused as children. *Journal of Nervous and Mental Disease, 182,* 145–150.

Rogers, R., Bagby, R. M., & Dickens, S. E. (1992). *Structured Interview of Reported Symptoms professional manual.* Odessa, FL.: Psychological Assessment Resources.

Rorschach, H. (1981). *Psychodiagnostics: A diagnostic test based upon perception* (P. Lemkau & B. Kronemberg, Eds. & Trans., 9th ed.). New York: Grune & Stratton. (Original work published 1921)

Rorty, M., Yager, J., & Rossotto, E. (1994). Childhood sexual, physical, and psychological abuse in bulimia nervosa. *American Journal of Psychiatry, 151,* 1122–1126.

Ross, C. A. (1989). *Multiple personality disorder: Diagnosis, clinical features, and treatment.* New York: Wiley.

Ross, C. A., Anderson, G., & Clark, P. (1994). Childhood abuse and the positive symptoms of schizophrenia. *Hospital and Community Psychiatry, 45,* 489–491.

Ross, C. A., Anderson, G., Heber, S., & Norton, G. (1990). Dissociation and abuse among multiple personality patients, prostitutes, and exotic dancers. *Hospital and Community Psychiatry, 41,* 328–330.

Ross, C. A., Heber, S., Norton, G. R., Anderson, G., & Barchet, P. (1989). The Dissociative Disorders Interview Schedule: A structured interview. *Dissociation: Progress in the Dissociative Disorders, 2,* 169–189.

Ross, C. A., Joshi, S., & Currie, R. (1990). Dissociative experiences in the general population. *American Journal of Psychiatry, 147,* 1547–1552.

Ross, C. A., Miller, S. D., Reagor, P., Bjornson, L. , Fraser, G. A. , & Anderson, G. (1990). Structured interview data on 102 cases of multiple personality disorder from four centers. *American Journal of Psychiatry, 147,* 596–601.

Ross, C. A., Norton, G. R., & Wozney, K. (1989). Multiple personality disorder: An analysis of 236 cases. *Canadian Journal of Psychiatry, 34,* 413–418.

Roth, S., Wayland, K., & Woolsey, M. (1990). Victimization history and victim–assailant relationships as factors in recovery from sexual assault. *Journal of Traumatic Stress, 3,* 169–180.

Rothbaum, B. O., Foa, E. B., Riggs, D. S., Murdock, T., & Walsh, W. (1992). A prospective examination of post-traumatic stress disorder in rape victims. *Journal of Traumatic Stress, 5,* 455–475.

Rowan, A. B., Foy, D. W., Rodriguez, N., & Ryan, S. (1994). Posttraumatic stress disorder in a clinical sample of adults sexually abused as children. *Child Abuse and Neglect, 18*, 51–61.

Ruch, L. O., & Chandler, S. M. (1983). Sexual assault trauma during the acute phase: An exploratory model and multivariate analysis. *Journal of Health and Social Behavior, 24*, 184–185.

Ruch, L. O., & Leon, J. J. (1983). Sexual assault trauma and trauma change. *Women and Health, 8*, 5–21.

Runtz, M. R (1987). *The psychosocial adjustment of women who were sexually and physically abused during childhood and early adulthood: A focus on revictimization.* Unpublished master's thesis, University of Manitoba, Winnipeg, Manitoba, Canada.

Runtz, M. (1990). *The influence of coping strategies and social support on recovery from child abuse.* Unpublished doctoral dissertation, University of Manitoba, Winnipeg, Manitoba, Canada.

Runtz, M., Roche, D., & Embree, J. (1996, June). *Validation of the Trauma Symptom Inventory (TSI) in a Canadian sample.* Paper presented at the annual symposium of the American Professional Society on the Abuse of Children, Chicago, IL.

Russell, D. E. H. (1983). The incidence and prevalence of intrafamilial and extrafamilial sexual abuse of female children. *Child Abuse and Neglect, 7*, 133–146.

Saigh, P. A. (1989). The validity of the DSM–III posttraumatic stress disorder classification as applied to children. *Journal of Abnormal Psychology, 98*, 189–192.

Sales, E., Baum, M., & Shore, B. (1984). Victim readjustment following assault. *Journal of Social Issues, 40*, 17–36.

Salley, R., & Teiling, P. (1984). Dissociated rage attacks in a Vietnam veteran: A Rorschach study. *Journal of Personality Assessment, 48*, 98–104.

Sanders, B., McRoberts, G., & Tollefson, C. (1989). Childhood stress and dissociation in a college population. *Dissociation: Progress in the Dissociative Disorders, 2*, 17–23.

Sanders, S. (1986). The perceptual alteration scale: A scale measuring dissociation. *American Journal of Clinical Hypnosis, 29*, 95–102.

Sargant, W., & Slater, E. (1941). Amnestic syndromes of war. *Proceedings of the Royal Society of Medicine, 34*, 757–764.

Saunders, B. E., Arata, C. M., & Kilpatrick, D. G. (1990). Development of a crime-related Post-Traumatic Stress Disorder scale for women within the Symptom Checklist–90—Revised. *Journal of Traumatic Stress, 3*, 267–277.

Saunders, B. E., Villeponteaux, L. A., Lipovsky, J. A., Kilpatrick, D. G., & Veronen, L. J. (1992). Child sexual assault as a risk factor for mental disorders among women: A community survey. *Journal of Interpersonal Violence, 7*, 189–204.

Saunders, E. A. (1991). Rorschach indicators of chronic childhood sexual abuse in female borderline patients. *Bulletin of the Menninger Clinic, 55*, 48–71.

Schlenger, W. E., Kulka, R.A., Fairbank, J. A., Hough, R. L., Jordan, B. K., Marmar, C., & Weiss, D. S. (1989). *The prevalence of post-traumatic stress disorder in the Vietnam generation: Findings from the National Vietnam Veterans Readjustment study.* Research Triangle Park, NC: Research Triangle Institute.

Schulman, M. (1979). *A survey of spousal violence against women in Kentucky.* Washington, DC: U.S. Department of Justice, Law Enforcement.

Schwartz, M. D. (1987). Gender and injury in spousal assault. *Sociological Focus, 20,* 61–74.

Scott, R. L., & Stone, D. A. (1986). MMPI measures of psychological disturbance in adolescent and adult victims of father–daughter incest. *Journal of Consulting and Clinical Psychology, 42,* 251–259.

Scotti, J. R., Sturges, L. V., & Lyons, J. A. (1996). The Keane PTSD scale extracted from the MMPI: Sensitivity and specificity with Vietnam veterans. *Journal of Traumatic Stress, 9,* 643–650.

Searles, P., & Berger, R. J. (1987). The current status of rape reform legislation: An examination of state statutes. *Women's Rights Law Reporter,* 25–43.

Segal, J., Hunter, E. J., & Segal, Z. (1976). Universal consequences of captivity: Stress reactions among divergent populations of prisoners of war and their families. *International Journal of Social Science, 28,* 593–609.

Selzer, M. L. (1971). The Michigan Alcoholism Screening Test: The quest for a new diagnostic instrument. *American Journal of Psychiatry, 127,* 89–94.

Sewell, J. D. (1993). Traumatic stress of multiple murder investigations. *Journal of Traumatic Stress, 6,* 103–118.

Sharpe, L., Tarrier, N., & Rotundo, N. (1994). Treatment of delayed posttraumatic stress disorder following sexual abuse: A case example. *Behavioral and Cognitive Psychotherapy, 22,* 233–242.

Shedler, J., Mayman, M., & Manis, M. (1993). The illusion of mental health. *American Psychologist, 48,* 1117–1131.

Shepard, M. F., & Campbell, J. A. (1992). The Abusive Behavior Inventory: A measure of psychological and physical abuse. *Journal of Interpersonal Violence, 7,* 291–305.

Shilony, E., & Grossman, F. K. (1993). Depersonalization as a defense mechanism in survivors of trauma. *Journal of Traumatic Stress, 6,* 119–128.

Shore, J. H., Tatum, E. L., & Vollmer, W. M. (1986). Psychiatric reactions to disaster: The Mount St. Helens experience. *American Journal of Psychiatry, 143,* 590–595.

Siegel, J. M., Golding, J. M., Stein, J. A., Burnam, M. A., & Sorenson, S. B. (1990). Reaction to sexual assault: A community study. *Journal of Interpersonal Violence, 5,* 229–246.

Siegel, R. K. (1984). Hostage hallucinations. *Journal of Nervous and Mental Diseases, 172,* 264–272.

Simons, R. C., & Hughes, C. C. (1993). Culture-bound syndromes. In A. Gaw (Ed.), *Culture, ethnicity, and mental illness* (pp. 75–79). Washington, DC: American Psychiatric Press.

Singer, M. I., Petchers, M. K., & Hussey, D. (1989). The relationship between sexual abuse and substance abuse among psychiatrically hospitalized adolescents. *Child Abuse & Neglect, 13,* 319–325.

Skinner, H. A. (1992). The drug abuse screening test. *Addictive Behaviors, 7,* 363–371.

Sloan, I. H. , Rozensky, R. H., Kaplan, L., & Saunders, S. M. (1994). A shooting incident in an elementary school: Effects of worker stress on public safety, mental health, and medical personnel. *Journal of Traumatic Stress, 7*, 565–574.

Sloan, P. (1988). Post-traumatic stress in survivors of an airplane crash-landing: A clinical and exploratory research intervention. *Journal of Traumatic Stress, 1*, 211–229.

Smith, D. W., & Frueh, B. C. (1996). Compensation seeking, comorbidity, and apparent exaggeration of PTSD symptoms among Vietnam combat veterans. *Psychological Assessment, 8*, 3–6.

Smith, E. M., North, C. S., McCool, R. E., & Shea, J. M. (1990). Acute postdisaster psychiatric disorders: Identification of persons at risk. *American Journal of Psychiatry, 147*, 202–206.

Solkoff, N. (1992). The Holocaust: Survivors and their children. In M. Basoglu (Ed.), *Torture and its consequences: Current treatment approaches* (pp. 38–55). Cambridge, England: Cambridge University Press.

Solomon, S. D., Keane, T. M., Newman, E., & Kaloupek, D. G. (1996). Choosing self-report measures and structured interviews. In E. B. Carlson (Ed.), *Trauma research methodology* (pp. 56–81). Lutherville, MD: Sidran Press.

Solomon, S. D., & Smith, E. M. (1994). Social support and perceived control as moderators of response to dioxin and flood exposure. In R. J. Ursano, B. G. McCaughey, & C. S. Fullerton (Eds.), *Individual and community responses to trauma and disaster: The structure of human chaos* (pp. 179–200). Cambridge, England: Cambridge University Press.

Solomon, Z. (1993a). *Combat stress reaction: The enduring toll of war.* New York: Plenum Press.

Solomon, Z. (1993b). Immediate and long-term effects of traumatic combat stress among Israeli veterans of the Lebanon War. In J. P. Wilson & B. Raphael (Eds.), *International handbook of traumatic stress syndromes* (pp. 321–332). New York: Plenum Press.

Solomon, Z., & Mikulincer, M. (1990). Life events and combat-related posttraumatic stress: The intervening role of locus of control and social support. *Military Psychology, 2*, 241–256.

Solomon, Z., Mikulincer, M., & Bleich, A. (1988). Characteristic expressions of combat-related posttraumatic stress disorder Israeli soldiers in the 1982 Lebanon war. *Behavioral Medicine, 14*, 171–178.

Solomon, Z., Mikulincer, M., & Waysman, M. (1991). Delayed and immediate onset posttraumatic stress disorder: The role of life events and social resources. *Journal of Community Psychology, 19*, 231–236.

Somasundaram, D. J., & Sivayokan, S. (1994). War trauma in a civilian population. *British Journal of Psychiatry, 165*, 524–527.

Southwick, S. M., Krystal, J. H., Morgan, A., Johnson, D., Nagy, L., Nicolaou, A., Henninger, G. R., & Charney, D. S. (1993). Abnormal noradrenergic function in post traumatic stress disorder. *Archives of General Psychiatry, 50*, 266–274.

Speed, N., Engdahl, B. E. Schwartz, J., Eberly, R. E., & Raina, E. (1989). Posttraumatic stress disorder as a consequence of the POW experience. *Journal of Nervous and Mental Disease, 177*, 147–153.

Spitzer, R. L., Williams, J. B., Gibbon, M., & First, M. B. (1990). *User's guide for the Structured Clinical Interview for DSM-III-R*. Washington, DC: American Psychiatric Press.

Stamm, B. H. (Ed.). (1996). *Measurement of stress, trauma, and adaptation*. Lutherville, MD: Sidran Press.

Steinberg, M. (1994a). *Interviewer's Guide to the Structured Clinical Interview for DSM-IV Dissociative Disorders—Revised (SCID-D-R)*. Washington, DC: American Psychiatric Press.

Steinberg, M. (1994b). *Structured Clinical Interview for DSM-IV Dissociative Disorders—Revised (SCID-D-R)*. Washington, DC: American Psychiatric Press.

Steinberg, M. (1994c). Systematizing dissociation: Symptomatology and diagnostic assessment. In D. Spiegel (Ed.), *Dissociation: Culture, mind, and body* (pp. 59–88). Washington, DC: American Psychiatric Press.

Steinberg, M., Cicchetti, D.V., Buchanan, J., Hall, P. E., & Rounsaville, B. J. (1989–1993). *NIMH field trials of the Structured Clinical Interview for DSM-IV Dissociative Disorders (SCID-D)*. Unpublished manuscript, Yale University School of Medicine, New Haven, CT.

Steinberg, M., Rounsaville, B. J., & Cicchetti, D. V. (1990). The Structured Interview for DSM–III–R Dissociative Disorders: Preliminary report on a new diagnostic instrument. *American Journal of Psychiatry, 147*, 76–82.

Steketee, G., & Foa, E. B. (1987). Rape victims: Post-traumatic stress responses and their treatment: A review of the literature. *Journal of Anxiety Disorders, 1*, 69–86.

Stermac, L., Sheridan, P. M., Davidson, A., & Dunn, S. (1996). Sexual assault of males. *Journal of Interpersonal Violence, 11*, 52–64.

Stordeur, R.A., & Stille, R. (1989). *Ending men's violence against their partners: One road to peace*. Newbury Park, CA: Sage.

Straus, M. A. (1979). Measuring intrafamily conflict and violence: The Conflicts Tactics (CT) Scales. *Journal of Marriage and the Family, 41*, 75–88.

Straus, M. A., & Gelles, R. J. (1985, November). *Is family violence increasing? A comparison of 1975 and 1985 national survey rates*. Paper presented at the meeting of the American Society of Criminology, San Diego, CA.

Straus, M. A., Gelles, R. J., & Steinmetz, S. (1980). *Behind closed doors: Violence in the American family*. Garden City, NY: Doubleday.

Surrey, J., Swett, C., Michaels, A., & Levin, S. (1990). Reported history of physical and sexual abuse and severity of symptomatology in women psychiatric outpatients. *American Journal of Orthopsychiatry, 60*, 412–417.

Tan, C., Basta, J., Sullivan, C. M., & Davidson, W. S. (1995). The role of social support in the lives of women exiting domestic violence shelters: An experimental study. *Journal of Interpersonal Violence, 10*, 437–451.

Taylor, A. J. W., & Frazer, A. G. (1982). The stress of post-disaster body handling and victim identification work. *Journal of Human Stress, 8*, 4–12.

Tellegen, A., & Atkinson, G. (1974). Openness to absorbing and self-altering experiences ("absorption"), a trait related to hypnotic susceptibility. *Journal of Abnormal Psychology, 83*, 268–277.

Tennant, C. G., Goulston, K. J., & Dent, O. F. (1986). The psychological effects of being a prisoner of war: Forty years after release. *American Journal of Psychiatry, 143*, 618–622.

Thom, D. A, & Fenton, N. (1920). Amnesia in war cases. *American Journal of Insanity, 76*, 437–448.

Thompson, S. C. (1985). Finding positive meaning in a stressful event and coping. *Basic and Applied Social Psychology, 6*, 275–285.

Timnick, L. (1985, August 26). Of those surveyed, 22% were child abuse victims. *Los Angeles Times*, p. A1.

Tolman, R. M. (1989). The development of a measure of psychological maltreatment of women by their male partners. *Violence and Victims, 4*, 156–177.

Toomey, T. C., Hernandez, J. T., Gittelman, D. F., & Hulka, J. F. (1993). Relationship of sexual and physical abuse to pain and psychological assessment variables in chronic pelvic pain patients. *Pain, 53*, 105–109.

Torrie, A. (1944). Psychosomatic casualties in the Middle East. *Lancet, 1*, 139–143.

Trimble, M. R. (1981). *Post-traumatic neurosis*. Chicester, England: Wiley.

Tromp, S., Koss, M. P., Figueredo, A. J., & Tharan, M. (1995). Are rape memories different? A comparison of rape, other unpleasant, and pleasant memories among employed women. *Journal of Traumatic Stress, 8*, 607–627.

True, W. R., Rice, J., Eisen, S. A., Heath, A. C., Goldberg, J., Lyons, M. J., & Nowak, J. (1993). A twin study of genetic and environmental contributions to liability for posttraumatic stress symptoms. *Archives of General Psychiatry, 50*, 257–264.

Tsai, M., Feldman-Summers, S., & Edgar, M. (1979). Childhood molestation: Variables related to differential impacts on psychosexual functioning in adult women. *Journal of Abnormal Psychology, 88*, 407–417.

Ursano, R. J., Fullerton, C., Kao, T., & Bhartiya, V. (1995). Longitudinal assessment of posttraumatic stress disorder and depression after exposure to traumatic death. *Journal of Nervous and Mental Disease, 183*, 36–42.

Ursano, R. J., Fullerton, C., Kao, T., Bhartiya, V., & Dinneen, M. P. (1992, April). *PTSD in community samples: Development of a self-report instrument*. Paper presented at the meeting of the International Society for Traumatic Stress Studies, World Conference, Amsterdam, Netherlands.

Ursano, R. J., Fullerton, C. S., & McCaughey, B. G. (1994). Trauma and disaster. In R. J. Ursano, C. S. Fullerton, & B. G. McCaughey (Eds.), *Individual and community response to trauma and disaster: The structure of human chaos* (pp. 3–27). Cambridge, England: Cambridge University Press.

Ursano, R. J., & McCarroll, J. E. (1990). The nature of a traumatic stressor: Handling dead bodies. *Journal of Nervous and Mental Desease, 178*, 396–398.

Ursano, R. J., & McCarroll, J. E. (1994). Exposure to traumatic death: The nature of the stressor. In R. J. Ursano, C. S. Fullerton, & B. G. McCaughey (Eds.), *Individual and community response to trauma and disaster: The structure of human chaos* (pp. 46–71). Cambridge, England: Cambridge University Press.

U.S. Department of Health and Human Services, National Center on Child Abuse and Neglect. (1996). *Child maltreatment 1994: Reports from the states to the National Center on Child Abuse and Neglect.* Washington, DC: U. S. Government Printing Office.

Valent, P. (1984). The Ash Wednesday bushfires in Victoria. *The Medical Journal of Australia, 141*, 291–300.

van der Hart, O., Witztum, E., & Friedman, B. (1993). From hysterical psychosis to reactive dissociative psychosis. *Journal of Traumatic Stress, 6*, 43–64.

van der Kolk, B. A., & Ducey, C. (1984). Clinical implications of the Rorschach in post-traumatic stress disorder. In B. A. van der Kolk (Ed.), *Post-traumatic stress disorder: Psychological and biological sequelae* (pp. 29–42). Washington, DC: American Psychiatric Press.

van der Kolk, B. A., & Ducey, C. (1989). The psychological processing of traumatic experience: Rorschach patterns in PTSD. *Journal of Traumatic Stress, 2*, 259–263.

van der Kolk, B. A., Hostetler, A., Herron, N. & Fisler, R. E. (1994). Trauma and the development of borderline personality disorder. *Psychiatric Clinics of North America, 17*, 715–730.

van der Kolk, B. A., Pelcovitz, D., & Roth, S. (1995). *Disorders of extreme stress: Results of the PTSD field trial for the DSM-IV.* Manuscript submitted for publication.

van der Kolk, B. A., Perry, J. C., & Herman, J. L. (1991). Childhood origins of self-destructive behavior. *American Journal of Psychiatry, 146*, 490–494.

van IJzendoorn, M. H., & Schuengel, C. (in press). The measurement of dissociation in normal and clinical populations: Meta-analytic validation of the Dissociative Experiences Scale (DES). *Clinical Psychology Review.*

Van Velsen, C., Gorst-Unsworth, C., & Turner, S. (1996). Survivors of torture and organized violence: Demography and diagnosis. *Journal of Traumatic Stress, 9*, 181–193.

Veronen, L. J., & Kilpatrick, D. G. (1980). Self-reported fears of rape victims: A preliminary investigation. *Behavior Modification, 4*, 383–396.

Vesti, P., & Kastrup, M. (1995). Refugee status, torture, and adjustment. In J. R. Freedy & S. E. Hobfoll (Eds.), *Traumatic stress: From theory to practice* (pp. 213–235). New York: Plenum Press.

Vrana, S., & Lauterbach, D. (1994). Prevalence of traumatic events and post-traumatic psychological symptoms in a nonclinical sample of college students. *Journal of Traumatic Stress, 7*, 289–302.

Vreven, D. L., Gudanowski, D. M., King, L. A., & King, D. W. (1995). The Civilian Version of the Mississippi PTSD Scale: A psychometric evaluation. *Journal of Traumatic Stress, 8*, 91–109.

Wakefield, H., & Underwager, R. (1992). Uncovering memories of alleged sexual abuse: The therapists who do it. *Issues in Child Abuse Accusations, 4*, 197–213.

Walker, E. A., Katon, W. J., Hansom, J., Harrop-Griffiths, J., Holm, L., Jones, M. L., Hickok, L. R., & Jemelka, R. P. (1992). Medical and psychiatric symptoms in women with childhood sexual abuse. *Psychosomatic Medicine, 54,* 658–664.

Walker, E. A., Katon, W. J., Neraas, K., Jemelka, R. P., & Massoth, D. (1992). Dissociation in women with chronic pelvic pain. *American Journal of Psychiatry, 149,* 534–537.

Walker, E. A., Katon, W. J., Roy-Byrne, P. P., Jemelka, R. P., & Russo, J. (1993). Histories of sexual victimization in patients with irritable bowel syndrome or inflammatory bowel disease. *American Journal of Psychiatry, 150,* 1502–1506.

Walker, L. E. (1984). *The battered woman syndrome.* New York: Springer.

Walker, L. E. (1991). Post-traumatic stress disorder in women: Diagnosis and treatment of battered woman syndrome. *Psychotherapy, 28,* 21–29.

Waller, N. G. (in press). The Dissociative Experiences Scale. In *Twelfth mental measurements yearbook.* Lincoln, NE: Buros Institute of Mental Measurement.

Watson, C. G. (1990). Psychometric post-traumatic stress disorder measurement techniques: A review. *Psychological Assessment, 2,* 460–469.

Watson, C. G., Plemel, D., DeMotts, J., Howard, M. T., Tuorila, J., Moog, R., Thomas, D., & Anderson, D. (1994). A comparison of four PTSD measures' convergent validities in Vietnam veterans. *Journal of Traumatic Stress, 7,* 75–82.

Weathers, F. W., Blake, D. D., Krinsley, K., Haddad, W., Huska, J., & Keane, T. M. (1992, October). *The Clinician-Administered PTSD Scale—Diagnostic Version (CAPS-1).* Paper presented at the annual meeting of the International Society for Traumatic Stress Studies, Los Angeles.

Weathers, F. W., Blake, D. D., & Litz, B. T. (1991, August). *Reliability and validity of a new structured interview for PTSD.* Paper presented at the 99th Annual Convention of the American Psychological Association, San Francisco, CA.

Weathers, F. W., Litz, B. T., & Keane, T. M. (1995). Military trauma. In J. R. Freedy & S. E. Hobfoll (Eds.), *Traumatic stress: From theory to practice* (pp. 103–128). New York: Plenum Press.

Weaver, T. L., & Clum, G. A. (1993). Early family environments and traumatic experiences associated with borderline personality disorder. *Journal of Consulting and Clinical Psychology, 61,* 1068–1075.

Weiss, D. S. (1993). Structured clinical interview techniques. In J. P. Wilson & B. Raphael (Eds.), *International handbook of traumatic stress syndromes* (pp. 179–187). New York: Plenum Press.

Weiss, D. S. (1996). Structured clinical interview techniques. In J. P. Wilson & T. Keane (Eds.), *Assessing psychological trauma and PTSD* (pp. 493–511). New York: Guilford Press.

Weiss, D. S., & Marmar, C. R. (1996). The Impact of Event Scale—Revised. In J. P. Wilson & T. Keane (Eds.), *Assessing psychological trauma and PTSD* (pp. 399–411). New York: Guilford Press.

Weiss, D. S, Marmar, C. R., Metzler, T., & Ronfeldt, H. (1995). Predicting symptomatic distress in emergency services personnel. *Journal of Consulting and Clinical Psychology, 63,* 361–368.

Weissberg, M. (1993). Multiple personality disorder and iatrogenesis: The cautionary tale of Anna O. *International Journal of Clinical and Experimental Hypnosis, 41*, 15–34.

West, L. (1967). Dissociative reaction. In A. M. Freedman & H. I. Kaplan (Eds.), *Comprehensive textbook of psychiatry* (pp. 885–898). Baltimore, MD: Williams & Wilkins.

Wetter, M. W., Baer, R. A., Berry, D. T. R., & Reynolds, S. K. (1994). The effect of symptom information on faking on the MMPI-2. *Assessment, 1*, 199–207.

Wetter, M. W., Baer, R. A., Berry, D. T. R., Robinson, L. H., & Sumpter, J. (1993). MMPI-2 profiles of motivated fakers given specific symptom information: A comparison to matched patients. *Psychological Assessment, 5*, 317–323.

Wetter, M. W., Baer, R. A., Berry, D. T. R., Smith, G. T., & Larson, L. (1992). Sensitivity of MMPI-2 validity scales to random responding and malingering. *Psychological Assessment, 4*, 369–374.

Wilkinson, C. B. (1983). Aftermath of a disaster: The collapse of the Hyatt Regency Hotel skywalks. *American Journal of Psychiatry, 140*, 1134–1139.

Williams, L. M. (1994). Recall of childhood trauma: A prospective study of women's memories of child sexual abuse. *Journal of Consulting and Clinical Psychology, 62*, 1167–1176.

Williams, L. M. (1995). Recovered memories of abuse in women with documented child sexual victimization histories. *Journal of Traumatic Stress, 8*, 649–673.

Wilson, J. P. (1994). The historical evolution of PTSD diagnostic criteria: From Freud to DSM-IV. *Journal of Traumatic Stress, 7*, 681–689.

Wilson, J. P., & Keane, T. M. (Eds.). (1996). *Assessing psychological trauma and PTSD*. New York: Guilford Press.

Wilson, J. P., & Walker, A. J. (1990). Toward an MMPI trauma profile. *Journal of Traumatic Stress, 3*, 151–168.

Wind, T. W., & Silvern, L. E. (1992). Type and extent of child abuse as predictors of adult functioning. *Journal of Family Violence, 7*, 261–281.

Winfield, I., George, L. K., Swartz, M., & Blazer, D. G. (1990). Sexual assault and psychiatric disorders among women in a community population. *American Journal of Psychiatry, 147*, 335–341.

Wolfe, J., Brown, P. J., & Bucsela, M. L. (1992). Symptom responses of female Vietnam veterans to Operation Desert Storm. *American Journal of Psychiatry, 149*, 676–679.

Wolfe, J., Brown, P. J., Furey, I., & Levin, K. B. (1993). Development of a wartime stressor scale for women. *Psychological Assessment, 5*, 330–335.

Wong, M. R., & Cook, D. (1992). Shame and its contribution to PTSD. *Journal of Traumatic Stress, 5*, 557–562.

World Health Organization. (1993). *ICD-10 classification of mental and behavioural disorders: Diagnostic criteria for research*. Geneva: Author.

Wyatt, G. E. (1985). The sexual abuse of Afro-American and White American women in childhood. *Child Abuse and Neglect, 9*, 231–240.

Wyatt, G. E., Newcombe, M. D., & Riederle, M. H. (1993). *Sexual abuse and consensual sex: Women's developmental patterns and outcomes*. Newbury Park, CA: Sage.

Yehuda, R., Kahana, B., Southwick, S. M., & Giller, E. L. (1994). Depressive features in Holocaust survivors with posttraumatic stress disorder. *Journal of Traumatic Stress, 7,* 699–704.

Yehuda, R., & McFarlane, A. (1995). Conflict between current knowledge about posttraumatic stress disorder and its original conceptual basis. *American Journal of Psychiatry, 152,* 1705–1713.

Yehuda, R., Southwick, S. M., Krystal, J. H., Bremner, D., Charney, D. S., & Mason, J. W. (1993). Enhanced suppression of cortisol following dexamethasone administration in post traumatic stress disorder. *American Journal of Psychiatry, 150,* 83–86.

Yule, W. (1992). Post-traumatic stress disorder in child survivors of shipping disasters: The sinking of the "Jupiter." *Psychotherapy and Psychosomatics, 57,* 200–205.

Zaidi, L. Y., & Foy, D. W. (1994). Childhood abuse experiences and combat-related PTSD. *Journal of Traumatic Stress, 7,* 33–42.

Appendix

A Case Example of a Trauma-Relevant Assessment

Diana M. Elliott, PhD

Introduction

This Appendix illustrates some of the assessment principles outlined in this book. First, background information received by the evaluator prior to seeing the client is given. It is followed by all relevant test data and a brief commentary on the data where appropriate. Finally, the actual report is provided. The data are a composite of clients who presented with very similar histories and levels of functioning. However, the composite history and test data have remained faithful to the original dynamics of a specific case. Because this case involves clinical, forensic, vocational, and neuropsychological issues, the resultant report is likely to be more complex than would be true for the typical trauma victim appearing for assessment.

Background Information

Katie is a 24-year-old Caucasian female referred for a full psychological assessment by the therapist who had seen her for an initial intake. Katie had sought treatment because she felt she was "going to lose it." Although oriented in all spheres and nonpsychotic, Katie was particularly afraid that she might hurt her 6-year-old daughter. An assessment of Katie's potential and intent to harm her daughter was conducted by the therapist, who judged the imminent risk to be low. Katie felt overwhelmed with life and unable to cope, but did not voice suicidal ideation.

Katie's assessment and treatment were being paid for by her father. Five years earlier, he was in a near-fatal car accident while driving under the influence of alcohol. As a result of the accident, he entered a recovery program for alcoholics, and soon thereafter he admitted to chronic sexual abuse of Katie throughout her childhood. Until then, she had not disclosed the abuse.

At that time, Katie had no relationship with her father. Although he wanted her to receive treatment, she did not see the need for it. She did, however, agree to an evaluation to placate her father. The psychologist who evaluated Katie when she was 20 was not trained in the assessment of trauma. An interview was conducted and Katie completed the Minnesota Multiphasic Personality Inventory–2 (MMPI-2) and the Millon Clinical Multiaxial Inventory–II (MCMI-II). She acknowledged the sexual abuse but minimized its extent and frequency. No other traumas were asked about or reported, although it later became apparent the she was being physically assaulted by her boyfriend at the time of that evaluation.

The previous psychologist judged Katie to be nonpsychotic and oriented in all spheres. Katie indicated that her most significant difficulties were financial stress and raising her then 2-year-old daughter. The psychologist indicated that Katie was functioning adequately given her circumstances based on the interview and psychological testing, both of which were judged to be normal. He recommended that she receive short-term treatment for stress management and that she engage in family therapy with her parents to improve their communication. Katie declined treatment. The issue was dropped until recently, when Katie, through her mother, sought her father's financial assistance in obtaining individual psychotherapy.

The current evaluator reviewed the old test data and noted the following. On the MMPI-2, Katie had an L scale T score of 66, an MF of 69, Paranoia of 35, Mania of 65, and O-H of 70. Additionally, there were several 10+ point differences between the Subtle–Obvious scales, with the subtle greater than the obvious. On the MCMI-II, Katie had a Desirability BR score of 80, Compulsive of 84, Avoidant of 74, Antisocial of 70, and Somatoform of 75. Combined, the data suggest that Katie was quite defensive in her approach to the original evaluation. It suggests an undercurrent of agitation and possible hostility that may have been contained through a rigid approach to her life and the expression of conflict through somatic complaints. Additionally, the extremely low MMPI-2 Scale 6 may have indicated that she was quite secretive, withdrawn, and suspicious of others.

Current Test Results

Wechsler Adult Intelligence Scale—Revised (WAIS–R)

Verbal Subtests		Performance Subtests	
Information	7	Picture Completion	12
Digit Span	14	Picture Arrangement	17
Vocabulary	11	Block Design	13
Arithmetic	7	Object Assembly	12
Comprehension	11	Digit Symbol	13
Similarities	12		

VERBAL 103   PERFORMANCE 125   FULL SCALE 113

The data from the WAIS–R suggest an overall IQ that is above average with average verbal abilities and superior visual–spacial capacities. There is a significant difference (22 points) between her verbal and performance IQ. Significant intersubtest scatter on her Verbal subtests suggests that it is probably not helpful to interpret the Verbal IQ of 103 in isolation. The difference in the verbal and performance scale scores appears primarily due to the significantly low scores on Information and Arithmetic in the Verbal domain and the perfect score on Picture Arrangement in the Performance domain. The low scores on I and A point to limited factual knowledge, inadequate ability in mental arithmetic, and poor school achievement (the origins of which are not clear from testing), while the perfect score on PA suggests an excellent ability to anticipate what might result from various behaviors in social situations.

Wechsler Memory Scale—Revised (WMS–R)

Verbal Memory Index	116
Visual Memory Index	133
General Memory Index	124
Attention/Concentration Index	122
Delayed Recall Index	116

The results of the WMS–R suggest that all aspects of Katie's memory abilities are above average. There is a significant difference between the verbal and visual memory scores, with the visual area being superior. However, research by Loring, Lee, Martin, and Meador (1989) suggest that this difference alone cannot be used with any confidence to infer lateralization of brain difficulties. The Attention/Concentration Index, which typically correlates highly with general intelligence, is superior. The test strongly suggests against organic difficulties being the cause of Katie's memory and concentration problems.

Peabody Individual Achievement Test—Revised (PIAT–R)

General Information	87
Total Reading	111
Mathematics	87
Spelling	112
Total Test	101

Overall, Katie's achievement is average, but there is a significant difference between her information and mathematic performance compared to her reading and spelling performance. In addition, the PIAT–R very quickly reaches its ceiling. The scores of 111 on Reading and 112 on Spelling reflect nearly perfect performance.

The data on the PIAT–R and WAIS–R raise a concern about the possibility of a learning disability in the area of arithmetic, given her overall adequate intelligence. To rule out a learning disability, it must be clear that the discrepancy between her arithmetic skills and overall intellect is not due to emotional or environmental difficulties. Thus, the client's history and psychological status will provide important information in this regard.

Peabody Picture Vocabulary Test—Revised (PPVT–R)

Standard Score = 115   Percentile Ranking = 84%

The results of the PPVT–R suggest above-average receptive language abilities.

Trailmaking Test

A: 19 s; 0 errors   B: 42 s; 0 errors

The Trailmaking test was used to assess Katie's speed for visual search, attention, and mental flexibility. She scored at better than the 90th percentile on both A and B.

Minnesota Multiphasic Personality Inventory—2 (MMPI–2)

L (raw = 0)	33	FB (raw)	12
F (raw = 13)	82	VRIN	54
K (raw = 18)	56	TRIN	58
F-K (raw)	− 5		

1. Hypochondriasis	64	6. Paranoia	78
2. Depression	70	7. Psychasthenia	79
3. Hysteria	64	8. Schizophrenia	80
4. Psychopathic	66	9. Hypomania	71
5. Masculinity/ Femininity	67	10. Social Introversion	51

Anxiety	72	O-H	33
Repression	45	PTSD (K)	78
Mac-R	67	PTSD (S)	81
Ego Strength	33	Responsibility	30

Harris–Lingoes

Depression		*Hysteria*	
Subjective Depression	66	Denial of Social Anxiety	45
Psychomotor Retardation	51	Need for Affection	34
Physical Malfunctioning	70	Lassitude-Malaise	75
Mental Dullness	53	Somatic Complaints	65
Brooding	70	Inhibition of Aggression	39

Psychopathic Deviate

Familial Discord	56
Authority Problems	59
Social Imperturbability	42
Social Alienation	70
Self-Alienation	68

Paranoia

Persecutory Ideas	68
Poignancy	78
Naivete	41

Hypomania

Amorality	45
Psychomotor Acceleration	70
Imperturbability	43
Ego Inflation	62

Schizophrenia

Social Alienation	78
Emotional Alienation	61
Lack of Ego Mastery, Cognitive	80
Lack of Ego Mastery, Conative	69
Lack of Ego Mastery, Defense Inhibition	72
Bizarre Sensory Experience	61

Social Introversion

Shyness/Self-Conscious	55
Social Avoidance	47
Alienation, Self & Other	58

The results of the MMPI-2 revealed a moderately elevated F score, suggesting that she may have exaggerated her symptoms or was in a fair amount of distress and aware of her own distress. Katie shows significant elevation on the 8 scale, with several other clinical scales elevated above 65 (including 2, 4, 6, 7, and 9). The 8-7-6 profile suggests that Katie is in a great deal of turmoil and probably lacks adequate defenses to keep herself psychologically comfortable. With the relative elevations on these three scales, overt psychosis is not likely, particularly given her scores on the Harris–Lingoes subscales and her responses to critical items. The subscales suggest the elevation on Scale 8 is primarily related to lack of ego mastery and social alienation. Although unlikely to be clearly psychotic, her thinking may appear fragmented, tangential, and circumstantial when stressed. At a minimum, she is apt to distort perceptions, but she may also have delusions of persecution. She may appear confused and in a state of panic. Because of these findings, suicidal ideation should be evaluated, especially given the mildly elevated 2 (suggesting depressive symptoms) and 9 (suggesting the propensity for impulsive acting-out behavior). The subscales provide important information regarding the specifics of Katie's symptom constellation. For example, the elevation on Scale 4 appears most related to alienation from self and others rather than authority problems, imperturbability, or family discord. The elevated subscales on Scale 6, combined with the diminished score on naiveté, suggest she is quite cynical, feels misunderstood, does not trust others, and may engage in tension reduction behaviors as a means of decreasing emotional pain. The elevation on Scale 9 may be related to psychomotor agitation, or alternatively, may reflect the hyperarousal found in chronic trauma survivors. The Mac-R suggests she has a number of personality characteristics that have been associated with substance abuse problems. Both post-traumatic stress disorder (PTSD) scales are elevated above 70. Although the raw score cutoff of 28 recommended by Keane and his colleagues is not met on the P-K scale, Katie's score of 27 suggests a great deal of distress commonly seen among individuals with PTSD.

Millon Clinical Multiaxial Inventory—III (MCMI–III)

Personality Patterns		*Validity Scales*	
Schizoid	67	Disclosure	79
Avoidant	89	Desirability	43
Depressive	88	Debasement	80
Dependent	85		
Histrionic	60	*Clinical Symptom Syndromes*	
Narcissistic	52	Anxiety	76
Antisocial	85	Somatoform	72
Aggressive	63	Bipolar	64
Compulsive	43	Dysthymic	78
Passive–Aggressive	65	Alcohol Dependence	59
Self-Defeating	87	Drug Dependence	81
		Post-traumatic Stress	65
Schizotypal	65	Thought Disorder	63
Borderline	73	Major Depression	82
Paranoid	65	Delusional Disorder	65

As with the MMPI-2, the MCMI-III suggests that Katie may have a tendency to magnify her distress, suggesting either a characterological inclination to complain or feelings of vulnerability associated with an episode of acute turmoil. Given the results of the MMPI-2 and MCMI-II 4 years earlier, the data are not likely to represent the former. There are significant elevations on the Avoidant, Depressive, Dependent, Antisocial, and Self-defeating scales, all of which are within 5 points of each other. Interestingly, in contrast to the MMPI, the PTSD scale in this test is not significantly elevated. This may reflect a lack of the disorder or point to limitations of this scale as outlined in this text, with fewer than 50% of the items tapping posttraumatic symptomatology. There is no indication of a thought or delusional disorder in this test. Mild elevations are noted on the Anxiety, Dysthymia, Drug Dependence, and Major Depression scales. These data are consistent with studies that point to diffuse personality difficulties among sexual abuse survivors. Although often elevated in the testing of sexual abuse survivors, Katie's borderline scale is not significantly elevated.

Personality Assessment Inventory (PAI)

Inconsistency	52	Negative Impression	75
Infrequency	51	Positive Impression	31
Somatic Complaints	64	Paranoia	64
Conversion	63	Hypervigilance	89
Somatization	65	Persecution	51
Health Concerns	54	Resentment	49
Anxiety	79	Schizophrenia	87
Cognitive	78	Psychotic Experience	64
Affective	73	Social Detachment	79
Physiological	72	Thought disorder	84
Anxiety-Related Disorders	79	Borderline Features	86
Obsessive–Compulsive	59	Affective Instability	76
Phobia	59	Identity Problem	86
Traumatic Stress	65	Negative Relations	91
		Self-Harm	68
Depression	88	Antisocial Features	71
Cognitive	79	Antisocial Behavior	75
Affective	80	Egocentricity	59
Physiological	77	Stimulus-Seeking	64

Mania	52	Aggression	49
Activity Level	65	Aggressive Attitude	50
Grandiosity	50	Verbal Aggression	48
Irritability	50	Physical Aggression	46
Alcohol Problems	56	Nonsupport	77
Drug Problems	84	Treatment Rejection	40
Suicide Ideation	61	Dominance	37
Stress	65	Warmth	37

On the PAI, Katie endorsed items that present an unfavorable impression, raising the possibility of exaggeration of symptoms. A review of the critical items of this test (as well as those of the MMPI and MCMI) do not indicate an endorsement of extremely bizarre symptoms, but rather symptoms of confusion and chaos. The configuration of the clinical scales also suggests a person who is confused, emotionally labile, and angry. Her profile is very much like the PTSD group in Morey's (1991) study. Her ARD–Traumatic Stress scale is elevated along with confusion (SCZ–Thought Disorder), social estrangement (SCZ–Social Detachment and BOR–Negative Relations), and problems with anger control (BOR–Affect Instability). Overall, it suggests marked interpersonal dysfunction and significant problems in thinking and concentration. The elevation on the Anxiety-Related Disorder scales appears to be specifically related to PTSD. Although the overall Paranoia scale is *not* elevated, the Hypervigilance subscale therein is markedly high, further suggesting a possible diagnosis of PTSD. The elevation on the schizophrenia scale is less related to psychotic experiences than social detachment and problems in her thought processes. She admits to a history of antisocial behaviors including substance abuse, but does not appear to have the personality characteristics that typically accompany antisocial personality disorder. All aspects of the borderline scale are elevated. This is in contrast to the results of the MCMI, which does not strongly suggest a diagnosis of borderline personality disorder. Her depression and anxiety pervade the cognitive, affective, and physiological domains.

Trauma Symptom Inventory (TSI)

ATR	68	Trauma Factor	80
RL	41	Self Factor	76
INC	43	Dysphoria Factor	71
Anxious Arousal	72	Dissociation	85
Depression	69	Sexual Concerns	84
Anger/Irritability	66	Dysfunctional Sexual Behavior	67
Intrusive Experiences	80	Impaired Self Reference	73
Defensive Avoidance	71	Tension Reduction Behavior	70

The results of the TSI are valid, and items suggestive of a psychotic thought process were not endorsed. All scales are elevated above the clinically significant level, with the highest levels found on the Dissociation, Sexual Concerns, and Intrusive Experiences scales. This consistent elevation, especially with very high dissociation, intrusive and reliving symptoms, and sexual concerns, is described in the TSI manual as suggestive of a posttraumatic response to sexual victimization.

Impact of Event Scale (IES)

Sexual Abuse by Father	Sexual Abuse at 12 by 30-yr-old	Domestic Violence
Intrusion = 29	Intrusion = 4	Intrusion = 22
Avoidance = 29	Avoidance = 3	Avoidance = 27

Although the IES is a research measure, it is helpful in evaluating intrusive and avoidance symptoms of PTSD. The maximum score for Intrusion is 35; for Avoidance, the maximum score is 40. Although no standardization data exist on this instrument, mean scores in the general population (Briere & Elliott, 1996a) are 7.0 (SD = 8.7) for Intrusion and 7.3 (SD = 9.1) for Avoidance. Katie's scores are above the 95th percentile on both Intrusion and Avoidance with reference to sexual abuse by her father and above the 90th percentile for Intrusion and 95th percentile for Avoidance related to her history of partner assault.

Dissociative Experiences Scale (DES) Score=23

Although not a normed clinical instrument, the DES can provide information regarding the presence of symptoms associated with dissociative identity disorder. Research suggests that the score obtained by Katie (23) is rarely obtained by individuals with dissociative identity disorder or other extreme dissociative disorder, but more typical of individuals with borderline personality or posttraumatic stress.

Child Abuse Potential Inventory (CAP)

Lie	Normal	Faking Good	Normal
Random	Normal	Faking Bad	Normal
Inconsistency	Normal	Random Response	Normal
Abuse	Elevated	Problems with child	Normal
Distress	Elevated	Problems with family	Elevated
Rigidity	Normal	Problems with others	Elevated
Unhappiness	Elevated		

The results of the CAP Inventory are valid, with all validity scales in the normal range. The data indicate that Katie has characteristics similar to individuals who are known physical abusers at the time of testing. The risk factors for her appear to be related to her level of psychological distress, unhappiness with life, and lack of family and other social support systems.

Rorschach Inkblot Test (selected responses)

I. __ A lot of faces; not sure if they are animal or human ([outlines 4 faces] here's the eyebrows like they are looking at something. See it, here in the shading. [outlines the faces again] . . . probably animals . . .)
__ A skeleton of a pelvis ([outlines the shape] The shape of the bones here and the black and white make it look like an x-ray)

II. This picture is weird. It looks angry. Very angry. (It's dark and very drastic . . . the way the darkness and the redness are pushing together)

III. 2 people, not sure if they are men or women. ([Outlines shape])

IV. This one is scary; a gigantic monster, you are looking up at it though, it's towering over you. (The feet, the arms. They are small cause you're looking up at it . . . It's scary because the feet are so much larger like they could step on you any minute.)

VI. A canyon, like you are looking over it and down into it, like it's endless. (Look down into it. This is the land and as it gets darker, you're looking farther and farther into it.)

VIII. This looks like a skeleton of a dog's face, very scary, very angry. ([outlines the dog's face] The eyes are so big and there's nothing in back. That why it looks like a skeleton because of the holes . . . It looks angry because these look like teeth were clamping down on something before it died [outlines]. It makes it look very mean and vicious.)

IX. A skeleton of something, the pelvic area ([outlines] The backbone is here. This is the pelvis.)

```
==================RATIOS, PERCENTAGES, AND DERIVATIONS================

R=24        L = 0.5                   FC:CF+C=3:3        COP=3    AG=2
------------------------------------  Pure C =  2       Food     = 1
EB=4:5.5    EA= 9.5   EBPer=N/A        SumC':WSumC=2:5.5 Isolate/R =0.08
eb=5:9      es=14        D=-1.0        Afr     =0.50     H:(H)Hd(Hd) = 3:3
       Adj es= 9  Adj D= 0             S       = 2       (Hhd):(AAd) = 1:3
------------------------------------  Blends:R=6:24     H+A:Hd+Ad  =11:5
FM=3   :  C'=2   T=0                   CP      = 0
 m=2   :  V =2   Y=6
                        P  =5          Zf     = 10      3r+(2)/R=.29
a:p      =7:2   Sum6 =1  X+%=0.33      Zd     =+1.5     Fr+rF    = 0
Ma:Mp    =4:0   Lv2  =0  F+%=0.33      W:D:Dd=7:10:7    FD       = 1
2AB+Art+Ay=4    Wsum6=2  X-%=0.29      W:M    = 7:4     An+Xy    = 4
M-       = 0    Mnone=1  S-%=0.12      DQ+    = 5       Mor      = 2
                        Xu%=0.29       DQ v   = 2
====================================================================
SCZI = 3    DEPI = 5*   CDI = 1    S-CON = 4    HVI = no    OBS = no
====================================================================
```

Katie's unstructured color responses, traumatic content, and poor form quality on the Rorschach may be indicative of post-traumatic intrusion. Additionally, her $T = O$ is consistent with traumatic avoidance. The elevated depression constellation suggests that Katie has intense affective experiences that make it difficult for her to maintain consistent adjustment over time. D-1 combined with an AdjD of 0 suggests that she currently has limited resources available to form and implement decisions but that this is likely to be situationally based. This stress increases the likelihood of impulsive thinking, emotion, and behavior. Katie appears to be experiencing a good deal of helplessness and powerlessness (m and Y). Her three color–shade blends, two pure C responses (in blends) with negative form quality, an EB of 4:5.5, and an Afr of .50, suggest that her emotions are not consistent in their impact on her thinking. The pure C responses are consistent with other test data suggesting that Katie is at risk for acting without thinking. Although at times she can modulate her affect, she lapses in her control, during which her behavior is likely to be maladaptive. She appears confused by emotion, experiences both positive and negative feelings in response to the same situation, and may have difficulty bringing emotional situations to closure. Katie's V and FD scores suggest that she engages in self-inspection more often than most people and that much of this is excessively ruminative feelings of guilt and shame. Her poor perceptual accuracy limits the potential benefits of her introspective nature. The lack of texture responses suggests that she has lower expectations regarding closeness in relationships than most people, although she has retained a template that positive interactions with others can exist (3 cop). The data suggest that Katie is willing to engage in complex thinking regularly; however, some of her processing is not very thorough. Katie has serious problems concerning perceptual accuracy that contribute significantly to difficulties in reality testing (X+%, F+%, X−%, Xu%). Her problems in this area appear to be both chronic and pervasive. The frequency with which she distorts reality is considerable and suggests she will have great difficulty maintaining adequate adjustment in most situations for any extended period. As with the MCMI and TSI, the Rorschach does not indicate a psychotic disorder.

CONFIDENTIAL—FOR PROFESSIONAL USE ONLY

PSYCHOLOGICAL EVALUATION

Client Name: Katie
Date of Birth:
Referred by:
Referred on:
Dates of Evaluation:
Date of Report:
Evaluator: Diana M. Elliott, PhD

Informed Consent

The examiner informed Katie of the purpose of the evaluation and intended use of its results. Katie gave written consent to the evaluation, to verbal communication with her therapist, and to the writing of a summary report to her therapist. Consent is limited in the use of this report by her therapist and therapist consultants. Specific consent of the client is needed to release the report to any other person or agency. This report contains sensitive information subject to misinterpretation by untrained individuals.

Collateral Contacts

Katie gave informed consent to have the evaluator speak with her mother and father, who were spoken with separately on the telephone, each for approximately 45 minutes. Additionally, the evaluator observed Katie with her daughter through a one-way mirror for approximately 90 minutes and briefly interacted with Katie's male companion, who cared for Katie's daughter while she was in the evaluation.

Documents Reviewed

Evaluation notes provided by _____ _____, Ph.D.

Intake notes provided by _____ _____, LCSW
Medical Records from _____ Medical Center
Millon Clinical Multiaxial Inventory–II given in 199_
Minnesota Multiphasic Personality Inventory–2 given in 199_

Referral Questions

Psychological testing was requested by Katie's therapist after an initial intake interview. Assistance was requested in order to better understand the client's level of distress, self and trauma difficulties, interpersonal functioning, parenting skills, diagnosis, and treatment planning. A request was also made to evaluate the client's goal to attend college in the fall. Finally, there was a question of possible organicity based on the client's report of chronic memory and concentration problems and a history of multiple episodes of unconsciousness caused by physical assaults.

Identifying Information, Mental Status, and Symptomatology

Katie is a 24-year-old Caucasian female, who is above-average in height and slender in stature (reported height and weight are 5' 9", 120 pounds). She is single (never married) and the mother of a 6-year-old daughter who was present during one of the evaluation sessions. She has been employed as a nanny for the past 4 years in the same home. Katie was casually dressed, alert, and oriented in all spheres throughout the evaluation. Her affect in the interview was congruent with her mood. She was cooperative with the evaluation process and appeared to exert a great deal of effort in every task required of her.

Katie reported fearing that she was losing her mind. She stated that her mind sometimes raced and at other times was completely blank. She reported chronic concentration and memory problems as well as frequent tension headaches. She typically felt calm when working alone or with her daughter. When "forced" to interact socially, she became highly anxious and heard voices in her head. When asked to describe these voices, she identified the voices as her own or as her memory of words her former boyfriend or father said to her. Thus, she described symptoms consistent with cognitive intrusion rather than psychosis. She became particularly anxious when she thought about her life history and described intrusive, avoidant, and hyperarousal symptoms often associated with trauma. These symptoms were reported to be primarily related to childhood sexual abuse and secondarily related to partner assault. They appear to have begun 2 years prior to the current evaluation and had markedly increased in the last 6 months. Despite a high level of symptomatology, she denied suicidal ideation, intent, or plan. Additionally, although Katie reported a chronic fear that she would harm her daughter, she reported no history of abuse and no desire, intent, or plan to do so. She reported that she sometimes felt full of rage. At those times she either exercised or "exploded." She denied that her daughter was ever present when she was rageful.

Although she denied depressive symptoms of sadness and suicidal ideation, she reported that she had no expectation that she would ever enjoy life, had poor concentration, and generally lacked hope about her future. She reported that this state was the only state she could remember for herself other than when she was abusing drugs and alcohol during her teenage years. She denied any current misuse of drugs or alcohol. She experienced significant confusion over her sexuality. Although she desired sexual contact, she withdrew from any relationship in which she might be approached sexually. She reported marked anxiety when the issues of sexual contact was raised either in her thoughts or in conversation with another. She denied symptoms of any eating disorder and indicated that she stayed slim because she exercised "to an extreme" when she was upset. She denied pervasive sleep disturbance but reported that she was sometimes awakened by nightmares with diffuse violent or sexual content.

Relevant Psychosocial History

Katie is an only child, born into a two-parent home. Katie's birth and early childhood development were reported to have been normal. However, her parents fought constantly throughout the first 3 years of Katie's life. They divorced when she was 3 years of age, because her mother was having an extramarital affair. Her father allowed no subsequent contact with her mother until Katie was 18. After the divorce, Katie was cared for by nannies, most of whom were employed for less than 6 months. Her father was an alcoholic, whose consumption of alcohol increased after the divorce. He never remarried, but he had numerous relationships with particularly young women (aged 18–25), none of whom were reported to have been abusive toward Katie. However, between age 4 and 7 she observed her father beating at least one of his female lovers. Her father was never physically abusive toward her, but she reported chronic psychological abuse by him.

Katie's father began sexually abusing her when she was approximately 8 years of age. The abuse began with fondling, progressed to vaginal and anal intercourse, and occurred multiple times per week. Katie reported that initially she enjoyed the touch and that by the time she was 10, she became sexually aroused during the contact but felt "grossed out" after he left the room. As she reached her teenage years, she became angry at her father for the abuse and wanted the contact to stop. When she protested, her father physically restrained her during the contact. Katie reported guilt over the physical pleasure she experienced during the abuse, felt betrayed by her body, and believed she must have encouraged her father to abuse her.

During her first 3 years of school, Katie obtained straight As. She tested above the 95th percentile nationally in all areas of scholastic achievement in grades 2 and 3. She had a B–C average throughout the remainder of grammar and high school. She began displaying behavioral problems in fifth grade, which persisted throughout high school. Most of the difficulties in grammar school were related to inattention and underachievement. She was suspended on more than one occasion during high school for cutting classes and physical altercations with peers. She reported that when not out with her friends, she spent hours alone in her bedroom reading.

Katie began having sexual contact with teenaged boys when she was in the seventh grade. At that same time, she began drinking alcohol excessively and smoking marijuana. At age 12, she had sexual contact with a 30-year-old man who provided her with drugs. She characterized the contact as consensual, despite the nearly 20-year age discrepancy. After he left the geographic area, Katie had sexual contact with multiple partners, none of which was protected. At the age of 16, she began a long-term relationship with an 18-year-old male. Very early on, physical altercations occurred between the two and continued throughout their relationship. She reported that the fights were sometimes started by her, but that once started, she would be beaten until she was unconscious.

The sexual abuse of Katie by her father continued until she was 17 years old. At that time, she actively refused to engage in the contact. Because her father continued to pursue her, she ran away from home with her boyfriend. She informed her father that if he reported her to the police or attempted to make her come home, she would report the ongoing sexual abuse. She had had no regular contact with her father since that time and reported no desire to see him at the time of the evaluation.

When Katie left home, she was a senior in high school; she dropped out during her last semester. A few months later, she was beaten so badly by her boyfriend that she needed medical care. While in the emergency room, she was found to be approximately 5 months pregnant. Katie reported that she did not know who the father of her child was. She had been having consensual contact with two peers and was being sexually abused by her father at the time she was impregnated. She indicated that she had no desire to know the father's identity. Katie went home to her boyfriend's after the assault but stopped consuming alcohol or illegal drugs because of the pregnancy. The physical assaults continued for two more years. She ultimately left the relationship, when he assaulted her in front of her daughter and her daughter attempted to intervene on her behalf.

Katie soon found a job as a nanny in an upper middle class home. She has lived in her employer's guest house with her daughter since that time. Approximately 3 years ago, she studied for and passed her GED. She has enrolled in college three times, but dropped out each time. Her goal was to become an attorney, but she feared she did not have the mental capacity to achieve it.

Katie indicated that she has had no problems in her job as a nanny. She had few friends and reported a general mistrust of others. She has had no sexual partners since she left her abusive boyfriend, but had been involved in a relationship with a 27-year-old male for approximately 9 months. She viewed the relationship as platonic, but knew that he wanted more. She indicated that her symptoms began to feel unmanageable as she grew closer to this man, but she did not see any causal connection between the status of the relationship and her psychological distress. She refused to date him even though she was attracted to him. She indicated that when she thought of dating, "all I see is my father fucking me or my boyfriend pounding the shit out of me." Katie was aware of her need for help, but was skeptical of the probable efficacy of treatment.

Medical History

Katie had no unusual childhood illness or hospitalization. Her first hospitalization occurred when she was 18 due to physical assault by her former boyfriend. She was treated for two fractured ribs and released. She had two subsequent emergency room visits, also caused by partner battery. Each of these involved trauma to the head. After the first, a CAT scan revealed no subdural hematomas or residual traces of blood. An EEG revealed a borderline abnormality with some spike waves seen in the right frontal region. However, she had a normal CAT scan and EEG after her second head trauma. This may suggest that there was transitory damage to the right frontal area that resolved over time. Alternatively, the original EEG findings may have been artifactual. Katie also was hospitalized for the birth of her daughter, which was a full-term, vaginal delivery.

Legal History

Katie had three juvenile arrests for physical altercations and shoplifting. In each case, no charges were filed and she spent no time in juvenile hall. She had one adult arrest which occurred a few days after she left her abusive boyfriend. She had stolen food from the grocery store and the owner wanted her prosecuted for shoplifting. She pleaded guilty to a misdemeanor theft charge. Additionally, Child Protective Services had intervened on one occasion because of an allegation of child neglect. Katie had left her daughter with a babysitter, who subsequently left the minor alone. The case was closed as unfounded without any court involvement.

Treatment History

Katie was seen by a psychologist for an evaluation when she was 20 years old after her father confessed to sexually molesting her throughout her childhood. The data suggested she was quite defensive throughout the evaluation. The therapist recommended stress management and family therapy, but she refused both.

Psychological Tests Administered

Child Abuse Potential Inventory (CAP)
Diagnostic Interview
Dissociative Experiences Scale (DES)
Impact of Events Scale (IES)
Millon Clinical Multiaxial Inventory–III (MCMI-III)
Minnesota Multiphasic Personality Inventory–2 (MMPI-2)
Peabody Individual Achievement Test—Revised (PIAT-R)
Peabody Picture Vocabulary Test—Revised (PPVT-R)
Personality Assessment Inventory (PAI)
Rorschach Inkblot Test (Exner Scoring System)
Trauma Symptom Inventory (TSI)
Traumatic Events Survey (TES)
Trailmaking Test (A & B)
Wechsler Adult Intelligence Scale—Revised (WAIS-R)
Wechsler Memory Scale—Revised (WMS-R)

Cognitive Functioning

The data from the Wechsler Adult Intelligence Scale (WAIS-R) suggest a Verbal IQ of 103, a Performance IQ of 125, and a Full-Scale IQ of 113. Her overall intellectual capacities exceed that of 81% of the individuals in the United States within her age bracket. There is, however, a significant difference between her verbal and performance abilities, with greater capacities demonstrated in her visuo–spatial–motor abilities.

The results of verbal tests indicate that Katie's abilities in this domain exceed 58% of individuals in her age bracket, although they were not evenly developed. Abilities that rely heavily on school-related learning (e.g., Information, Arithmetic) are relatively diminished. In tasks less affected by school learning, her performance is at or above average. These latter skills suggest that Katie's ability to attend to and memorize rote verbal data, her receptive and expressive language abilities, the ability for conceptualization, abstract thinking, verbal reasoning, and the use of practical information to solve problems are adequately developed. In cases of child abuse, the deficits in school-related tasks may reflect the effects of traumatic events on the learning process during school years rather than innate discrepancies in abilities.

The data indicate that Katie's nonverbal comprehensive ability and perceptual organizational ability are superior, exceeding 95% of individuals in her age bracket. She is alert to visual stimuli, has very adequate visual–motor–spatial integration, is readily able to differentiate essential from nonessential details, and is able to synthesize concrete parts into meaningful wholes. She has a particular strength in her ability to perceive nonverbal social cues in the environment—a skill that is apt to assist the chronic abuse survivor in avoiding abuse under certain circumstances.

The results of the Wechsler Memory Scale—Revised (WMS-R) suggest a similar pattern as seen on the WAIS–R. Her visual memory (MQ = 133; 99%) is better developed than her verbal memory (MQ = 116; 86%). However, for both verbal and visual memory, Katie is able to recall information that had been attended to and encoded better than the average individual (delayed recall = 116; 86%). Additionally, her ability to attend and concentrate appear to be superior (122; 93%). Thus, although Katie complained of concentration and memory difficulties, when given structured tasks, she has superior abilities in this domain. However, her ability to perceive things accurately is apt to decrease when she is presented with more ambiguous stimuli.

Katie's academic achievement is consistent with the scores obtained on her verbal intelligence testing (Total Test = 101; 53%). Although her achievement in the areas of math and acquisition of factual information is below average, her reading and spelling skills are above.

Katie's test data, history of As early in school, and superior performance in national achievement testing in the 2nd and 3rd grades (prior to the onset of abuse) suggest that it is unlikely that she has a learning disability in arithmetic. Her normal CAT scan and EEG suggest that no organic problems are present. Taken together, the WAIS, WMS, PPVT, PIAT, and Trails A&B suggest that failed attempts at college studies are apt to have causes that are nonorganic in nature. These may include psychological distress or an attempt to take college classes that rely heavily on basic skills that were not obtained during childhood (such as arithmetic). Under normal circumstances, Katie may be able to do quite well in academic pursuits, although she will need remedial assistance in basic math skills not previously acquired. At the present time, she is apt to experience greatest difficulties in abstract intellectual tasks such as those found in the study of law. Any decision to pursue a college degree at this time should be based on her psychological status and other resources to do so.

Affecting Functioning

Although valid, the MMPI-2, MCMI-III, and PAI suggested that Katie is sending a "cry for help." The psychological test data are marked by significant elevations across a broad range of clinical features, which increases the probability of multiple concurrent diagnoses. Profile patterns of this type are usually associated with marked acute distress and severe impairment in psychological, interpersonal, and behavioral functioning.

One of five measures suggest the possibility of a psychotic disorder. Her thought processes are likely to be marked by confusion, distractibility, and some peculiarities. She may experience her thoughts as being somehow blocked or disrupted. However, active psychotic symptoms such as hallucinations were not noted in the interview, critical items, or content sub-scales. She is apt to display a higher than usual frequency of behaviors that disregard social demands or expectations. This appears to be related to an overpersonalization of environmental stimuli, rather than to be psychotic in nature. It is likely that in obvious situations, acceptable social responses will occur. The probability of less conventional or disorganized responses occur in more ambiguous situations.

Katie reports a high level of anxiety that is apt to constrict her life and create difficulty meeting minimal expectations without feeling overwhelmed. She monitors her environment in an un-usually vigilant fashion. She presents with classic posttraumatic symptomatology, including intrusive experiences, avoidance, and hyperarousal and meets the diagnostic criteria for PTSD. It is likely that these symptoms have become more or less integrated into her personality. Her history of multiple trauma predisposes her to dissociative symptoms. Those most regularly used in-clude "spacing out," disengaging, detachment, and depersonal-ization, which serve to pull her away from her strong affect. She is particularly apt to engage in dissociative behaviors in either interpersonal situations or when painful affect triggers memo-ries of her childhood. Despite these symptoms, however, she does not meet the criteria for a dissociative disorder.

It is likely that Katie's emotions are inconsistent in terms of their impact on her thinking and problem-solving and decision-making behaviors. In one instance, thinking may be strongly influenced by feelings, whereas in a second similar situation, emotions may play only a peripheral role. Katie is often con-fused by her emotions and may experience positive and nega-tive feelings in response to the same circumstance. She has some potentially serious problems concerning the way in which she displays her feelings. Her emotions are at times quite intense when they are released and appear to come out of nowhere. There is an undercurrent of moodiness and anger, distrust, and resentfulness of others. Ordinarily she keeps her anger under tight control. However, when she feels particularly overwhelmed, she is apt to engage in tension reduction behaviors that are po-tentially self-injurious, such as excessive exercise and rageful outbursts.

Katie has a number of personality characteristics that have been associated with the abuse of drugs or alcohol. Individuals with similar data are often actively misusing mood-altering substances and have little ability to control the habit. In the clinical interview, Katie denied current drug usage but acknowledged a history of chronic abuse. It may be that the test data reflect Katie's propensity to abuse drugs, despite currently being clean. Alternatively, Katie may be denying the extent of current use of mood-altering substances. In the latter case, some of her seemingly psychotic symptoms may be at least partially drug or alcohol related.

Interpersonal Functioning

Problematic relationships are apt to be characteristic for Katie. She is apt to relate to others ambivalently. Although she can engage in cooperative activities with others, she never fully trusts or loves those with whom she is involved, and as a result, never establishes lasting, intimate relationships. Katie's interpersonal style is likely to be the result of a history of disappointments in relationships rather than a basic compositional shyness; that is, her social isolation is not apt to arise because of intrinsic emotional deficits, but as an active means for controlling the expression of intense affect and as protection against humiliation and rejection from others.

There is an intense conflict between a desire to withdraw from others (because of anticipated humiliation) and a need for interpersonal contact. Whereas it is likely that she, at one time, sought closeness and affection, she has learned to anticipate ridicule and pain in relationships. She therefore tends to retreat, becoming increasingly removed from potential sources of interpersonal gratification. Her interpersonal needs and concomitant fear may result in periods of acute emotional turmoil, despondency, and occasional irrational thinking.

It is likely that others have disapproved of Katie's past attempts at autonomy. As a result, she tends to remain dependent on a few people, but resents doing so. This internal conflict may erupt in an unpredictable or passive–aggressive manner. Recognizing she might lose the support of the few people close to her, she tends to control her anger by withdrawing. Her outbursts are likely to evoke rejecting responses, which in turn reinforce her self-protective social withdrawal. It is likely that when she does enter relationships, she experiences exploitation and abuse. Given her history, current symptoms, and pattern of interpersonal functioning, it is likely that the onset of Katie's acute psychological distress was precipitated by her emotional ambivalence regarding increased involvement with her male companion; she is both attracted to him but fears intimacy with him.

Katie describes behaviors that are consistent with antisocial personality traits. She has a history of antisocial behavior and is likely to have manifested a conduct disorder during adolescence. However, other features of the antisocial personality, such as competitiveness, egocentricity, impulsivity, disregard for others, disloyalty, vindictiveness, and recklessness, do not appear to be particularly prominent parts of Katie's clinical picture.

Parenting Capacity

Katie reports no prior abuse of her child. Additionally, an observation of her with her daughter indicates that the two are well-bonded and have good communication and that Katie is not intrusive or insensitive toward her. Nevertheless, Katie is fearful that she will abuse her child. Psychometric data likewise indicates that she is at risk for using physically abusive parenting practices. This risk appears to be primarily related to her psychological distress and unhappiness with herself, rather than an excessively rigid approach to parenting or particular problems with her child. Factors including her distress, low sense of self-worth, relative absence of social relationships, hypersensitivity to critical feedback, and difficulty in resolving conflict increase the probability of role reversals and inappropriate demands in the parent–child relationship. If she were to abuse her child, it is most likely to occur in a dissociated rageful state. Such states, by their very nature, are difficult to predict but are more apt to occur as external and internal stress increase.

Summary of Test Results

Katie is a 24-year-old Caucasian female with a GED. She is a single mother of a 6-year-old girl, who may be the product of incest or consensual contact with a peer. The client described a childhood history of maternal abandonment (from ages 3 to 17), emotional abuse and intrafamilial sexual abuse by her father (from ages 8 to 17), sexual abuse at age 12 by a 30-year-old man, and peer-aged physical assaults throughout her teen years. As an adult, she was involved in a battering relationship that resulted in multiple emergency room visits. She is seeking outpatient treatment because of feelings that she will lose control with her daughter, a fear of decompensation, and symptoms of PTSD. Despite her feelings of overwhelming emotional pain, in the client's favor is her consistent work history and consistent provision of adequate care to her daughter.

The WAIS-R indicates that cognitively Katie is functioning in the high-average range. Her overall capacities exceeds 82% of individuals in her age bracket, although this may be an underestimation of her true cognitive ablilities. Her memory and concentration abilities are superior, exceeding 95% of individuals in her age bracket. Her scholastic achievement level is mildly depressed compared to her overall intellectual capacities, but is relatively consistent with her verbal IQ. She tends to perform better on visuospatial tasks than verbal ones. This difference appears to be more related to a scholastic underachievement than a true deficit in her cognitive abilities. This pattern has been noted clinically among individuals who experience trauma during their school years. Such children frequently exhibit avoidance symptoms to cope with the abuse, which disrupts the normal acquisition of basic scholastic information.

No sign of psychotic thought processes was noted in the clinical interview, and critical items suggestive of psychosis were not endorsed in the test data. Although Katie does display some peculiarity in her thinking and is prone to morbid ruminations, this appears to be the result of a basic lack of trust in her own perception of reality combined with a lack of trust in those who would interpret reality for her. This leaves her in a state of cognitive indecisiveness and makes her vulnerable to errors in judgment.

Currently, Katie is experiencing acute turmoil and lacks resources for dealing with it. This appears most related to symptoms of chronic PTSD. Multiple dissociative symptoms are engaged in as a means of dealing with triggers of her past trauma.
An undercurrent of depressive symptoms date back to early
childhood and include decreased capacity to experience pleasure, low self-esteem, and feelings of hopelessness. She is fearful
of and avoids sexual contact with others, although she desires
such contact. She has a strong undercurrent of anger that she
typically keeps under tight control but that is apt to erupt at
times of stress. She uses tension reduction behaviors to deal with
her stress. Test data suggest that, statistically, Katie is at risk for
using physically abusive practices with her daughter, primarily
as a result of her distress, unhappiness, and social isolation.

Interpersonally, she is apt to vacillate between wanting acceptance and fearing rejection and humiliation. She is fearful of
others and does not trust that they will treat her fairly. When
she does engage in relationships, she is apt to be involved with
people who treat her abusively. She is likely to be easily hurt by
criticism and disapproval and is unwilling to get involved with
people unless she is certain of being liked. To defend against the
possibility of rejection, Katie tends to isolate herself socially. Her
unwillingness to engage in normal social interactions may prevent her from getting the necessary feedback needed to correct
her perception of both herself and the world around her.

Diagnostic Impressions (*DSM–IV*):

AXIS I	309.89	Post-Traumatic Stress Disorder: chronic, with delayed onset
	300.40	Dysthymia: early onset
	302.79	Sexual Aversion Disorder: acquired, generalized, and due to psychological factors
AXIS II	301.82	Avoidant personality disorder with prominent dependent and borderline traits
AXIS III		Deferred to primary physician
AXIS IV		Problems with primary support group

	Problems related to social environment
	Other psychosocial and environmental problems
AXIS V	Current GAF: 35
	Highest GAF past year: 50

Recommendations and Treatment Considerations

1. Katie should be referred for a medical consult with a psychiatrist familiar with posttraumatic states. Psychotropic medication is apt to reduce emotional pain such that Katie can work in therapy. However, it should be carefully monitored, given her history of chronic substance abuse. PRN medications are typically contraindicated in similar cases.

2. Despite Katie's denial of substance abuse, every test that evaluated for such abuse suggested that she may be currently abusing drugs or alcohol. The therapist should be aware of the client's propensity in this area. Involvement with 12-step programs, such as Alcoholics Anonymous, Narcotics Anonymous, and/or Alonon, should be discussed with the client in conjunction with individual treatment.

3. Katie's fear of harming her daughter in the context of an emotional outbreak appears warranted, although her parenting skills appear adequate. Katie needs to establish a plan for her daughter's care should she ever fear that she might imminently harm her. She also needs to understand and begin to predict when she is at greater risk for emotional dyscontrol in order to activate the needed support and care for her daughter. Katie may benefit from involvement in a single-parents' support group where she can make contact with others in similar situations as her own and learn complex parenting skills. Finally, Katie's remaining abstinent from mood-altering substances is a crucial component of her ability to continue to provide appropriate care for her daughter.

4. Clinical experience suggests that individuals with psychosocial histories and test data similar to Katie have long-term adjustment problems that are resistant to change. Katie should be made aware that it is not uncommon for such treatment to last

several years and to include some exacerbation of symptoms, particularly during the early stages of treatment. Her expectation for positive change as a result of treatment is low. Addressing this belief in session will be important in helping her activate energy to participate.

5. Katie is at risk of decompensation into anxious and depressive episodes. Environmental pressures that aggravate her anxieties should be controlled to the extent possible. Taking on additional pressures is contraindicated at this time. Thus, Katie's plans to begin university should be discussed in terms of her psychological distress and the added stress that such an endeavor would inevitably create. Continued employment will be important in order that Katie's self-esteem not decrease further.

6. Psychotherapy could increase her already elevated avoidant symptoms if the therapist does not monitor the balance between her self capacities and level of traumatic stress. Although Katie makes considerable effort in processing information, she has strong tendencies to ruminate. She is not likely to do well, at least initially, in unstructured therapy and may actually deteriorate if her introspection increases without any increase in ability to access psychological resources. Goal-directed, cognitive treatment is most appropriate at this time.

7. Because of her intense ambivalence between wanting help and yet mistrusting the intentions of others, Katie will have difficulty sustaining a therapeutic relationship. She may be inconsistent in her session attendance, and her withdrawal may increase as she confronts painful memories. Predicting such withdrawals may provide some sense of sanity and predictability. The therapist should not set goals too high or press changes too fast because Katie does not tolerate demands or expectancies well.

8. At the request of Katie and her treating therapist, these test results were verbally explained to the client. Should further questions arise, Katie should be referred back to this evaluator for consultation.

_____

Signature

Index

About the Author

John Briere, PhD, is an associate professor in the Departments of Psychiatry and Psychology at the University of Southern California School of Medicine and a clinical psychologist in the Division of Emergency Psychiatry of Los Angeles County–University of Southern California Medical Center. His primary research and clinical interests are in the areas of child abuse, psychological trauma, interpersonal violence, and research methodology. Dr. Briere is author, editor, or co-editor of several books, including *Therapy for Adults Molested as Children: Beyond Survival, 2nd Edition*, *Child Abuse Trauma: Theory and Treatment of the Lasting Effects*, *Assessing and Treating Victims of Violence*, and the *APSAC Handbook on Child Maltreatment*. He has authored two psychological tests: the Trauma Symptom Inventory and the Trauma Symptom Checklist for Children, published by Psychological Assessment Resources. He consults and provides workshops to government and law enforcement agencies and clinicians in the areas of violence and psychological trauma.